THE LOST WORLD OF THE
KALAHARI

THE LOST WORLD

"Pass world!: I am the dreamer
that remains;
The man clear cut
against the last horizon."

ROY CAMPBELL

OF THE

KALAHARI

LAURENS VAN DER POST

A Harvest/HBJ Book
Harcourt Brace Jovanovich
New York and London

Printed in the United States of America

Harvest/HBJ edition published by arrangement
with William Morrow and Company

Library of Congress Cataloging in Publication Data
Van der Post, Laurens.
The lost world of the Kalahari.
(A Harvest/HBJ book)
Reprint of the ed. published by Morrow, New York.
1. San (African people) 2. Kalahari Desert.
I. Title.
[DT737.V36 1977]   968'.1   77-4292
ISBN 0-15-653706-0

HBJ

First Harvest/HBJ edition 1977

A B C D E F G H I J

To the memory of Klara who had a Bushman

mother and nursed me from birth;

And to my wife, Ingaret Giffard, for saying

without hesitation when I mentioned the

journey to her: "But you must go and do it

at once."

CONTENTS

Chapter

1. The Vanished People   3

2. The Manner of Their Going   35

3. The Pact and the Random Years   54

4. The Break-Through   68

5. The Shadow In Between   83

6. Northern Approaches   102

7. The Swamp of Despond   130

8. The Spirits of the Slippery Hills   188

9. The Hunter at the Well   218

10. The Song of the Rain   254

THE LOST WORLD OF THE
KALAHARI

Map of Southern Africa showing the main features mentioned in the story.

Chapter 1

THE VANISHED PEOPLE

THIS is the story of a journey in a great wasteland and a search for some pure remnant of the unique and
almost vanished First People of my native land, the Bushmen
of Africa. The journey in fact was accomplished barely a year
ago, but in a deeper sense it began long before that. Indeed,
so far back in time does all this go that I am unable to determine precisely when it did begin. I know for certain only that
no sooner did I become aware of myself as a child than my
imagination slipped, like a hand into a glove, into a profound
preoccupation with the little Bushman and his terrible fate.

I was born near the Great River, in the heart of what, for
thousands of years had been great Bushman country. The
Bushman himself as a coherent entity had already gone, but I
was surrounded from birth by so many moving fragments of
his race and culture that I felt him extraordinarily near. I was
always meeting him afresh on the lips of living men. Beside
the open hearth on cold winters' nights on my mother's farm

of Wolwekop, "the Mountain of the Wolves" (as my coun-trymen call the big striped hyenas), or round the campfire with the jackals' mournful bark raising an apprehensive bleat from a newly lambed ewe in the flock kraaled nearby, and with the night plover wailing over the black plain like a bo-sun's pipe, there the vanished Bushman would be vividly at the centre of some hardy pioneering reminiscence: a Bush-man gay, gallant, mischievous, unpredictable, and to the end unrepentant and defiant. Though gone from the land, he still stalked life in the mixed blood of the coloured peoples as subtly as he ever stalked the multitudinous game of Africa. He was present in the eyes of one of the first women to nurse me, her shining gaze drawn from the first light of some un-believably antique African day. Here a strain of Bushman blood would give an otherwise good Bantu face an odd Mon-golian slant, there turn a good central African black into an apricot yellow or just break out, like a spark of electricity, in the clicks of onomatopoeic invention which the Bushman had forced on an invader's sonorous tongue.

The older I grew the more I resented that I had come too late to know him in his natural setting. For many years I could not accept that the door was closed for ever on the Bushman. I went on seeking for news and information of him as if preparing for the moment when the door would open and he would reappear in our midst. Indeed I believe the first objective question I ever asked of life was, "Who, really, was the Bushman?" I asked it of people of all races and col-ours who might have had contact with him, to the point where many a patient heart must have found it hard to bear with the uncomprehended importunity of a child. They told me much. But what they told me only made me hunger for more.

They said he was a little man, not a dwarf or pigmy, but just a little man about five feet in height. He was well, sturdily and truly made. His shoulders were broad but his hands and feet were extraordinarily small and finely modelled. The oldest of our 'Suto servants told me that one had only to see his small precise footprints in the sand never to forget them. His ankles were slim like a race-horse's, his legs supple, his muscles loose, and he ran like the wind, fast and long. In fact when on the move he hardly ever walked but, like the springbuck or wild dog, travelled at an easy trot. There had never been anyone who could run like him over the veld and boulders, and the bones of many a lone Basuto and Koranna were bleaching in the sun to prove how vainly they had tried to outdistance him. His skin was loose and very soon became creased and incredibly wrinkled. When he laughed, which he did easily, his face broke into innumerable little folds and pleats of a most subtle and endearing criss-cross pattern. My pious old grandfather explained that this loose plastic skin was "a wise dispensation of Almighty Providence" to enable the Bushman to eat more food at one feasting than any man in the history of mankind had ever eaten before. His life as a hunter made it of vital importance that he should be able to store great reserves of food in his body. As a result, his stomach, after he had eaten to capacity, made even a man look like a pregnant woman. In a good hunting season his figure was like that of a Rubens' Cupid, protruding in front and even more behind. Yes, that was another of the unique characteristics of this original little Bushman body. It had a behind which served it rather as the hump serves the camel! In this way nature enabled him to store a reserve of valuable fats and carbo-hydrates against dry and hungry moments. I believe the first scientific term I ever learned was the name anatomists gave to this phenomenon of the Bushman body: "steatopygia." One night by the fireside I seem to remember my grandfather and the oldest of my aunts saying that in a lean time the Bushman behind would shrink until it was much like any normal behind except for the satiny creases where his smooth buttocks joined his supple legs. But in a good hunting season it would stick out so much that you could stand a bottle of brandy with a tumbler on it! We all laughed at this, not derisively but with affectionate pride and wonder that our native earth should have produced so unique a little human body. Somehow, my heart and imagination were deeply concerned with this matter of the Bushman's shape. The Hottentots, who were very like him, much as I loved them, could not excite my spirit as did the Bushman. They were too big. The Bushman was just right. There was magic in his build. Whenever my mother read us a fairy-tale with a little man performing wonders in it, he was immediately transformed in my imagination into a Bushman. Perhaps this life of ours, which begins as a quest of the child for the man, and ends as a journey by the man to rediscover the child, needs a clear image of some child-man, like the Bushman, wherein the two are firmly and lovingly joined, in order that our confused hearts may stay at the centre of their brief round of departure and return.

But the Bushman's appetite, shape and steatopygia were, though remarkable, by no means the only unique features of his body. His colour, I was told, was unlike that of any other of the many peoples of Africa, a lovely Provençal apricot yellow. The old Basuto I have quoted told me that one most remarkable thing about the Bushman was that although he wore no clothes his skin never burned dark in the sun. He moved in the glare and glitter of Africa with a flame-like flicker of gold like a fresh young Mongol of the central Mongolian plain. His cheeks, too, were high-boned like a Mongol's and his wide eyes so slanted that some of my ancestors spoke of him as a "Chinese-person." There is a great plain between blue hills in South Africa called to this day the Chinese Vlakte after the Bushman hunters who once inhabited it. His eyes were of the deep brown I have mentioned, a brown not seen in any other eye except in those of the antelope. It was clear and shone like the brown of day on a rare dewy African morning, and was unbelievably penetrating and accurate. He could see things at a distance where other people could discern nothing, and his powers of vision have become part of the heroic legend in Africa. The shape of the face tended to be heart-like, his forehead broad and chin sensitive and pointed. His ears were Pan-like, finely made and pointed. His hair was black and grew in thick round clusters which my countrymen called, with that aptitude for scornful metaphor they unfailingly exercised on his behalf, "peppercorn hair." His head was round, neatly and easily joined to a slender neck and throat on broad shoulders. His nose tended to be broad and flat, the lips full and the teeth even and dazzlingly white. His lips were narrow and, as my aunt said, "Lord, verily it has been a beautiful thing to see him move!"

But perhaps the most remarkable thing about the Bushman was his originality. Even in the deepest and most intimate source of his physical being he was made differently from other men. The women were born with a natural little apron, the so-called *tablier égyptien*, over their genitals; the men were born, lived and died with their sexual organs in a semi-erect position. The Bushman found dignity in this fact and made no attempt falsely to conceal it. Indeed he accepted it so completely, as the most important difference between himself and other men, that he gave his people the name of *Qhwai-xkhwe* which openly proclaims this fact. The sound of natural relish that the word *qhwai-xkhwe* makes on his lips is a joy to hear, and the click of the complex consonants flashes on his tongue as he utters them like a sparkle of sun on a burst of flower from our sombre mountain gorse. He has even painted himself all over the rocks of Africa in naked silhouette plainly demonstrating this distinguishing feature of his race, not with the obscene intent which some European archaeologists have projected into him, but simply because his God, with care aforethought, in the great smithy of Africa had forged him naked and unashamed just like that.

Only one thing seems really to have worried the Bushman regarding his stature and that was his size. Often I have been impressed by the extraordinary energy of revolt I have encountered in the spirit of many little men and have seen something of its exacting consequences in their own and other lives. Nor have I forgotten how disastrously this revolt can be orchestrated in the complexes and policies of whole races. When a prisoner of war of the Japanese, I was punished at times, I am certain, for no other reason than that I was often taller than those who had me in their power. Yet I have a suspicion that the Bushman's reaction to his smallness was of a different kind and brought about solely by his helplessness to repel the ruthless invasion of his country by men so much taller than he—men who seemed, in fact, so tall that he painted them on the rocks like giants! There was no doubt in the minds of those who had known him that his spirit was raw and vulnerable regarding his size. According to my mother's elder sister, our favourite aunt (who could count up to ten in Bushman and utter his formal greeting for our delight, although she invariably went dangerously purple in the process), it was fatal to remark on the Bushman's smallness in his presence. More, it was often perilous to show in one's bearing that one was aware of dealing with a person smaller than oneself.

Our old 'Suto hands strongly supported my aunt with their own colourful illustrations. They said they had always been warned never to show any surprise if they unexpectedly came upon a Bushman in the veld in case he took it to imply they could have seen him sooner had he not been so small. When, unexpectedly, one ran into a Bushman, the only wise thing to do was promptly to blame oneself for the surprise and say, "Please do not look so offended. Do you really imagine a big person like you could hide without being seen? Why we saw you from a long way off and came straight here!" Immediately the fire in those shining eyes would die down, the golden chest expand enormously, and gracefully he would make one welcome. In fact, the oldest of the old Basutos once told me one could not do better than use the Bushman's own greeting, raising one's open right hand high above the head, and calling out in a loud voice, "*Tshjamm:* Good day! I saw you looming up afar and I am dying of hunger." Europeans so often use a diminutive for that which they want to endear. But with the Bushman this mechanism is reversed. The pitiless destructive forces sent against him by fate seemed to mock his proportions until he sought perhaps to appease his sense of insecurity with a wishful vision of a physical superlative he never possessed. So, in his rock paintings the Bushman depicts himself in battle as a giant against other giants to such a degree that, were it not for his *qhwai-xkhwe,* he would be hardly distinguishable from his towering enemies.

But, I was told, this little man before all else was a hunter. He kept no cattle, sheep or goats except in rare instances where he had been in prolonged contact with foreigners. He did not cultivate the land and therefore grew no food. Although everywhere his women and children dug the earth with their deft grubbing sticks for edible bulbs and roots and, in season, harvested veld and bush for berries and fruit, their lives and happiness depended mainly on the meat which he provided. He hunted in the first place with bow and arrow and spear. The heads of his arrows were dipped in a poison compounded from the grubs, roots and glands of the reptiles of the land, and he himself had such a respect for the properties of his own poison that he never went anywhere without the appropriate antidote in a little skin wallet tied securely to his person. My grandfather and aunt said that he was so natural a botanist and so expert an organic chemist that he used different poisons on different animals, the strongest for the eland and the lion, and less powerful variants for the smaller game. His arrow points were made of flint or bone until he came to barter for iron with those about to become his enemies.

As an archer he was without equal. My grandfather said he could hit a moving buck at 150 yards, adding that he would not have liked to expose any part of himself in battle to a Bushman archer under 150 yards' range. But he not only hunted with bow and arrow. In the rivers and streams he constructed traps beautifully woven out of reeds and buttressed with young karree wood or *harde-kool* (the "hard-coal" wood my ancestors used in their nomadic smithy fires) and so caught basketfuls of our lovely golden bream, or fat olive-green barbel with its neck and huge head of bone and moustaches, greased and pointed like those of "a soldier of the Victorian Queen." The baskets at the end of the traps were like the eel-baskets of Europe but never so bleakly utilitarian. They were woven of alternate white and black plaits not because they were better that way but, my aunt said with great emphasis, because the Bushman wanted to make them pretty. Hard by, among the singing reeds, he dug pits with a cunningly covered spike in the centre in order to trap the nocturnal hippopotamus, whose sweet lard meant more to him than *foie gras* to any gourmet.

When my grandfather first crossed the Orange River, or the Great River as the Bushman and we who were born close always called it, there were still many of those big game-pits left. The trekkers, or covered-wagon pioneers of my people, kept patrols of horsemen scouting well ahead of the lumbering convoys to look out for these holes and, on a signal, someone would go to the front of the large span of oxen and lifting the lead rope from the horns of the two guide-oxen, march carefully at their head. My grandfather often said he wished he had a dollar for every mile he had led his span by the head through the veld. Once in very early childhood, on one of our spring hunting and fishing excursions in the deep bed of the Great River, I saw some of those holes. The spikes in the centre and the top cover were gone, but I remember the sensation of wonder that came over me as one of the elder men said, "That's how he did it! That's how fat old tannie sea-cow found her way into the pot." "Old tannie sea-cow" was our endearing way of naming the hippopotamus, so called because it was there in the surf of the sea to welcome my people when they first landed in Africa. Between the sea and the Great River of my childhood lay hundreds of difficult miles, and it was impossible to find a place of water and reeds not associated in local legend and story with the sea-cow. However, long before this day of which I am speaking, "fat little old aunt sea-cow" had vanished like the Bushman who had so admired her waistline and so loved her lard.

In the tracks between water-holes and rivers the Bushman spread snares of tough home-made rope. The snares, according to my grandfather, were made of several kinds but the favourite was the classical hangman's noose. The noose was spread round the rim of a hole delicately covered over with grass and sand. Its end was tied to a tense spring made of the fiercely resilient stem of blue-bush wood. This stem was doubled over into the sand and so triggered that, however deft a buck's toe or crafty a leopard's paw, the merest touch would release the spring. The noose would instantly be jerked tight and the straightened stem hang the lively animal in the air by paw or throat.

So skilful and confident a hunter did the Bushman become that he did not hesitate to match himself in the open against the biggest and the thickest-skinned animals. For instance my grandfather said he would provoke the male by darting in and out of a herd of elephant, or teasing the smaller crashes of rhinoceros, relying only on his knowledge of their ways and his own supple limbs for survival. He would contrive to do this until an angry elephant bull or some never very enlightened rhinoceros father would charge out to deal with him. Twisting and turning and shrieking a charm of magic words, the Bushman would flee until the animal was involved in a baffling pursuit. Then a companion could run up behind, unperceived, to attack the only place where such a rampant animal was vulnerable to Stone Age weapons. Smartly he would slice through the tendons above the heel. The animal now helpless on its haunches, the Bushman could close in to finish him off with spears and knives.

On top of his great daring and resource as a hunter, he was also subtle. That was a quality stressed by all those who had known him. He never seems to have attempted to accomplish by force what could be achieved by wit. The emphasis in his own natural spirit was on skill rather than violence. I can remember my grandfather saying with a note of admiration, if not envy, strangely alive on his pious Calvinist tongue, "Yes! he was clever, diabolically clever." The Bushman would, for example, use the lion as his hunting dog. When his normal methods of hunting failed him he would frighten the game in the direction of a hungry lion. He would let the lion kill and eat only enough to still its hunger but not enough to make it lazy. Then the Bushman would drive the lion off with smoke and fire and move in to eat the rest of the kill. In this way he would follow a favourite lion about from kill to kill and it was extraordinary how he and the lion came to respect their strange partnership. My grandfather said there was something uncanny about it. He remembered, too, his father telling him that when they first felt their way into the country across the Great River they found that all the lions were man-eaters. The many thousands of dead bodies left on the veld after a generation of massacre and counter-massacre by Koranna, Griquas, Mantatees, Zulu, Matabele and Barolong had given the lions such a taste for human flesh that they ignored the herds of game whenever it was possible to go after human prey. Yet oddly enough they never seemed to go after the Bushmen. It was said that the Bushmen smeared themselves with an ointment whose smell so offended the lions' sensitive nose that it would not come near them. But whatever the reason the Bushmen would come and go fearlessly and unscathed through lion country wherein a man armed with a gun was barely safe.

My aunt was more impressed by the Bushman's way with the ostrich. She said he used it, without its knowledge, as his hen and chicken. He never cleared a nest of all its eggs but always left one for the bird. When I asked the reason she said the Bushman knew that the ostrich, although the greatest in size of all birds was also the stupidest, and so unless he left one egg in the nest to remind it what it was supposed to be doing, it would forget its job and stop laying! She also gave me wonderful imitations of how the hunter covered himself with the wings and feathers of a dead ostrich and then, with the neck and head of the bird held erect by a stick, set out to stalk a flock of birds with inevitable success.

But perhaps my favourite of all the Bushman stories came from a very old 'Chuana cattle-herder who had been raised in superb giraffe country. I remember him today mainly for two reasons: for the beating I got from one of my elder brothers because one day I addressed that crumpled old body directly by his first name and omitted the respectful "old father" which should have preceded it; and also for this story. The Bushman, this old father told me, knew only too well that all giraffe were women at heart, utterly inquisitive and completely incapable of resisting a pretty thing. Moreover the

Bushman knew from long experience what hard and thank-
less work it could be stalking one who looked down on life
from so great a height and out of such far-seeing eyes. So he
thought up a wonderful plan. He took out a glittering magic
stone he always carried on him and crawled into a bush which
was just in sight of a troop of giraffe. He held the stone in
his hand in the sun at the side of the bush, constantly turning
it in the bright light so that the giraffe could not fail to see it.
At first they thought nothing of it, dismissing it as a sparkle
of sun on dew or an effect of the mirage of the heat-mounting
distortion and hallucination in the quicksilver light of day.
But as the sun climbed higher and this sparkle followed them,
so prettily, wherever they moved, they began to get curious.
"And there, little master," the old father would always exclaim, "the fat was in the fire!" I could see the giraffe, vivid
in the mirror of the old man's words, their timid hearts, despite all their other instincts and whatever they had of reason
in their shapely Victorian heads, drawn slowly toward the
concealed hunter. They would come so near that the Sche-
herazade pattern in the silk of their clothes would be distinct
and visible, and their wide slanted eyes, perhaps the loveliest
of all animal eyes in the world, would shine behind their long
dark lashes like wild honey deep within the comb. For a moment they would stand there in the hypnotic sparkle of so unusual and pretty a thing—and then the Bushman would send
his arrows trembling like tuning forks into the tender place
below the shoulder because, much as he loved the lard of "fat
little old aunt sea-cow," he loved more the marrow in the
long giraffe bone.

Yet with all this hunting, snaring and trapping, the Bushman's relationship with the animals and birds of Africa was
never merely one of hunter and hunted; his knowledge of the
plants, trees and insects of the land, never just the knowledge
of a consumer of food. On the contrary, he knew the animal

and vegetable life, the rocks and the stones of Africa as they
have never been known since. Today we tend to know statis-
tically and in the abstract. We classify, catalogue and sub-
divide the flame-like variety of animal and plant according to
species, sub-species, physical property and use. But in the
Bushman's knowing, no matter how practical, there was a
dimension that I miss in the life of my own time. He knew
these things in the full context and commitment of his life.
Like them, he was utterly committed to Africa. He and his
needs were committed to the nature of Africa and the swing
of its wide seasons as a fish to the sea. He and they all participated so deeply of one another's being that the experience
could almost be called mystical. For instance, he seemed to
know what it actually felt like to be an elephant, a lion, an
antelope, a steenbuck, a lizard, a striped mouse, mantis, baobab
tree, yellow-crested cobra or starry-eyed amaryllis, to mention only a few of the brilliant multitudes through which he
so nimbly moved. Even as a child it seemed to me that his
world was one without secrets between one form of being
and another. As I tried to form a picture of what he was
really like, it came to me that he was back in the moment
which our European fairy-tale books described as the time
when birds, beasts, plants, trees and men shared a common
tongue, and the whole world, night and day, resounded like
the surf of a coral sea with universal conversation.

I do not want to trouble a picture of the beginnings with
wisdom after the event. But I am trying to articulate now
what was then too deep for the powers of expression of a
boy on the veld. What drew me so strongly to the Bushman
was that he appeared to belong to my native land as no other
human being has ever belonged. Wherever he went he contained, and was contained, deeply within the symmetry of the
land. His spirit was naturally symmetrical because moving in
the stream of the instinctive certainty of belonging he re-

mained within his fateful proportions. Before we all came to
shatter his natural state, I have never found true evidence that
he exceeded his proportions. His killing, like the lion's, was
innocent because he killed only to live. He never killed for
fun or the sake of killing, and even when doing it, was curiously apprehensive and regretful of the deed. The proof of
all this is there in his paintings on his beloved rock for those
who can see with their hearts as well as their eyes. There the
animals of Africa still live as he knew them and as no European or Bantu artist has yet been able to render them. They
are there not as quarry for his idle bow or food for his
stomach but as companions in mystery, as fellow pilgrims
travelling on the same perilous spoor between distant life-
giving waters. And there is proof, too, of the balance and
rough justice of his arrangements in the fact that when my
ancestors landed on the southern tip of the continent three
hundred years ago, Africa was nearly bursting its ancient
seams with riches of life not found in any other land on earth.
Even I, who came on the scene so long after the antique lock
was picked and the treasure largely plundered, can still catch
my breath at the glimpses I get, from time to time, of the
riches that remain. Whenever I do so, one vision of the little
hunter, who alone is missing from the privileged scene,
comes urgently to my mind because it illustrates with delicacy
as well as clarity what I am trying to convey of his poignant
standing with nature.

The Bushman loved honey. He loved honey with a passion
that we, with a sweet-shop on every corner, cannot hope to
understand. Bitterness is to the tongue what darkness is to the
eye; darkness and bitterness are forms of one another. And the
taste of honey to the Bushman was like the light of the fire to
his eye, and the warmth of its ruby flame in the black night of
Africa. His bees' nests, like his springs and water-holes, were
almost the only things in the land about which he felt posses-

sive. He cared for the wild nests and collected his honey from
them in such a way that the bees were not disturbed. He knew
how to calm and secure a swarm on the wing, and his nests
were passed down from father to son. One of the many tragic
sights of the closing phase of his history in the country
wherein I was born was the reappearance, at odd moments, in
the bed and valleys of the Great River of some wrinkled old
Bushman body come from afar to harvest the honey passed on
to him by a line of ancestors, only to be shot down in his efforts by some Griqua or European invader. Indeed, the taste
of the honey on his tongue drove the Bushman to do many
reckless things. He would scale great cliffs to get at honey in
places where only "the people who sit on their heels" (as is
his dignified name for the baboons) would dare to go. I had
one such place pointed out to me which I would not have attempted without rope and climbing boots. Yet the Bushman
had climbed it regularly on bare hands and feet, driving pegs
of wood for a grip into the fissures of the cliff face. At the
top he had only a narrow ledge on which to stand while he
made his special herbal smoke to drug the bees before he
dared reach out for the honey in the hole in the damp overhanging rocks. For the wild bees of Africa are the most formidable bees I have ever encountered. They are smaller than
most but quick, fearless and quite unpredictable. In the village
where I was born no hive was allowed by special by-law
within four miles of the township because one sleepy summer's afternoon all the bees had carried out a combined oper-
ation against everything that moved in the streets and sun-
filled courtyards and paddocks. I have forgotten the precise
extent of the casualty list, but I remember there were two
little coloured boys, pigs, hens, sheep, goats, dogs and several
horses among the dead. To this day the bees, the mosquito and
the tsetse fly are among the stoutest defenders of ancient
rights in Africa. They resent strangers, black as much as

white. But for the Bushman they had no such antipathy. They appear to have known from his colour and his smell that he too was part of the necessity of Africa and to have stung him only perfunctorily, as if merely to save their sensitive, jet-eyed and oddly oriental little faces!

Whenever some disaster overwhelmed his bees the Bushman would set out to look for a new swarm. He would be up early in the morning, hoping to find the black water-carrier bees among the dew, and with his eyes would follow them and their silver burden in the slanted light back to their base. Or he would stand still in some fragrant spot at sunset, comforted by the tall shadow beside him, and wait for an illumination of wings to draw a bee-line home. It was quite unbelievable, my aunt said, how far those slanted, oddly Mongolian eyes of his could follow the flight of a bee. Long after the European or black man lost sight of it he would still be there marking the flight. When he failed to follow the bee he would go to the spot where the bee had vanished, mark the place, returning the next day and thereafter as long as was necessary to determine the exact whereabouts of the swarm. But most wonderful of all, he had an ally in a little bird called *Die Heuning-wyser*, the honey-diviner, who loved honey as much as did the Bushman. It always had its bright little eyes wide open for a nest, and whenever it found a swarm at work it would come streaking back, its little wings whirring and starry in the shadows of the trees, to tell the Bushman of its discovery.

"Quick! Quick! Quick! Honey! Quick!" it would sing at the Bushman from the nearest bush, flapping its wings imperiously in the trembling air. "Quick! Quick!"

At once the Bushman would understand the bird's excited chatter and hasten to reassure it with a melodious call of his own: "Look, oh person with wings! Gathering my things and following thee quickly I come."

When at last he had drawn his amber ration he would never fail to reward the bird with honey and, on a point of mutual honour, share with it the royal portion of the harvest: a comb as creamy as the milk of Devon with its own cream made of half-formed grubs.

And there I must leave them in this moment of fair exchange and communion. I shall return later to the Bushman's relationship with the bees and birds and the significant role which honey and the bubbling mead he made from it plays in his spirit. But this seemed to belong here because it came to me in the very beginning, breaking out of the darkness of the past like moon-sparkle blown by the night wind from some startled water, a portion of the glory the Bushman trailed in his nakedness from the God and Africa that were his home.

Now, one of the many arguments used by his enemies to show that this little hunter and seeker after honey was really a very inferior person, was precisely the fact that he was utterly dependent on nature. He built no home of any durable kind, did not cultivate the land and did not even keep cattle or other domestic chattel, and this seemed to prove to his enemies that he was a human "untouchable" and not far removed from the beasts of the veld. The Hottentot, a devout pastoralist, the Bantu who was both pastoralist and tiller of the soil, and of course the white man were all rated much higher than the Bushman. Now, it is true that the shelters the Bushman built for himself when on the move after game were of the lightest possible structure. Home, for the greater part of the year, was wherever he made a major kill. Nonetheless, he had a permanent base on which his whole life swung. In my own part of the country he built round walls of stone on top of the hills near his permanent waters. The walls were from four to five feet high and, according to the local tradition, without opening or roof of any kind. At night he would merely climb over the wall, light a fire and cook his food out of the wind, and then curl up by the coals under a blanket of skin. Long after he had vanished from the land it was possible to see, within some crumbling circle of stone, the scorched earth and blackened pebbles where his fires had burned for centuries. Close by was the hollow he had scratched in the ground to ease the lying for his hips and which was the only bed he ever inherited from his fathers, or passed on to his sons.

I was shown the site of such a permanent base as soon as I could scramble up a hill. It was on the top of the hills at the back of the homestead on my grandfather's immense farm. The lovely place was made more attractive for me by its evocative name: Boesmansfontein, "the Fountain (or spring) of the Bushman." This name it possessed already when my grandfather bought the property, so casually, from its Griqua robbers nearly a century ago, and is enough to show that the fountain once was the permanent water of a Bushman. It came gushing out of the earth in a cleft overgrown and purple with the shadow of blue-bush, karree tree, wild poplar and African willow. It was unique among the springs in the area because it gushed simultaneously out of what we called "three-eyes," that is to say it had three distinct round openings for the urgent crystal water. The water was sweet and bubbled in the light with a noticeable rhythm, as if somewhere within the earth a caring heart was beating to pump it up to us. As a child who had participated already from birth in my native country's perennial anxieties about water, I never looked at it without feeling that I was in the presence of an Old Testament miracle. Yet, more unusual still, barely a quarter of a mile away the water of the spring joined naturally with other permanent waters in the bed of a stream always musical with bird-song and well clothed in silky reeds and tasselled rushes. This stream had the provocative name of Knapsack River, but it remains one of the minor disappointments of my life that I have never discovered the answer to the question, "Whose knapsack?" About six miles of this water flowed through my grandfather's farm and both it and the three-eyed fountain made the hills behind an apt site for a permanent Bushman base. It was far enough from the waters not to frighten the game from drinking there, and high enough for the Bushman to observe the movement of the buck below in the plains between the lone blue hills which we called vlaktes, and also to allow him to watch the passes against timely signs of invasion. There the Bushman certainly had neighbours to read his signals of smoke, to join in his celebrations and help in his troubles.

I remember when I first stood in the broken circle of stone on top of the highest hill, the permanent waters were pointed out to me. In the east, renowned for its bream and barbel and flashing with light, lay the Long Pool, and not far behind it rose the ridge of red rock on the edge of a pan of water at a place called Setting Sun. In the north, fifteen miles away, a long hill, which rose to the horizon against a sky so polished and shining that the hill's reflection stood upside down upon its own summit, marked the water called the Fountain of the Shooting, so named after some forgotten incident of our turbulent history. To the west, twenty-five miles away, a pinnacle of rock threw a clear shadow on the edge of the land's sudden drop into the deep bed of the Great River. Between me and the shadow rose a spire of devout poplar on the rim of the famous water Great Fountain; to the south-west, a bare three miles away, but blue already with distance, was a cloud of green curling over the place called Three Fountains; and due south was a glitter of the water dammed close to the Merchant's Fountain. There were other waters in the vicinity as well.

Watching the gypsy swing and flicker of the brilliant buck that remained in the plains mingling with the respectable huddles of imported sheep and cattle in their foreign wool and calico, the view was enough even for a child to realize how well the land had suited the little hunter. And yet there were other places that suited him better still. Wherever possible, he preferred to make his home under some huge overhanging rocks, the more inaccessible the better; or best of all, within the many caves such as those found not far from my home in the foothills of the Mountains of the Night, the gorges of the Great River and other cataclysmic rifts in the Dragon ranges.

There the Bushman felt at his safest. There his culture had its greatest continuity and flowering, and there he came to produce the purest form of a truly organic art the continent has yet known. There, too, when he had leisure from hunting and hunger, he made his music. No African music, so I was told from all sides, could compare with Bushman music. He had drums, rattles, stringed instruments from a single-stringed fiddle to a harp with four strings. For sounding boxes, he clamped the shell of the small veld tortoises on his single-stringed instruments; and for the equivalent of cello and bass violin he used the shell of our big, dark, mountain tortoises. To this day I am moved by the thought that a tortoise, also, was the inspiration of our European surrealist violins and cellos. For wind instruments the Bushman had flutes made out of a lesser bamboo that grew in our plains and river backwaters, and he played also, I was told, a double pipe like the authentic pipes of Pan. He had no bells, but he made a mould of stiff leather shaped like a bell with a stone clapper inside, tied it to his ankles and wrists, and so beat time to the music of his orchestras. He loved music for all occasions, even for games, and if there is truth in the suggestion that a culture expresses itself most creatively by stimulating in men the instinct to play, then this little man with his variety of games and complex music puts many other so-called "superior" cultures to shame.

But, above all, music served his dancing. He was born a

dancer and had a dance for everything. He danced birth; he danced adolescence; he danced his marriage and many another event of life and spirit; he danced the sun leaping into the sky; he danced for the moon under the moon; and finally he danced out the agony of dying. From all I was told, it seemed that he came alive in a different way when the sun went down, for he sang and danced the night through with a passion and energy which we could not hope to imitate. In that respect, too, I noticed he remained with us. Every night when our coloured servants withdrew to the far side of the stream which, by law, divided us after dark, instead of going to the rest which they had amply earned, they would invariably gather and dance and sing with a glitter that shone like burnt silver in the darkness around my bed. They would dance till the early hours of the morning even though they knew the difficulties wherein it landed them. I believe in that way alone could they endure our exacting presence and keep alive in their blood the natural Bushman which our wilful way of living inhibited in them by day.

In those caves and underneath those overhanging rocks, too, the Bushman told some of the greatest of his stories. I shall have to deal with this aspect of his spirit more fully later, so that it is enough to stress here how mistaken is the common assumption that literature exists only where there is a system of writing. Literature, surely, exists wherever the living word is spoken. All Africans, and the Bushman in particular, possess a great spoken literature of their own. To our everlasting reproach we know only the merest fragment of this meaningful activity in the little hunter's spirit, but there is no doubt that stories and story-telling were one of the great rewarding loves of his life. The proof of it is with me still in such stories as I know, as it was there in the light which burned suddenly in the dim accepting eyes of the old people who had once known the Bushman when I begged them to recall him telling his stories, even though the theme was sometimes beyond their power of recall.

But above all, on those walls of stone and among those rocks the Bushman engraved and painted. In this he was truly unique and assumed his full adult stature. All the races of Africa had some music, some dancing and their own special scheme of "literature." But none appear to have had this astonishing gift of painting. The Bushman seems to have discovered this rare visual talent very early in his history, how early it is impossible accurately to say. The estimates which experts have made of the age of the oldest of his paintings in southern Africa vary from 8000 B.C. to 1300 A.D., but there is circumstantial evidence to suppose that he may have been a painter long before then. Indeed, there is a growing feeling that he and the ancient Egyptians, who alone of the peoples attached to Africa practised the visual arts so extensively, together with the palaeolithic painter of the caves of the Dordogne and the Iberian Peninsula, were of the same origins. This feeling exists not merely because of the remarkable resemblances of subject matter and manner between the paintings in the Iberian, Egyptian and southern African worlds, but for other reasons as well. I have already mentioned the delicate matter of his *qhwai-xkhwe* and the *tablier égyptien* of his women. The *tablier égyptien* was so-called because the anatomical phenomenon to which it referred was a noted feature of the shape of the women of ancient Egypt and is referred to in records of the Second Dynasty. The Bushman's steatopygia, too, was shared by the same people, and I myself have noticed in copies of the paintings in the caves of Lascaux the presence of men with his shape and his *qhwai-xkhwe*. But however remote his discovery of painting and however widespread its practice, he appears never to have painted more consistently and better than he did in my part of Africa. Much of his painting has been thoughtlessly destroyed or has crum-

bled away from weather and time. Yet there is so much left
that to this day it is not difficult to imagine its scale before we
and the black man broke into the Bushman world. I myself
from childhood have followed his progress as a painter from
the Cape of Good Hope for about fifteen hundred miles north
into the hills of Rhodesia, and then west from the eastern
spurs of the Dragon ranges and stormy Outeniquas for close
on another fifteen hundred miles to the skeleton coast of the
Atlantic seaboard. Vast as that area is, it is not the whole of his
painter's story, but it is enough to indicate the size of his
practice.

I love my own time too much, and would not have chosen
to live in any other even if that had been possible, yet, if
forced to an alternative, I would choose to be the first European in Africa free to see, before we laid our blind, violent
hands upon it, the vast land glowing from end to end in the
blue of its madonna days, like some fabulous art gallery with
newly restored and freshly painted Bushman canvases of
smooth stone and honey-coloured rock. For so, apparently, it
existed for many centuries. As fast as a painting faded it was
either restored or a new theme painted over it. At the same
time, entirely new pictures were continually added to the
great store. It is astonishing how, in this late hour, they burn
within the aubergine shadows of cave and overhang of cliff
and krans, and what power they still possess to provoke an
almost unbearable nostalgia for the vanished painter and for
the spirit that possessed him. True, their fire is dying and the
ruby coals are blown silver with the ashes of time. But underneath there is enough authentic flame to show the Bushman
and his chosen companions on the enigmatic spoor as, with
mystery of life upon them, they spied out on the far side of
the desert a land of promise for the wandering hosts of God.

In the earliest of these paintings the subjects are almost all
animal. Where space is small the animals are painted singly,

such as the miniature head of a great classic antelope beauty I once saw staring with Byzantine eyes out of a frame of saffron rock on the edge of an old game track in the remote bush. Or, where there is room enough, in battalions, as in the cave above the White Kei River which contains a painting of a troop of 150 springbuck, each one individually appraised and respectfully portrayed; "little old aunt sea-cow"; the long-limbed giraffe with its shapely neck and ladylike droop of shoulder; the elegant blue crane on a mannequin leg; the hammerhead, messenger of death; pythons of a length and stature no more seen; the rhinoceros, angry like a pricked *toro* with the rosette of blood that comes to it in adolescence vivid on the flank; the elephant, Titan of his world; the mantis, incorrigible and indestructible; the lion, royal and unafraid; the leopard prince; the ostrich, great bird cruelly earth-bound for a Promethean sin; the crafty jackal; the star-like lynx and other lesser breeds of cats without the law; the hyena, the werewolf being of the half-light of his world; all varieties of buck and antelope; "the people who sit upon their heels"; these and many more of what the Bushman called not beasts, birds and insects but "persons of the early race" are there still accurately observed, inwardly shared and appreciated. Indeed, I know one painting where a frightened herd of running eland is shown with such a gift of movement that when I first experienced its impact I had the illusion, with all the vividness of reality, of seeing them suddenly charging across the rock and away over the side of the hill.

However, gradually the Bushman himself came to figure in the animal scene. Subjects became more complex and the theme more fully orchestrated. He is there as child, husband, hunter and fighter, his women always in close support. His domestic life and fighting intrude. The bees and honey appear, and he begins to dance. Now an inner vision emerges to join in the demands of the outer. Mysterious shapes in profile, human below, bird or beast above, like the gods of ancient Egypt, stand watching the everyday scene from a corner on the rock, deeply in a cave, or walk catfooted along a ledge on the brink of an abyss. At places of reeds and rushes, mysterious shapes appear, upside down, beneath the rare water. Somewhere in a cool gorge on the edge of a waste sparkling like broken glass in the hissing sun, a white lady, self-possessed, with a flower in her long hand, walks with a high step down a steep wall. Suddenly tall black men are splashed, like giant exclamation marks of printer's ink, all over the northern canvases. The Bushman raises himself to gianthood to meet them. The struggle becomes more desperate. Raid and counter-raid and massacre multiply; the security, inner certainty and sense of sharing that for so long sanctified the stone vanishes. The pools of blood on the rocks steadily grow bigger. A new invader with a gun intrudes on another far frieze of the canvas. In the Mountains of the Night hard by the Great River, paintings of an enemy in red coats and riflemen on horses are briefly seen. Then abruptly the antique art vanishes from the ancient land.

I wish I could present it in greater detail, but I have Bushman proportions to observe, and only enough is permitted here to give answer to the question posed in the beginning: What sort of a person was the Bushman? His paintings show him clearly to be illuminated with spirit; the lamp may have been antique, but the oil is authentic and timeless, the flame was well and tenderly lit. Indeed, his capacity for love shows up like fire on a hill at night. He, alone of all the races of Africa, was so much of its earth and innermost being that he tried constantly to glorify it by adoring its stones and decorating its rocks with painting. We other races went through Africa like locusts devouring and stripping the land for what we could get out of it. The Bushman was there solely because he belonged to it. Accordingly he endeavoured in many ways to express this feeling of belonging, which is love, but the greatest of them was in the manner of his painting.

The significance of all this, of course, did not escape the attention of his enemies. I repeat, their justification for exterminating him was always that he was no better than an animal. Whenever they captured him they called the process of bending him to their will "taming" him, just as if he were really a wild animal. As a child, over and over again I would hear the old people exclaim, the unpleasant ones with a terrifying bitterness and the others with an unwilling note of real regret, "But you see he just would not be tame!" Everything we did to him was excused on the grounds that he was a grossly inferior person impeding the progress of greatly superior races. As I see it, nothing throws that excuse more firmly back into the narrow lap of our conscience than his painting. An attempt even has been made to prove that he was not, after all, the painter of the caves and art engraver of the iron stone plates of my country. We are told they were the work of another people suppressed in their turn by the Bushman. This is argued with an obstinacy that would seem inexplicable did one not know how great and complex must be the private stirring of unrecognized conscience behind the specialized clamour. But apart from the mass of circumstantial evidence, there is the weight of European and Bantu tradition, eye witness accounts of persons who knew the Bushman, and, to me most important of all, the Bushman's word. The greathearted and dedicated George William Stow, to whom we owe so much of the little organized knowledge we have of the Bushman, collected much moving evidence from old survivors who, whenever he showed them one of his superb copies of cave paintings, expressed great delight and called them "their paintings," "their own paintings," the paintings of "their nation." Stow also tells how the last of the Bushman painters was shot down in a raid in the Basuto hills and picked up dead with a zebra thong round his middle to which were attached ten little horns, each filled with a different-coloured paint. The anecdote stirred me deeply when I first read it because there seemed to be a significant validity between it and an experience of my own childhood. Someone in my grandparents' family came back as a youth from a raid against the Bushman in the hills of the Great River with an account of how he had seen one of the dead with a dozen similar little horns strapped to his middle.

His critics also make much of the theory that he was not the first man of our land. Our uneasy national conscience, of course, would be relieved if it could be proved that the Bushman was not the orginal inhabitant but merely another invader like the black man and ourselves. Since the world is full of specialists who will seize on the discovery of yet another prehistoric half-bone to demolish the theories of our beginnings, as Samson did the jaw-bone of an ass to destroy the Philistines, they do not lack support. Other peoples and other cultures, they say, preceded the Bushman. Who knows but that they may well be right in a continent as old, vast and inscrutable as Africa? But I myself, being neither scientist nor specialist, have never been tempted to carry the argument beyond acknowledgement of its possibility. The point for me is over-refined. Whoever may have come before the Bushman in my native land, he is unremembered and, for all his magic, is now at one with the abundant dust which stains the African west ever redder at dusk. For me always, the fact of urgent practical consequence was the fact that the Bushman, unlike any possible predecessors, was a remembered, and remembering and living, link with human origin in my native land. Alive and living, he was accepted as the oldest inhabitant of the land.

When I was a child, no one among those who had known him doubted it. Many went further and said, as some specialists tend to agree today, that he was the hunter of palaeolithic

Iberia and shared a common ancestor with the ancient Egyptians. Apart from the evidence of his *qhwai-xkhwe, tablier égyptien* and painting, they quoted Herodotus's significant references to a "little people of adroit bow-and-arrow hunters" in the Libyan hinterland. They believed he was driven out of the Mediterranean and North African worlds many thousands of years ago by migratory hordes of stronger races from the East. Some even held firmly that he was the aboriginal of the Mediterranean world, the primordial prototype of the little man in European folk-lore and not only the first man of Africa but the oldest form of human life left in the world. I know for certain only that, whatever happened, no living evidence can prove that the Bushman had not always been in Africa. Indeed, one of the oldest traditions of history in Africa proclaims the origin of races to be in the far north with a subsequent and protracted period of migration of men south. The pattern of the tradition may be confused with eddies and swirls of terrified peoples doubling back or fanning out round obstacles east and west until they reach the oceans. But the broad flow of humanity was inexorably south, like burning lava sinking slowly from violent eruption down a volcanic slope into a broad plain.

I have yet to meet the African race or tribe that can say, "Here, where you see our people now, we have been since the beginning of memory." Everywhere tribal legend and history point to a remote beginning north and then a perilous descent into the blue and enigmatic south. There seems to have been only one exclusion from the tradition: the Bushman. In this, as in all else, he appears with ironic consistency to be the uncompromising outsider. Even the Hottentot, one of the oldest inhabitants in Africa and so close to the Bushman that my ancestors were, for long, confused into mistaking one for the other, is joined firmly in the common tradition. This is all the more remarkable considering the Hottentot had trav-

elled so far ahead of the descending hordes that when the
first Europeans landed at the Cape of Good Hope he was already in partial possession of the southern tip of the African
continent and already beginning to feel his way back north
along the East Coast. Centuries of destructive contact with
Europe, sustained effort by missionaries to reshape his mind
and spirit, and not a little intermarriage, did not shake the
Hottentot's version of his beginnings somewhere in the far
north. I came across an example of this once very early in
childhood.

When I was a child, every day a very old man came to our
home for food. As I sat in front of the old man, in a patch of
acacia shade which trembled like stricken water in the flaming
dust of our white-walled courtyard crackling with noonday
fire, I seem to remember someone saying behind me, "He
must be a hundred and ten if he is a day." To me, at that age,
the thought of a whole year between one birthday and
another was almost unendurable; that of a hundred and more,
like the numbers of sparks of dust wherein we sat, unimaginable. But the heart of a child is naturally antique and I needed
no arithmetic to know that history was alive and sanctified in
the bent body and unbelievably creased and wrinkled face
before me. He lived in a hut a mile away among the hundreds
of black and coloured peoples excluded by law from our
midst. Though he got up every day as soon as the sun was
warm, it took him from then until noon to get to us in time
for the midday meal, which my mother ("the Little Lamb,"
as he and we all called her) ordered for him daily to the day
of his death, out of her love for him and the indigenous past of
her country that he represented. He himself was a Griqua and
a descendant of one of the main branches of the Hottentot
race. They were moving, in their nomadic way, in the vicinity of the Cape of Good Hope when my ancestors landed
there, and were among the first to clash vainly with the

Europeans as they began to push ruthlessly inland. This old man's mind was still clear, and though he spoke no English he could repeat a hymn learned, parrot-like, from a great missionary divine nearly a hundred years before. Although his brown, slanted eyes were already blue with distance and his voice blurred, he spoke with authority, as one who never forgot that he was nephew of the last of the fantastic Griqua leaders who had appeared suddenly at the end of their ancient peoples' term of history, crowding the scene with the desperate profusion and brilliance of dream figures in a travellers' uneasy sleep toward morning.

Children very early on in life learn to mistrust the addiction of their elders to masterful pronouncements of the obvious. Nevertheless, over and over again, because the matter had begun to work on my imagination, I would ask this old Griqua, "But, old father, please, where did the Griquas come from in the very beginning?"

He would invariably turn his head to the side and slowly raise his hand to point to the north with so royal a gesture that, when I looked recently at a snapshot an elder brother had taken of him at the time, I was shocked to be reminded he had always been in rags. Then, calling on the first name of the god-hero of the Hottentots, *Heitse Eibib*, as Griquas invariably did when they were excited or anxious to emphasize the importance of what they were saying, and using in his address to me, the "sire" which his forefathers had picked up from the Huguenots centuries before, he would patiently repeat the old inherited story: "*Heitse*, small little sire, in the beginning the Griquas lived there far, far away. In the beginning, a long, long time ago, the Griquas lived on the other side of a great water and a broad river behind high mountains that blew out smoke."

"Blew out smoke!" I would interrupt, unfailingly startled and excited by the magic evoked in the vision.

"Yes! Small little sire, high mountains that blew out smoke and when angry made a noise like thunder and spat out fire. *Heitse!* I say to you that it was there that we came from in the beginning. I have spoken."

"But then, old father, please go on—how did you come from there?" I would plead, rather desperately because this was how it always seemed to end, the trail of this strange people of copper-coloured skins petering out like an old spoor in the hungry dust. But then the wrinkled face would go dull with the weight of irrevocable Hottentot travail and he would mumble more to himself than to me, "It was a long, long ago that we left there in the beginning. And who is this old Griqua who sits here now dying of hunger? *Heitse*, he is I. Please go and tell the Little Lamb he is I, and I am here."

He would then begin singing his one missionary hymn, less, I suspect, for the comfort he usually sought but rather to drive away from his mind the phantom of nothingness which stood between the long beginning of his race and his shrinking present like one of the ghosts of Africa which, as we all knew, walked not at midnight but noon. He would hardly have reached the end of the first line: "Lord! How does the light fall toward the sea?" before I would interrupt again.

"But the Bushman, old father, please where did he come from? From the same place?"

The word "Bushman" at once alarmed his memory. His voice sharpened and became firm with scorn. He spat into the brilliant dust. "The Bushman! That cursed thing! *Heitse!* He came from nowhere! He was like the tortoise and yellow-throated lizard and springbuck—just always there."

So there, first, I had it. After the Hottentot and the terrible and yet so disarmingly lovable Griqua branch of his race, I spoke to Namaqua mixtures, Koranna, Herero, Ovambo, Mambukush; the many tribes of Bechuana, the Thaba'nchu Barolong, Basuto, Tambuki, Tembu, Batlapin; also to the great warrior races whose names break the silence of the past like the crack of a whip, Amaxosa, Amazulu, Amaswazi, Amongwane, Amampondo; and scores of other subdivisions of the Bantu peoples of my native land. Yet one and all exclaimed, "The Bushman! Why, he was just always there."

Then, more impressive still, where tribal legend and story vanished into the turmoil and confusion of the terrible past, the cool objective evidence sealed in the earth firmly took over. Not far from my home, eight feet below the surface of a great pan, as we call those shallow round depressions in earth and sand encountered all over south-western Africa, the early prospectors for gold and diamonds once found characteristic Bushman beads made out of ostrich-egg shells. The accumulation of earth had been so gradual that numerous layers of shells of minute land animals which no longer exist were interspersed between the beads and the surface of the bed of the pan. The climate, too, had undergone a change since that remote day, for it was clear from the composition of the dry pan that it had not always been enclosed in arid earth but had been part of an immense system of vanished lakes. Again, in a bed of water-gravel, deep in what centuries ago had been the course of the Vaal or Grey River but fifty feet above the present level of the stream, Stow once uncovered unmistakable Bushman relics. I had only to remember how slowly water nibbled into stone to have some idea of the immense antiquity of the Bushman occupation of the land. The evidence was repeated all over the country, and as I grew up confirmed for me the belief to which I have clung gratefully ever since—that there is one thing of which no one can ever deprive the denied and rejected little hunter: the honour of being at the head of those men who have earned a cross for gallant and sustained conduct on active service of life in Africa, when the great campaign was blinder and the issue even more in doubt than in this split Atomic Age.

Chapter 2

THE MANNER OF
THEIR GOING

Barely had the first Europeans landed at the Cape in 1652 with the intention of staying there for good than they clashed with the Bushman. The Hottentot was there too, but warfare against the Hottentot was never quite so deadly. Perhaps the Hottentot was nearer to the invaders in time and therefore not entirely out of reach of their meagre understanding. The European values were so bound up with possessions and other material issues that perhaps they found some common ground in the fact that the Hottentot had an objective idea of property and owned cattle on which he doted. However ruthless their suppression and pursuit of the Hottentot, he was never entirely out of reach of some narrow compromise. But the Bushman apparently was beyond even the most elementary understanding. In the European sense of the word he owned nothing, and therefore was owed nothing. It never occurred to the invaders that he had, perhaps, some rudimentary rights by virtue of being in occupation. As they

pushed steadily inland, took over the vital waters handed on
to the Bushman by his long line of ancestors, killed off the
game which had sustained him unfailingly through the centuries, plundered his honey, destroyed the pastures of his bees,
dispersing the quick swarms, and systematically eliminated not
only the natural amenities of his life but also the necessities of
bare survival, they seem to have found it strange that he should
be angry and embittered and in his turn should resist, kill and
plunder. In fact, one of the most striking ironies of the many
ironic elements at this time is the hurt surprise of the Europeans that the little hunter did not fall flat on his face at their
appearance, like man Friday at the feet of Crusoe, and beg for
the privilege of being their slave. Instead he chose to stand up
and defend himself manfully. As I grew up I looked in vain for
some flicker of conscience in regard to this sombre picture
of our beginnings. If there was a conscience at work it was
submerged in the labyrinthine basement of the Calvinistic spirit
of my people and could be detected only in storms of abuse
and misrepresentation raised against the Bushman. For here
in my native country, too, the ancient law of human nature
holds good. First, one must vilify in one's own spirit what one
is about to destroy in others; and the greater the unadmitted
doubt of the deed within, the greater the fanaticism of the
action without. Ominously, from the start there was nothing
too bad to be said about the Bushman. He was, for instance,
not even a savage—he was no better than a wild animal and
he used such intelligence as he possessed merely to make himself a more dangerous and efficient animal. He was dirty even
beyond the bounds of savagery. This particular charge was
pressed home with great zeal and heat, and I have encountered
it now so often, not only in regard to the Bushman, but also
in regard to the other primitive peoples of Africa, that I could
write an essay on its dubious role in our spirit. However, it
is enough to say here that over and over again I found this

reproach of physical dirt used as a smoke screen to hide the naked humanity of the little hunter from the hearts of those about to crush him with their own inhumanity. Even that was not enough. Other charges made against him were that he was cruel, treacherous, vindictive, utterly useless and a subtle and incorrigible thief. There is no doubt that, in the moment of his final bitterness, deprived of his country, surrounded, doomed in time and with such little life as was left to him abstracted from the long rhythm of his past, the Bushman did do many terrible things to confirm the accusations made against him. My grandfather, when he spoke of the raid organized to kill off the last of the Bushmen in the hills of the Great River, always said with regret, "We could have overlooked the theft of cattle or horses. We knew he, too, had to eat to live. But what we could not forgive was that after taking what he needed he hamstrung all the animals within reach, out of spite, and then left them there, helpless, on the veld for us to shoot." The old Basuto said much the same, adding that the Bushman was always lying in wait for small parties of his people to shoot them down with poisoned arrows or stab them with spears. Invariably he, too, ended with the half-regretful exclamation, "You see, little master, he would not learn. He just wouldn't be tamed."

Yet there is ample evidence from the past that the Bushman was not always so aggressive. Tradition among many of the weaker tribes of southern Africa speaks of him as a generous host and loyal friend. When the first stragglers, fleeing from the vast black hordes pushing down from the north, appeared destitute and afraid in his midst, he gave them asylum. What added to his bitterness was that, almost without exception, the stragglers, when succoured and confident, united with other black men to dispossess and exterminate him. Again, even my own people, when they could begin to recollect the terrible past with some tranquillity, spoke of him as a trustworthy man of his word. I was told, for instance, that in early days the farmers on the frontier would often hand over hundreds of sheep to the Bushmen, who would vanish to graze them in the interior where the Europeans themselves dared not go. Many months later the Bushmen would return with the flock grown into fine condition and every head accounted for. And all for the reward of a little tobacco which the Bushman loved to smoke.

Nor, until invasion made him so, does he appear to have been a particularly quarrelsome and aggressive person. In his own society there were no traditions, legends or stories of great warfare. He seems to have been singularly peaceful, and such skirmishes as he had with close neighbours were rarely more than outbursts of his lively temper. Indeed he loved his ease and fun so much that he did not suffer quarrelsome people in his company unduly, and if they proved impervious to correction he quickly combined with his friends to remove them.

There is evidence, too, that he kept faith under fire, recognized a system of parley and respected, even under the most provocative circumstances, messengers of truce. Finally, even his bitterest enemies were forced reluctantly to admit his immense courage, and to pay belated tribute to the untarnished dignity with which the unwashed little body fought to the end. For me, one of the saddest of all the many tragic things about the Bushman's fate is that no one of stature outside the conflict was moved to defend him. There was no contemporary recognition of his qualities which might have consoled him even if it could not prevent his end. In time the Hottentot and other native races found formidable champions to plead their causes. The little Bushman, with a few exceptions from frontier farmers of my race and one distinguished minister of the Dutch Reformed Church, had no noteworthy champions. The missionaries who came flocking to my country filled with abhorrence of slavery, and fired with the new ideas regarding "the dignity of man" that were setting Europe aflame, hardly gave him a thought. Even the Aborigines Protection Society, which should have been the first to succour the Bushman— for who was aboriginal if he was not?—ironically sponsored missions that made pets of his most ruthless enemies and so contributed to his doom. From first to last he appears to have been abandoned until it must have seemed to him as if he had been abandoned as well by God. Indeed, he fought out his fate in the great ocean of land that had borne him with a depth of loneliness and anguish of spirit akin to that of the Ancient Mariner:

> . . . *this soul hath been*
> *Alone on a wide, wide sea;*
> *So lonely 'twas, that God himself*
> *Scarce seemed there to be.*

I have no intention of going into great detail about the terrible pattern of history woven tightly round the Bushman from the time we landed in Africa up to my grandfather's day 125 years ago. But some particulars are needed to show how the subject seized my emotions as a child. All the odds were against the little man and my sympathies have always been with those who fight back, without losing heart, though all the gods and life itself, seem against them. Our aboriginal hearts know no neutrality: we are all born either Greeks or Trojans. As a boy of six I helped, in my imagination, to man the walls of the doomed city in the Great Plain, for I was born a Trojan. From the start I was on the Bushman's side, and the moment I was old enough to contemplate the full spectacle of our conflict with the little hunter I found myself in passionate revolt against the consequences of the past.

I know it is useless to abstract people and events from the

context of their own time. Perhaps one of the most prolific sources of error in contemporary thinking rises precisely from the popular habit of lifting history out of its proper context and bending it to the values of another age and day. In this way history is never allowed to be itself but is given such a vicarious and negative extension that whole nations, classes and groups of individuals never really live their immediate present but go on repeating a discredited pattern of the past. Nowhere is such a negative entanglement with history greater than in my own country. On one side there are those of my countrymen who have made a determined effort to suppress and falsify the history of the Afrikaner people in order to show our forefathers establishing themselves as saviours in Africa. On the other side they are presented as a race of human monsters from which has sprung a monstrous generation in the present. Neither is right. But I am certain we shall never be free of the destructive aspects of our history until we can honestly look our past in the face and truly see ourselves for what we were: ordinary in our human fallibility, with much that was dishonourable and inadequate in our behaviour as well as a good deal that was brave, upright and lovable. Both black and white peoples could begin so healing an exercise in no better way than by pondering upon the ills we all inflicted on the first little man of Africa. There our mutual records could not be blacker.

While the giant hordes of black races in the far north had already fallen on the Bushman and were driving deeper into the heart of his ancient land along the East and West Coasts as well as down the centre of Africa, we landed at the Cape of Good Hope and seized him in the rear. From that moment it was a war of encroachment from all points of the compass with gathering retaliation on the Bushman's part. He asked for no quarter and was given none. He himself would go with gay defiance into the weighted battle, his quiver full of arrows and another supply handy in a band around his head, from which he deftly sent arrows whistling like a wild pigeon's wing with incredible rapidity at his enemies. They were terrified of his arrows. The old Basutos, who only finished their war of extermination in my grandfather's day, said that a wound from one of the Bushman's arrows unnerved the bravest of their warriors. The terrible pain caused by the poison made them hack with spears and knives at their wounds, slicing through veins and arteries in their panic and merely hastening their own end. This sort of scene is depicted in some of the greatest paintings of the Bushman twilight hour. My own people, thanks to their horses and guns, usually managed to keep out of range and fell only when ambushed. When they stormed the Bushman in his kranses and caves, they usually moved behind a screen made of their saddle-cloths and thick duffel coats. The Bushman never had a chance against them. His only hope lay in a compassion against which the heart of the European and the brutal hour were firmly shut. Yet even when surrounded and cut down by hosts armed with shields, clubs and assegais, or shot at from a safe distance by guns in the hands of a race of un-equalled marksmen, he never asked for mercy. Wounded and bleeding, he fought to the last. Shot through one arm, Stow says, the Bushman would instantly use his knee or foot to enable him to draw his bow with the uninjured arm. If his last arrow was spent he still struggled as best he could until, finding the moment of his end had come, he would hasten to cover his head so that his enemies should not see the agony of dying expressed upon his face. On all sides his enemies had just enough generosity to admit that he died royally. The same instinct which made Charles the First, on his last grey morning in Whitehall, ask for an extra shirt so that he might not shiver with cold and be thought by the crowd to be afraid came to crown also the Bushman's end. What, indeed, could be prouder than the Bushman's reply to young Martin du Plessis, a boy of fourteen who was sent into a great cave in a mountain near my home (blatantly miscalled Genadeberg, "Mountain of Mercy") where the Bushman was surrounded in his last stronghold by a powerful commando. The boy, almost in tears, beseeched him to surrender, promising to walk out in front of him as a live shield against any treacherous bullets. At last, impatient that his refusal was not accepted, the Bushman scornfully said, "Go! Be gone! Tell your chief I have a strong heart! Go! Be gone! Tell him my last words are that not only is my quiver full of arrows but I shall resist and defend myself as long as I have life left. Go! Go! Be gone!"

Again, what could have been more Spartan than his end among the rocks of the projecting shoulder of a great precipice in the Mountains of Snow in the Cape Province where, for the last time, he turned at bay with his kinsmen to face another murder commando. Bushmen, dead and dying, were piled high on a dizzy ledge; others in their death struggle had rolled over the edge and fallen into the deep crags and fissures that surrounded them. Still they resisted. At last only their leader remained, undaunted. Posting himself on the outermost point of the projecting ledge of the precipice, where no man dared to follow him, he defied his pursuers and plied his arrows with immense skill, all the time bearing what seemed to be a charmed life among the bullets flying about him. But inevitably the moment came when he held the last arrow in his bow. A feeling of compassion stirred the hearts of his pursuers. Someone called on him to surrender and promised him life. He sent his last arrow at the speaker with the scornful answer that "a chief knew how to die but never to surrender to the race who had despoiled him." Then, with a shout of bitter defiance, he turned round and jumped over the precipice to be shattered on the rocks far below.

But long before the Bushman made his last stand in the hills he was remorselessly driven from the great buck-bright plains below. For two hundred years and more, all along the steadily expanding European frontier, he was shot on sight and hunted down with horses, dogs and guns with as great ardour as the lion and other carnivorous animals of the veld. Even a professed philanthropist like François Le Vaillant tells without shame how he and his attendants pursued and tried to kill a party of thirteen Bushmen merely because they were seen near the area where he kept his stock.

Wherever the Bushman struck back, as he did with increasing bitterness and vindictiveness, my countrymen immediately banded together and went after him with their deadly guns and quick-footed horses. They would load the heavy muzzles with extra powder and special shot and, taking care to keep out of arrow range, provoke the Bushmen to charge them. Then they would open fire with terrible effect. One leader, Commandant Nel, alone on one small sector of the long frontier, in the thirty years from 1793 to 1823, served on thirty-two expeditions against the Bushman. On those raids great numbers of little men and their women were killed and their children carried back as slaves to the farms of the men on commando. One of Nel's expeditions massacred no less than two hundred Bushmen, and yet he himself seemed to have suffered no especial remorse for what he had done. Although he was in all other respects declared to be a God-fearing and benevolent man, he claimed ample justification for his deeds in the atrocities Bushmen had reputedly committed on farmers and their stock.

On the northern front the Bushman fared no better. I hope some day a historian from among my black countrymen will not shirk the full implications of their share in the over-all tragedy. The traveller James Chapman, for example, has several detailed stories of how Leshulatibi, a Bantu chief in

Ngamiland, persecuted the Bushman. On one occasion when two of the chief's horses had suffocated in a bog, he bound the two Bushman slaves in charge of them to the dead animals and thrust them back into the morass. Later, when another group of Bushmen carried off some of his cattle and vanished into the desert, he waited some months for revenge. Then he sent envoys with presents of tobacco and by various sustained acts of kindness lulled their suspicions and persuaded them to come to a great feast. There they were overpowered and brought to where he was sitting on a veld stool. From there he personally supervised the cutting of their throats, embellishing their last moments, it is said, by every taunt and sarcasm that came to his sinister imagination.

But as a child what shocked me most was the realization of what we had done to the Bushman's children. If we pause to reflect, our justification for eliminating him is revealed as guilt-laden hypocrisy in view of the extreme value we placed on his children. Everywhere they were in great demand as slaves because, when they survived captivity, they grew up into the most intelligent, adroit and loyal of all the farm servants. Even long after slavery was abolished, and until the supply dried up, their service was exacted under a system of forced labour. From the earliest days, all along the frontier the more desperate and adventurous characters among my countrymen added to their living by kidnapping Bushman children and selling them to the land- and labour-hungry farmers. Hardly a commando came back from an expedition without some children, and an early traveller speaks casually of seeing wagons full of children returning from a raid across the frontier. Many of the children died of the heart-ache, shock and the suspension of the only rhythm their little lives had known. Many tried to escape and if recaptured were flogged heavily for their pains. Others, more fortunate, once clear of the settlers, would try furtively to sig-

nal by fires to their own people. If they saw no answering
smoke in the land round about them, they would quickly
extinguish the fire for fear of attracting the attention of
their pursuers and move stealthily ever deeper into the interior. Then they would try to signal from another place. So
it went on until they either found some people of their own
race, or died of hunger, or were eaten by wild animals. Stow,
who learned all this from Bushman survivors when the last act
of the tragedy was barely over, suggests that far more children
died than ever got through to safety. His description of their
fate impressed me so deeply that sometimes as a boy when I
was alone on my pony below the hills at home where the
Bushman had lived, I thought that the wind coming up behind me through the pass brought the fading voice of doomed
lost children crying in the bleached grass between the iron-
stone boulders under an empty and unresponsive blue heaven.

This hopeless situation reached its climax and declined
swiftly into its fatal resolution between the years 1800 and
1860. Already, at the beginning of this period, the Bushman's
extensive hold on Africa had shrunk to the country along the
Great River, the southern and central water-points of what
was to become the Orange Free State, and some of the steeper
mountains and deeper gorges of the Dragon ranges and their
splintered spurs. He was still fighting back in tiny little pock-
ets all over the veld but only in these areas did he retain some
semblance of his former cohesion with his own kind and the
other natural children of Africa. But about the year 1800 all
that quickly changed. In that period pressure from the south
reached its greatest force, in the north, its starkest brutality. A
long process of demoralization of the spirit of the indigenous
peoples of Africa was fast approaching its climax. Already,
for centuries, human society in Africa had been society on the
run. But in this period the whirlwind welter of migratory
hordes having their violent way with weaker peoples, as well

as the systematic raiding, year in and year out, deep into the heart of the continent by the pitiless slave trader from Zanzibar armed with powder and shot, produced a convulsion and disruption of human life and spirit on a scale not seen before. Terror, destruction and disintegration, like the smell of the dead rotting on an apocalyptic battle field, stood high in the shining air. Almost every tribe of Africa picked up only what was negative in the situation. The weak lost the courage and wit that alone might have saved them and were ruled by blind terror. But they, too, whenever forced to flee into the country of someone even weaker than themselves, practised with all the ruthlessness of the convert the terror which had hitherto flayed them. The strong thought of little more than plundering and preying on the weak and making themselves ever stronger. Then they fell out among themselves, setting up rival combinations for loot and destruction.

Great and fantastic figures began to appear and to agitate even more the fearful scene. Chaka, the terrible, the beautiful, the wisely yet madly inspired, the victim caught, for all his magnificence and strength, as a fly in the web of the spider spinning that terrible hour, arose to take the glittering Amazulu in hand and sent his crescent impis to burn and loot Africa from the Indian Ocean to the Zambezi, and from the Umgeni to the Great Lakes. How many perished we shall never know, but the number has to be reckoned in tens of thousands. Even among his own followers the slaughter was immense. On the day of the death of his mother (whom, like many conquerors, he loved darkly and to excess) seven thousand people were killed so that she would have fitting company in the hereafter; and for a year following her death every woman found to be pregnant was put to death with her husband. What showed up the tragic darkness of this hour even more was the glimmer of a strange subliminal honour and belief which clung to slaughter of this kind like phosphorus to the tentacles of a giant octopus groping in the darkness of the oceans. After Chaka, others crowded fast to ruin more thoroughly the world of crumbling spirit. Dingaan, Sikonyella, Moselikatse, of the Matabele offshoot of the Amazulu, and the warrior-queen with thick, long, black hair who came like a comet in the night leading the dreadful hordes of Mantatees with their shields, spears and battle-axes. For years, unafraid and invincible, they advanced from one Bantu settlement to another, destroying all defenders and, after eating up grain and cattle, not staying to plant or husband but moving on, like locusts, to devour more.

All along the extremities of the zone of terror, packs of lesser tyrants and robbers formed and reformed like hyenas and jackals to quarrel over what was left by the pride of lions. Pushed out of the Cape by the fast-expanding European colony, the Hottentots, bands of bastards and outlaws of all sorts of colours, armed with European guns, moved in north to pick off whatever was left of life on the smoking and reeling veld. Away from the main routes of the murderous traffic there was no secluded place that did not conceal some group of broken people clutching at life like drowning men at straws. Food had become so scarce that far and wide the outcasts and survivors of disrupted tribes began to eat one another without shame. For two generations and more a phase of intensive cannibalism set in over all the unfamiliar parts of the land. Too weak and unequipped to hunt the by now thoroughly alarmed and athletic game of the veld, men made up packs to hunt, snare, trap, kill and eat other weaker men. Even the lions and leopards, it is said, gave up preying on game and indulged in a new and easier taste for the flesh of defenceless humans. When a whiff of a human being came to their noses, the terrible wild dogs broke off the hard chase of buck and, moaning with relish, went after some emaciated fugitive, while vultures became so gorged that they could scarce waddle fast enough to take to the air.

For some reason, which I suspect to be part of the general reluctance of us all to accept the unpleasant facts of the history of our beginnings in Africa, this phase is glossed over in our textbooks and I, myself, do not know of any specific research done in the matter. All I know is that these activities were carried on so intensively, and so close to my own day, that as a child I was possessed by the fear of being eaten by cannibals. All our old servants, black and coloured, spoke to me openly about it, and the horror of it had come down to them so vividly that many a time I shivered with them at the recollection. I met one very old 'Suto woman who frankly told me that in the time of the Great Hunger (as they call this period) she, as a child, came home one evening, after searching the veld all day for edible bulbs and tubers, to the cave which sheltered her family to be met by the unfamiliar smell of roasting meat. To her amazement she discovered that it came from a ham-of-man being grilled over the fire. Whenever my coloured nurses thought fear would be good for discipline, they threatened to send, not for a policeman, but for a cannibal, and for several years I believed the distant hills at home still contained men who lived off human flesh.

So great was the destruction let loose in this period over the central portion of South Africa that the wide-open plains were strewn with animal and human bones. One of my grandfather's elder kinsmen, who penetrated into the area at this time, threw a fearful glance at the scene as he hastened uneasily through it, and spoke later of the immense quantities of scattered bones. Again and again, he said, where some band of refugees had been forced to make a stand, the moon bone was scattered in hapless heaps like the splintered timbers of a single wreck swept by a vanished storm onto some deserted foreshore. Even in my childhood great quantities of bone, then almost entirely animal, were still a feature of the landscape. I still remember how the precise wind of our blue, transparent winters would sing a lyric of fate in the hollow bone left on the veld and how I shivered in my imagination.

This, then, was the setting for the final act of the drama of the little Bushman. By this time not only was every man against him but also he was against every man. Others, even the most miserable, seemed to find allies in their misery. But the Bushman had long since been forced to reject any idea of trust in other men. Yet, even in this moment of his greatest misery and isolation he seemed to retain intact a certain dignity abandoned by other races. He never took to eating his own kind. He and his lived or died together: there was no compromise. Knowing, as I do, how small a chance the human being in Africa has had to discover his dignity and develop a truly creative self, I marvel that he should have retained these essentials of human honour to the end, starving rather than prolonging his life by eating the flesh of fellow-men, dying without a whimper.

Some of the last of the Bushman's battles raged around the village where I was born and in the hills among which I grew up. There, largely at the inspiration of a minister of the Dutch Reformed Church, a final attempt was made by a few Europeans to succour him. But the land-hunger and the destructive forces were so great on all sides that the experiment was doomed before it began. The 'Suto people, one of the first to try to break out of the deadly cycle of destruction and to reintegrate the demoralized Bantu peoples, the moment they regained their strength hunted the Bushman down there. On my grandfather's farm in the little circle of stone on the hills above the Fountain of the Bushman, a nephew of Moshesh, the remarkable founder of the Basuto, and so ugly a person that he was known to my wry people as "Pretty Little Rose," one morning at dawn fell upon the Bushman there and destroyed him. My own father collected the skulls of the women and children and was moved to write a poem about them. I myself fingered a few of the broken beads buried in the rubble among the stones. Hardly had Pretty Little Rose withdrawn when the amoral Koranna came down out of the west. They found substantial groups of Bushmen concentrated on the neat cones of two hills standing side by side, like identical twins, near the Place of the Three Perennial Fountains and known to us children as the Hills of Weeping. The Koranna, who normally lusted greatly after Bushman women for most indigenous Africans were excited by their golden colour, on this occasion spared none, not even a child. On the heels of the Koranna came the Griquas, armed with European guns, and accompanied by the itinerant missionaries who pleaded their cause and justified their deeds to remote, unknowing governors. Soon the Bushman was cornered in the very places where he had known the greatest security and enjoyed the longest tranquillity. One by one his names for the caves, shelters and fountains were obliterated from memory, and in the centre of the area a new settlement was founded and called Philippolis, "the Town of Philip," after the eminent missionary divine who brought the Griquas there. I have never shared the hatred of my countrymen for the well-meaning Dr. Philip. But I have found it hard to forgive the naïve, wilful way in which he helped the Griquas to absolute power over the Bushmen at the most critical moment in their history. His behaviour, to say the least of it, appears as incongruous as the Macedonian-sounding "Philippolis" that was imposed, like a top-hat on a Hottentot, upon my native village in memory of him. For a brief period the Town of Philip became the capital of a fantastic kingdom from which the Griquas continued their war of extinction against the Bushman. One of them years later, speaking of Philippolis told a government commission, "We exterminated the Bushman, we shot him down and occupied the country." Another spoke openly of how one day, alone, he helped to cut the throats of thirty Bushmen. While all this was going on, commandos of European farmers appeared in the area to punish the Bushman for thieving across "their" frontiers. When the confusion, destruction and horror was at its greatest, the decisive complication developed.

One fine day the Afrikaner spirit erupted and the hungry European frontier, which had advanced steadily to a depth of miles since 1652, overflowed broadly. Impatiently loading their women, children and possessions into their large covered wagons, gathering together their movable stock and numerous half-caste servants, groups of Afrikaners everywhere abruptly turned their backs on the south and struck out north. Guns in one hand, Bibles in the other, singing their sombre battle hymns, like my grandfather's favourite:

> Rough storms may rage
> Around me all is night
> But God, my God, shall protect me

they penetrated deeply into the interior and took this nightmare of tribal warfare, like a bridal opportunity, into their arms. First they settled with the strongest of their black rivals for the country. They broke the Amazulu, repelled the Matabele, cowed many others and pinned down the formidable Basuto among the hills. Then, with some little barter fair enough, perhaps, according to the tight rule of the narrow day, a great deal of legal guile, natural cunning, bribery and corruption, all encouraged by supplies of the fiery Cape brandy known to us children as "Blitz" or "Lightning," they dispossessed the dispossessing Griquas. When all that was done they turned to the accepted refinement of conquest in Africa:

the extermination of the Bushman. They did this with greater dispatch and efficiency than any before them. Soon only a few names such as the Fountain of the Bushmen and the Hills of Weeping were left in that wide land to preserve his memory like broken-off spars above a sunken ship which mark the place and manner of her going.

For a while longer the Bushman made a desperate stand in the higher peaks of the Dragon ranges, but there, too, before the end of the century, the growing power of the Basuto silenced him for ever. Thereafter he was only to be recognized dragging out his diminished days in the harsh household of some conqueror, or working among the worst criminals on the breakwaters in Table Bay—a criminal, perhaps, because, starving, he had stolen one of the many sheep now owned by men who had stolen all his land. But even in these conditions, he stood out as an individual, despite his convict suit. I am told that his face, creased, lined and wrinkled, was unmistakable and like some Admiralty chart of the circumscribed sea of his time on earth. A sketch in colour of his old grey convict head shows his oddly slanted eyes filled with the first light of man and the last light of his race, both joined to make a twilight valediction to the land of his birth. At the back of his eyes is a look I found disturbing. It was not the calm acceptance of fate untroubled by hope or despair, but rather the certainty that, though he may vanish, his cause remains dynamic in the charge of life. I have been told by those who saw him thus that often the joyless warders guarding him with loaded guns would be startled by a gush of merriment that broke from him suddenly, like a fountain from the earth finding the freedom of air for the first time. A laugh of pure, unequalled clarity, like a call on the trumpet of a herald from afar, would ring out then among the hammers chipping at the convicts' stone. I did not know which perturbed me most, the look in his eyes or the description of his laughter. In such a time and place, the laughter could have come only as intimation of a future in which neither conqueror nor conquest could have place, and a reckoning of which we have not yet begun to be aware would be ready for presentation to all who have for so long so cruelly denied and rejected the Bushman.

Chapter 3

THE PACT AND THE
RANDOM YEARS

————

The older I grew the more concerned I became over the part my own family must have had in the extermination of the Bushman. That it was considerable I had no doubt. My mother's family had been in Africa since the European beginning. By all accounts more restless, bold and adventurous than most, they had always been in the forefront of what we called progress and expansion but what must have been retrogression and contraction to the Bushman. In fact my mother's own grandfather had been one of the very first to cross the Great River with a small band of kinsmen in covered wagons and to move north across the reeking and smoking cannibal plains of the centre. They were all soon observed, superbly stalked and finally massacred by the Matabele at dawn of a very still day, and only my mother's mother, her sister, brother, and coloured nurse miraculously survived to tell the tale. My mother's father's people too, as she once told me, had always lived naturally on frontiers, and he had been one of the earliest to settle north of the Great River. It seemed to me impossible along such an advanced line that they could have avoided taking part in extinguishing the Bushman. But when I asked for precise information I found the members of the family instinctively conspired to silence. They would answer questions in general readily enough, but when it came down to particulars of family history in this regard they were dumb. Their silence confirmed my worst suspicions. I sought comfort in the fact that I witnessed from birth daily manifestations of the capacity of love of my mother's people for everything that was indigenous and natural to our land. They were open-hearted, and although austere, their lives were lived justly according to their exacting lights.

All who worked for my grandfather, no matter whether Griqua, Hottentot, Bushman, Basuto, Bechuana, Cape—coloured or poor white, were ultimately held in equal affection as part of his family, and the relationship was nightly redeemed by calling them into his dining-room to share with his wife and children in his communion with his God. One can only realize how significant such an attitude was when one remembers that the descendants of men like my grandfather are today trying to exclude such people from common worship in the same churches. I concluded, therefore, that in a brutal age my mother's people might have been, perhaps, less brutal than most. That helped, though not overmuch, for I knew that with their deep Calvinist addiction to what they thought right, they would have done their duty conscientiously. Human beings are perhaps never more frightening than when they are convinced beyond doubt that they are right. Fearful, I was certain they would have persuaded themselves that it was right to punish the Bushman and so would have joined in his killing, no matter how reluctantly.

It is true that when my grandfather bought his vast estate around the Fountain of the Bushman from the Griquas, Pretty

Little Rose had already cleared the area of the little hunter. But there were still isolated bands out in hills of the Great River. They had all been proclaimed, as we put it, "Bird-Free" by the government of the day. That meant every burger was permitted, if not actually enjoined, to shoot a Bushman on sight. The Bushman raids and those of others against the Afrikaner settlements that were being fast consolidated finally were found to be so provocative that a great commando was assembled to deal with them. The fact that my grandfather played a prominent role in that expedition was known, but what precisely happened remains hidden to this day. All I know is that in the colourful background of the wonderful home my remarkable grandfather had made of the Fountain of the Bushman, two little old Bushman men moved like twilight shadows. My grandfather, I believed, had found them as children whimpering among the boulders and taken them home to the Fountain of the Bushman to grow up in his service. But found them where? What were they? Survivors? But survivors of what? Another Bushman tragedy in the long series of tragedies? And which particular one? Now I shall never know because the people who could speak of it with authority are dead. But I can only say that the whole of the Bushman past came to a point for me in those two little men. They confirmed all that I vaguely feared and wondered at, and the world of the past which I came to recreate for myself in my imagination spun on into the future and gathered substance with those two little men always at the imponderable centre.

From these two old men and others left in my native village I learned something of the imagination of the Bushman and his knowledge of the inmost life of Africa. That was another aspect of the past that confounded me. How little we ourselves knew of the Bushman's mind and spirit! We had killed him off after nearly 250 years of contact without really knowing whom we had exterminated. True, an old German professor had tried to reconstruct Bushman lore and grammar from a few convicts working on the breakwater in Table Bay, and a British geologist had tried to gather together the threads of remembrance still adrift on the sterile winds of our history and to weave them into some coherent design of the past. But what was known was a fragmentary and, to me, reproachful residue which made my slight contact with the few survivors all the more meaningful, since it gave me the actual feel of the living texture and quality of the vanished people.

In this way, for instance, as children we learned where to find and how to distinguish the edible from inedible tubers and roots of the veld and made good use of our knowledge. In winter our colds were doctored effectively by our parents with medicine brewed from a wild herb to which the Bushman had introduced us. I learned how to extract a thick milky liquid from a plant with the shape of an elephant's ear and the hide of a hippopotamus, which was what the Bushman used as glue for the poison on his arrows, and later learned how to make a sticky paste of it, spread it on traps baited with corn and so catch the birds who, attempting to feed, found their claws held fast by the glue. In summer we children descended into the deep bed of the Great River, threw off our clothes and lived there as the Bushman had done before us, naked. At evening we would stand as the Bushman had taught us to watch the bees flying home on burning wings. At dusk we were up in the wreath of purple rocks high above the gleaming river, where the bees had vanished, and listening, in the prescribed Bushman manner, for the bees' hymn of thanksgiving to die down in the amber catacombs of some tired nest, while baboon sentinels on the peaks around boomed out a challenge to warn their sleepy kinsfolk that we, the humans, were still near. Finally, making smoke "the Bushman way," we would extract our prize and come down in the dark to our campfires with buckets full of fragrant black honey.

Often at dawn we stood still in the shallows among the rocks above the rapids armed with long, supple blue-bush wands. When the golden bream on their way up-stream rose to the surface, a surface so filled with the light of the opening sky that they might have been birds with folded wings swooping out of the blue, we would smack the water smartly over their heads just as the River Bushman had done, and the shock would turn the fish over on their backs to drift helplessly into our clutches. At home our coloured and Bushman nurses would send us to sleep with stories of animals, birds, streams and trees, which were part of the response of the Bushman's creative imagination to the reality of his great Mother Earth. Somehow, in imagination, the Bushman was always with us even when the two little old men were no longer there to represent him. And in an even more subtle way the earth, too, participated profoundly in the process. Ever since I can remember I have been struck by the profound quality of melancholy which lies at the heart of the physical scene in southern Africa. I recollect clearly asking my father once, "Why do the vlaktes and koppies always look so sad?" He replied with unexpected feeling, "The sadness is not in the plains and hills but in ourselves."

This may be true for others, but it was not true for me. For me, the country in its own melancholy right was sad and in a deep mourning.

As a young boy I came to believe that some knowledge of the tragedy of the Bushman was always deeply implicit in the physical scene, making the blue of the uplands more blue, the empty plains more desolate, and adding to the voice of the wind as it climbed over the hill-tops and streaked down lean toward the river, the wail of the rejected aboriginal spirit cry-

ing to be reborn. It seemed to me that both the earth and I
were aware that spread out before us was the scene of a great
play in which the principal actor was absent, and He who
first created it missing.

I soon came to believe, too, that the country was haunted.
Late at night on lonely journeys when I climbed out of cart or
wagon to open a gate in a pass, I would suddenly tremble with
fear for the nearness and certainty of unacknowledged being.
It was not just a normal fear of darkness. Often I would find
the horses sharing my feeling and shivering deeply under my
hand as I laid it on their necks, as much to comfort myself as
to calm them. Sometimes when the sense of a presence in the
dark was at its most acute, a silent jackal would let out a yelp
of pain as if one of the arrows that fly by night had suddenly
hit it. Another time, out with a Hottentot groom on the veld
many miles from any habitation in a night as black as an Old
Testament Bible, our horses reared, stopped dead and stood,
legs wide apart, heads up, snorting with terror and trembling
all over. The Hottentot groom, who believed as do all his
kind that horses have second sight, cried hysterically, "Please,
little master, let's turn back! Please don't go on!" But he
would never say what he thought he had seen. I have seen
black women come screaming back to their homesteads in the
dying fire of dusk sobbing that they had been beckoned by a
compelling "little man" who had suddenly risen up from the
river reeds.

Ghosts in the conventional semblance of themselves may
not exist, but looking back at moments like these I am certain
that the pattern which makes the use of a ghost in Macbeth so
meaningful is constant in the spirit of all persons and countries
who have perpetrated a crime against life which they refuse to
acknowledge. I am certain it was the mechanism of a spirit
haunted in this sense that was so intensely at work among us
all, no matter what our race or colour. However, the climax

in childhood awareness came for me when the two little old men died, one I believe of pneumonia, the other, soon after, of a broken heart. I was inconsolable and lay awake at night close to tears because I was convinced that now, never again, would the Bushman and his child-man shape be seen upon the earth.

For some years I grieved secretly in this manner, until one day a man more picturesque than most appeared among the many colourful people who were always passing through our ample home. He was tall, lean, burnt almost black by the sun, and his skin the texture of wild biltong. His grey eyes in a dark face glittered so that I could not take mine from his. He had just come from some far northern frontier and had been everywhere in Africa. Our rebel community frowned upon him because he was thought to be on his way to join the British in their Great War. Then one day I heard him volunteer casually that on a recent journey to an oasis in the Kalahari Desert he had found the authentic Bushman living there as he had once lived in the country around us. After that, I could think of nothing else. Later in the afternoon I locked myself in the study of my father, who had died some weeks before, and took out a diary in which secretly I had begun to write poetry and record my thoughts. The day was October 13, 1914, and in High Dutch I wrote: "I have decided today that when I am grown-up I am going into the Kalahari Desert to seek out the Bushman."

Many years went by and the impact of remorse and resolution became obscured. I never lost my preoccupation with the Bushman and his fate, but my interest lost its simplicity and therefore much of its force. Part of the explanation, of course, is that like all of us I had to live not only my own life but also the life of my time. Today we overrate the rational values and behave as if thinking were a substitute for living. We have forgotten that thought and the intuition that feeds it only become whole if the deed grows out of it as fruit grows from the pollen on a tree, and so everywhere in our civilized world there tends to be a terrible cleavage between thinking and doing. Something of this dividing power of my time helped to separate the deepest impulses of the child from the calculated behaviour of the man. Also, there were the obvious difficulties. I had to make my own way in life. I had a living to earn and other compelling urges to satisfy. Nonetheless I never entirely forgot the pact with myself. In my twenties I made two attempts to keep faith with it and go into the Kalahari to find the Bushman, but neither was served with enough imagination nor pressed with sufficient energy to succeed. What I saw, too, of the sad mixtures of races that pass for "Bushman" on the fringes of the Great Thirstland, as my countrymen call the Kalahari, were so unlike the true Bushman that they prompted me to doubt whether he could still be found in his aboriginal state. Yet I saw enough of the Kalahari to be drawn to it as to no other part of the country, and to realize that if there were one place left in the world where the true Bushman might still be living it could only be there.

Then the Second World War was upon us and all else was forgotten. Yet that is not altogether true. One of the most moving aspects of life is how long the deepest memories stay with us. It is as if individual memory is enclosed in a greater, which even in the night of our forgetfulness stands like an angel with folded wings ready, at the moment of acknowledged need, to guide us back to the lost spoor of our meanings.

All the time I was on active service I do not remember giving the Bushman a thought. But this other memory, the keeper of the original blue-print of my being, never forgot. I discovered this the night I was thrown into a Japanese cell and the sentry with a grin assured me, as he turned the key on me, that my head would be cut off in the morning. That night I had a dream. I dreamt I saw my mother as a young girl. Her hair fell to her knees from underneath a chintz voortrekker sunbonnet and looked as if it was made of strands of light. She knelt by the water of the three-eyed Fountain of the Bushman. Opposite her was one of the little old Bushman men, also as a child. They both dipped their hands, cupped to-gether, into the fountain and then held them out, full of clear water, toward me. Smiling my mother said, "This is the be-ginning."

I woke up certain not only that I would live but also with the whole of the lost world which had revolved around the little Bushman once more made accessible to me, as fresh and unimpaired as if no long years of neglect lay in between.

After this I wish I could say the way was open, but I came out of three years of prison under the Japanese to go straight back on active service. I did not get leave until some years after the Japanese war had ended. I came back then to find the associations which had sustained me in war and prison ir-revocably dissolved, and I wandered, like a kind of Rip van Winkle, into a strange new world with nine years of unshared and incommunicable experience separating me from it. I al-ternated between Africa and Europe in a state of suspended being like a ghost from some unquiet grave, shocked almost as much by the ruthlessness and brutalities of peace as I had been by those of war, deeply aware only of how privileged I was in being, even so uneasily, alive.

In this mood I volunteered for work of national importance in Africa, and before long, guided like a sleep-walker in his dream, I found myself committed to a series of missions, the first of their kind, which led to my systematic exploring of the Kalahari. Then suddenly one night round our first camp-fire on my first post-war expedition, I found myself and my companions talking about the Bushman with great animation. In a flash the grim, inarticulate years between the confused

soldier and the child ceased to exist. And the scene was repeated night after night in every camp as we went deeper and
more widely into the Kalahari. Soon the newcomers to the
land caught the fever, and I was struck by their spontaneous
interest because it seemed to confirm that my interest was not
purely subjective but valid also in the natural imagination of
other men. Although none of my missions had anything to do
with the Bushman, finding him became important to us all.
Yet weeks passed before we saw any sign of him.

As we navigated our vehicles, like ships by the stars, across
the sea of land I felt deeply it was not as empty of human beings as it looked. Our black servants and companions had the
same feeling. Six weeks went by in which we covered some
thousands of miles without meeting the Bushman. Then one
evening at sundown, 150 miles from the nearest known water,
I came to a deep round pan in the central desert. It had obviously held water some weeks before and there, clear-cut in
the blue clay of the dried-up bottom, was a series of tiny
human footprints leading up the steep sides and vanishing in
the sand underneath a huge storm-tree. As I stood there in the
violet light looking at the neat little casts in clay, I seemed to
hear the voice of the old 'Suto herder of my childhood saying
again, close to my listening ear, "His footprint, little master,
is small and like no other man's, and when you see it you
know it at once from those of other men."

It was clear that some weeks previously a party of authentic
Bushmen had come to water at the pan. But though we
camped there that night and in the days that followed ex-
amined the country around, we saw no further sign of them.
Sometimes, far from river, fountain or well, in the bed of
steep old watercourses that have not run for centuries, we
found the Bushman's light grass shelters leaning empty against
banks of crimson sand, or one of his game-pits neatly dug and
the sands littered with the hair and bone of the animal. Once,

some miles away from our camp, deep in the desert a fire suddenly flared up in the dark, was caught by the sterile west wind and went flying past us like an overland night express. "*Massarwa!* Bushman!" the cry went up among our startled black companions. But as the weeks went by, still we did not see him.

One evening, in a camp hurriedly pitched for shelter against the first violent storm of summer, I was watching the Gothic lightning strike at the reeling earth around us when, against a flash of flame on the horizon, I saw a movement above the line of bushes. I watched carefully, and when the sheet-lightning flared purple in the smoking rain again, I saw the silhouettes of two little heads peering intently at us.

Instantly I left the camp in the opposite direction, crept out into the storm and worked my way around to the line of the bushes. I came out about thirty yards beyond the place I had marked. The noise of thunder, wind and rain was at its height and greatly helped me. I rose carefully. Between me and the light of our fires were indeed two little Bushman heads. I crept up quietly, suddenly put my hands on their shoulders, said loudly, "Good day. I saw you from afar."

The two little men fell over backwards with astonishment and, far from being upset, began laughing so much that they wriggled helplessly in the wet sand, for a while unable to stand up. I took them into my camp, and though none of us could speak their dialect we spent one of the happiest evenings I have ever known. I watched them eating the huge meal of roast springbuck, rice and raisins which my wonderful old safari cook and friend, Simon Marenga, a Northern Rhodesian, had cooked for us, and the sight of their pure Bushman faces and bodies sent a warm feeling to my heart. I looked forward to days of their company. But when morning came the pair had vanished with not a footprint left by wind and rain to show which way they had gone.

Another time, during a halt to mend a wheel, on a day of steel heat, two little hunters suddenly appeared like reflections in a distorting mirror on the far face of the shining ridge. They trotted easily toward us in the manner my aunt had described so well, and came straight into our midst holding out before them the buckskins they wanted to exchange for tobacco. We took them on with us in our trucks for a while but again were unable to speak except by signs. The use and shape of our trucks was a complete puzzle to them so we had to lift them, like babies in arms, in and out of the vehicles. One of them, excited by a herd of buck he wanted to chase, hurled himself from the vehicle, which was going at full speed, to fall onto the sands, apparently knowing no other way of leaving it! Surprised, by signs, we asked if they never climbed the great desert trees to spy out game. They seemed astonished and indicated clearly that they would never do anything so unnecessary while the spoor of game was printed plainly in the sand for them to read. We then shot some game for them and saw them throw themselves, helpless with laughter, upon the sand when the first of the guns went off. As the sun began to sink, though we beseeched them to stay, they insisted on leaving us. I longed to accompany them but my mission was too exacting to allow it. Full of chagrin I watched them, each carrying a buck across his firm little shoulders, walk gracefully away from us into the sunset.

One afternoon, on another expedition, at a time of terrible drought we came across the footprints of one grown-up person and two small children. The manner of the spoor perturbed me greatly. I showed it to my tracker. He confirmed my fears, saying, "People in trouble." We instantly followed the spoor for six miles, while it became more faltering and desperate. At the edge of a great pan I felt certain it was made by people half-dead by thirst. We searched the hollow depression. It was waterless, and the dried-up mud in the bottom was cracked and dull like the scales of a dead fish. Then far away in the white flame of heat we saw three little blobs of brown fluttering like wounded birds. We found a Bushman woman with a baby strapped to her side and two little boys nearly dead of thirst staggering about. We gave them water. The woman drank nearly three gallons though she was careful to ration the children. Again we could not speak her dialect and had to make signs to her inviting her to stay. However she steadfastly refused. As soon as she had eaten, she filled all the empty ostrich-egg shells she carried in a leather shawl with water. I offered to come with her but, in a fever of agitation, she signed refusal. Then, apparently fully recovered, she picked up her baby and set off with the little boys, to vanish into the sand and the bush on the far side of the pan.

In the years that followed I had other brief and tantalizing encounters with the genuine Bushman. But I was too busy to pursue the matter independently to its own lawful conclusion. Instead I tried to persuade more fully qualified people—scientists, anthropologists and psychologists—to follow up this line of living research and go and live with the Bushman in order to find out before it was too late his way of spirit and life. It seemed a strange paradox that everywhere men and women were busy digging up old ruins and buried cities in order to discover more about ancient man, when all the time the ignored Bushman was living with this early spirit still intact. I found men willing enough to come with me to measure his head, or his behind, or his sexual organs, or his teeth. But when I pleaded with the head of a university in my own country to send a qualified young man to live with the Bushman for two or three years, to learn him and his ancient way in the whole, he exclaimed, surprised, "But what would be the use of that? The Bushman would just fill him up with lies!"

So for many precious years I cast around to find someone

with more than a sharply sided interest in the Bushman. But it was a vain search. Yet all over the world whenever I spoke of the Bushman a look of wonder would come into the eyes of ordinary people and I took heart from that. I believe one cannot fully know people and life unless one knows them also through the wonder they provoke in one. Without a sense of wonder one has lost not only the spoor of life but the power of true increase.

Increasingly, my own imagination became troubled with memories of the Bushman, and in particular with the vision of the set of footprints I had found in the pan in the central desert at the foot of a great storm-tree. It was almost as if those footprints were the spoor of my own lost self vanishing in the violet light of a desert of my own mind. I found myself compelled against my conscious will toward the conclusion that, ridiculous as it might seem, I myself ought perhaps to take up the spoor where it vanished in the sand. Then one morning I awoke to find that, in sleep, my mind had been decided for me.

"I will go and find the Bushman," I told myself, suddenly amazed that so simple a statement had never presented itself to me before.

The difficulties were obvious. I was not qualified. I had no training. I was not a scientist. The demands on my time were many and exacting, and I could not possibly afford it.

But there was this pact I had made with myself in childhood. I could no longer ignore it and somehow felt the difficulties would resolve themselves.

Chapter 4

THE BREAK-THROUGH

THE WORLD I grew up in believed that change and development in life are part of a continuous process of cause and effect, minutely and patiently sustained throughout the millenniums. With the exception of the initial act of creation (which as every good Afrikaner boy knew was accomplished with such vigour that it took only six days to pass from chaos to fig-leaves and Adam), the evolution of life on earth was considered to be a slow, steady and ultimately demonstrable process. No sooner did I begin to read history, however, than I began to have my doubts. Human society and living beings, it seemed to me, ought to be excluded from so calm and rational a view. The whole of human development, far from having been a product of steady evolution, seemed subject to only partially explicable and almost invariably violent mutations. Entire cultures and groups of individuals appeared imprisoned for centuries in a static shape which they endured with long-suffering indifference, and then suddenly, for no demonstrable cause, became susceptible to drastic changes and wild surges of development. It was as if the movement of life throughout the ages was not a Darwinian caterpillar but a startled kangaroo, going out toward the future in a series of unpredictable hops, stops, skips and bounds. Indeed, when I came to study physics I had a feeling that the modern concept of energy could perhaps throw more light on the process than any of the more conventional approaches to the subject. It seemed that species, society and individuals behaved more like thunder-clouds than scrubbed, neatly clothed and well-behaved children of reason. Throughout the ages life appeared to build up great invisible charges, like clouds and earth of electricity, until suddenly in a sultry hour the spirit moved, the wind rose, a drop of rain fell acid in the dust, fire flared in the nerve, and drums rolled to produce what we call thunder and lightning in the heavens and chance and change in human society and personality.

Something of this sort, in a small way, had happened to me overnight. I who had been going round in circles for twenty long years in the particular matter of the Bushman had now not only found my way but wanted to go it at once. Before I was dressed I knew exactly what I had to do and how to do it.

I decided I would go to the Kalahari at the worst time of the year. I would aim to set out at its most northerly frontier on the Zambezi River at the end of August. I decided to do this entirely because I felt it was the only way to make sure that the Bushman, if I found him, would be pure. There are many peoples of mixed Bushman blood all around the fringes of the Kalahari, and from experience I knew that all these people would penetrate deeply into the Kalahari immediately after the rains had fallen. For the miraculous thing about the Kalahari is that it is a desert only in the sense that it contains no permanent surface water. Otherwise its deep fertile sands are covered with grass glistening in the wind like fields of gallant corn. It has luxuriant bush, clumps of trees and in places great strips of its own dense woods. It is filled, too, with its own varieties of game, buck of all kinds, birds and lion and leopard. When the rains come it grows sweet-tasting grasses and hangs its bushes with amber berries, glowing raisins and sugared plums. Even the spaces between the satin grass are filled with succulent melons and fragrant cucumbers, and in the earth itself bulbs, tubers, wild carrots, potatoes, turnips and sweet potatoes grow great with moisture and abundantly multiply. After the rains there is a great invasion of life from the outside world into a desert which produces such sweetness out of its winter travail of heat and thirst. Every bird, beast and indigenous being waits expectantly in its stony upland for the summer to come round. Then, as the first lightning begins to flare up and down below the horizon in the west as if a god walked there swinging a storm lantern to light his great strides in the dark, they eagerly test the winds with their noses. As soon as the air goes dank with a whiff of far-off water, they will wait no longer. The elephant is generally the first to move in because he not only possesses the most sensitive nose but also has the sweetest tooth. Close on his heels follow numbers of buck, wildebeest, zebra and the carnivorous beasts that live off them. Even the black buffalo emerges from the river-beds and swamps, shaking the tsetse fly like flakes of dried clay from his coat, and grazes in surly crescents far into the desert. When this animal movement is at its height and all the signs confirm that a fruitful summer is at last established, the human beings follow. What I feared was that this invasion into the normal life of the desert would make the genuine Bushman shyer and more than ever difficult to contact. I feared also that the return to the desert in summer of the so-called "tame" Bushman, who is reared in the service of the tribes and colonists impinging on the Kalahari, might complicate my task. For the "tame" Bushman, no matter how irrevocably wrenched from the pattern of his past, cannot entirely live without the way of his fathers. From time to time he refreshes his spirit by going back into the desert. Through the spring, as rain and electricity accumulate along the vibrant horizon, a strange tension mounts in his blood. He becomes moody and preoccupied until suddenly he can bear it no longer. Throwing away his clothes of service he commits himself naked to the desert and its ancient ways like a salmon from a remote river backwater coming to the open sea. Those who have inflicted a feudal vassalage on the Bushman wake up one morning to find him vanished. They do not see him again until summer is over. I knew from others who had already been seduced by his plausible recapitulation of the aboriginal way that the "tame" Bushman would only be distinguishable from the genuine Bushman by a protracted probe into both mind and history. I could not afford any confusion or delays of this kind. But I knew also that it was only the genuine Bushman who would stay deep in the desert through the worst time of the year. In those uncertain months between winter and the breaking of the rains, all fair-weather life quickly withdraws from the desert, and only the desert's own carefully selected and well-tried children like the genuine Bushmen remain to endure the grim diet of heat and thirst. It was their tiny feet that had left in the pan, far from water and habitation, the set of footprints that now drew my thoughts as a magnet draws the dust of sawn steel.

Long as it takes to define and explain all this, it was clear to me and decided in one vivid moment. How it was to be done hardly took any longer. I had led so many other expeditions to the Kalahari that the physical means came instantly to my mind. I knew at once the kind of vehicles I would use. I saw precisely where and how I would have to arrange refuelling and water-points in and around the desert. I knew the kind of people I would need if the search I had in mind was to be successful, as well as the individuals I would ask first to accompany me. I had a rough idea of how long it all would take. I knew exactly the amount of money I myself could spend on such an expedition. It was obviously not going to be enough, and no sooner did I realize that than I saw what I had to do to get the rest. In fact all the aspects of the plan that were within reach of my own hand were worked out and determined there and then. What took longer, of course, was the part which depended on the decisions of others and on circumstances beyond my own control. Yet even there I was amazed at the speed with which it was accomplished. I say "amazed," but it would be more accurate to say I was profoundly moved, for the lesson that seemed to emerge for a person with my history of forgetfulness, doubts and hesitation was, as Hamlet put it so heart-rendingly to himself: "the readiness is all." If one is truly ready within oneself and prepared to commit one's readiness without question to the deed that follows naturally on it, one finds life and circumstance surprisingly armed and ready at one's side. In fact, I would say now that the tragedy of Hamlet was precisely that he always found a reason for not obeying the readiness of his own spirit. I say this, not because I raised my own small problem to Shakesperian proportions, but merely for the order that the parallel helped to bring to the perplexities of my own mind and for something else that it revealed beyond: how what we sentimentalize as forgiveness is an iron exactment of life. Indeed, life does not merely exact but sets the example. Vengeance, revenge, forgiveness and bitterness are all reactions of the retarded Corsican in ourselves: they play no role in the abiding assertion of life. It is too urgent for that, and in order not to stand still in mere action and reaction, it moves on only with the effect that has freely forgiven its cause. The fact, I believe, will one day be capable of mathematical as well as emotional expression. Meanwhile, here was one more proof of it for me in that if anyone had deserved a rebuff from life after so many fumbled years, I had. Yet I found myself pardoned and my plan welcomed as an old friend.

There was, for instance, the response to the many letters I wrote that morning. I wrote first to Wyndham Vyan in East Africa, because there is no man in Africa whose friendship and judgement I value more. Our friendship goes back to my first major Kalahari expedition after the war, and since then we have served on several other missions in the same area. He is older than I, and yet I have never been conscious of the difference in years between us. I think that is due to the way he has lived. He has never sidestepped his problems but always lived them out in the circumstances wherein he encountered them, so there is no drag of the past holding him back from my own day. I never felt him to be anything but a truly contemporary person. This is all the more remarkable because he belonged to the generation which lost its finest flower in the First World War. He himself came out of it so old with killing and so sick at heart that he had only one clear instinct and that was to get away from the scene as quickly as possible. He went out to East Africa to one of its remote frontier areas and started a ranch of his own. He spent a great deal of money in stocking it with some of the finest sheep and cattle from Britain. Then, for years, with increasing dismay he watched Africa defeat his privileged and well-born stock. As fast as they withered and were stricken down he replaced them. He fought back with all the resources of European science and spent the rest of his money. But the campaign steadily went against him. A world slump joined in the formidable physical forces ranged against him. Then, one day, when his fortunes were at their lowest, he was out among his shrinking herds in the heat of the day and noticed that while his own herd, their eyes red, sore, blinking at the sun, lay with heaving flanks in the shade of thorn-trees, some native cattle of his Somali herdsmen grazed eagerly in the open close-by, untroubled by heat or sunlight, their eyes clear, and serene, and their furless coats sleek and shining. He stood still with amazement that he had not seen the meaning of it before. He realized at once that all these years he had been trying to impose Europe on Africa without regard to its own conditions of being. He there and then turned round, not only on his heel, but in his mind. He got rid of all his over-refined European stock and replaced it with what he could buy, or barter, from Somalis. He then devoted the same methods, care and sense of purposeful selection, which is one of the European's great gifts to my native continent, to the cattle forged in the fire of Africa. The response of Africa, he says, was truly staggering, and today he has one of the largest and most successful ranches in the country. More, in winning his own battle, he won also a battle for Africa because he has given it a vigorous cattle that can rival any other in the world. To hear him talk about cattle is to hear an artist in flesh and blood discussing his works. This interest has absorbed all his peacetime life. He has been to Europe only once between wars and that visit endeared Africa all the more to him. He has stayed unmarried and I have teased him saying he has not a pin-up girl but a pin-up heifer beside his bed. He loves his cattle so much that he hates selling them. He knows them individually, despite their thousands, and one of the most resolved moments I have ever spent in Africa was sitting with him in the grass while he smoked a pipe of Magaliesberg and watched his great white, humpback cows with their purple eyes and gentle ways grazing around us. Once when I stood with him by the walls of a ruined city of another vanished race in Southern Rhodesia, he took his pipe out of his mouth and said slowly, "I bet whoever built these walls built them to keep their cattle safe at night." He was with me deep in the Kalahari when Mau Mau struck and knew at once how serious it was. His own ranch was in the heart of Mau Mau country and he had close on two hundred Kikuyu working for him. From the start he saw the tragedy and its causes in all their complex wholeness. His imagination made straight for the centre of the storm and stood fast there. He was another confirmation, for me, of how one is free of the tyranny of the many in life only by committing oneself totally to the service of the one. Because Vyan had mastered his own job in such a living way, he had been rewarded with a capacity for understanding much besides. From the start of the Mau Mau trouble his main concern was that his countrymen of all races and colours, and not least the people who had produced Mau Mau, should not compromise such honour as was left to them, and should emerge from the disaster with hope of a greater future.

In writing to Vyan now I was certain that he, more than any other, would appreciate fully what I had in mind. I hoped also that my letter might coincide with his need for a respite. I got an immediate airmail letter in reply, saying among other things: "How odd that you should write just now. Things are somewhat better in the country but I need a break and was about to write to you to suggest it was time we did another safari together. Thank you. I'll be delighted to come. Let me know what I can do and bring to help."

At the same time I wrote to Ben Hatherall. Although he had a name with an Elizabethan ring to it and was obviously of English descent, he and his family had become so identified with my own countrymen that they regarded themselves as Afrikaners. His father was one of a small group of hardy and restless frontiersmen whom Cecil Rhodes persuaded to settle at Ghanzis, a small oasis in the western Kalahari, to act as buffer against the German expansion which he feared from South-West Africa. They had hardly settled there, when the

Jameson Raid, and then the Boer War, came to shatter Rhodes' political power and influence in my country for good. The little community, hundreds of waterless miles between them and the nearest railway and a thousand from their capital, was forgotten. The climate was against them, but with the help of friendly groups of Bushmen they managed to survive and to establish themselves austerely in the desert. Ben was born there and as a little boy had to bear a man's burden of deprivation and tribulation. His nurses and playmates were Bushmen. He learned their language and their ways and acquired much of their unique knowledge of the life of the desert. As a boy of nine, barefoot in the full heat of summer, he had to help his stern father drive the cattle that was their livelihood from one precarious water-hole to another for hundreds of miles across the burning desert to a disdainful market in Mafeking. At night he took a man's turn to defend the uneasy cattle from lion. I don't know whether it was then that he learned to shoot with a man's rifle but it was early in life. As a young man his exploits as a shot, hunter, tamer of horses and pioneer in the desert were legendary. His parents, with the Boers' immense respect of learning, skimped themselves and saved every penny to send him, for a few years, to school in Kimberley. When he returned to the Kalahari, he became schoolmaster to the children of the desperate little community because the greatest Empire on earth, in its moment of supreme prosperity, had turned down a petition for a school on the grounds that it could not afford it. For twelve years, too, he represented his people on the advisory council of a well-meaning but impoverished administration far away in Mafeking and fought a hard, and largely vain, battle for their rights. He, too, had accompanied me on my first post-war expedition and from the start we were friends. He was, for me, an Afrikaner version of Allan Quatermain and embodied much of what was best in our national character before power over the defenceless, and the arrogant political intellectualism of the Cape, had corroded it. He was self-reliant, resourceful, unafraid of man, beast or opinion; patient, generous, with boundless capacity for endurance and the manners of an aristocrat.

From him, too, I heard by return airmail, saying among other things: "It is strange I was about to write and ask how you were. We had not heard for so long and felt you should come to us soon again. Of course, I am with you all the way. But I have just started a new farm. So would you please remember, I should get back, God willing, when the rains break to do my ploughing. And, Colonel, if we are going back to the Kalahari in the summer, don't you think you should bring a hat with you for once?"

I took such swift and characteristic responses from Vyan and Hatherall to be what the ancient Chinese would call "confirmatory signs," and as they had it, that it "would further to continue." Vyan and Hatherall, too, had formed a friendship firmly based on a wide, shared experience and a deep love of natural Africa. They enjoyed each other's company so much that I had often seen a camp, sulky with fatigue at the end of a hard day, recover grace just by watching the two of them, smoking and talking imperturbably together. I felt with their acceptance the foundations of the expedition were laid on rock—though it was as well, perhaps, that I did not know then how severely that structure was to be tested.

I wrote on the same day to the Rover Company. On a previous government mission I had tried out a Land-Rover and had been impressed with its performance. There were disadvantages, of course, compared to the heavy three- and six-ton vehicles that had been provided for me by the government. The Land-Rover's carrying capacity was smaller, but they consumed less and, in comparison, skimmed lightly over the deep sand. In the past, one of my great problems had been that my trucks devoured almost as much as they carried. To cool their overheated engines they used more rare and precious water than fuel. But the Land-Rover, on my previous expedition, had not boiled once and its fuel consumption had been only one-third that of the other vehicles. It was far more manoeuvrable and its daily range, as a result of all these factors, far greater. The saving in time and weight of water, containers and fuel I believed would more than offset their lesser carrying capacity. My only fear was that, because of import control in South Africa and the long waiting list for Land-Rovers in the country, I would be unable to get the vehicles I needed in time. But I had an immediate and courteous reply and within a few days a meeting, first with John Baldwin, and then with Geoffrey Lloyd Dixon, of the headquarters staff of the company. I explained what I had in mind and, although I know the English so well, even I was surprised by the imaginative consideration they gave to my problem. They instantly promised me priority on any vehicles I needed and offered to build extra petrol and water tanks into the vehicles I chose before they were dispatched to Africa.

The next step was concerned with matters of which I had no experience. Part of my plan was to make a documentary sound film of the life of the Bushman. It seemed to me there could be no quicker, surer and more complete way of recording his life for the future. Moreover, I had a hunch that such a film could also be made into an original television series and some of its rights sold in advance to help me pay my way. Unhappily, I knew nothing of the technique of films and could hardly operate a Brownie. Before I could go any further, therefore, I had to do three things: (1) find out whether any television authority would be interested in such a plan; (2) if so, get hold of suitable technicians to accompany me; (3) work out with my own technicians what we would need in equipment and transport.

So I went first to the B.B.C. because I believe it to be the best medium of its kind in the world. In the war I remembered how its quality got through even to the illiterate southeast Asians in a Japanese prison camp. If they wanted to stress to me that a rumour was really true, the Asians always added, "This, Tuan, is B.B.C." In my own contacts over many years I had always found it searching, accessible and imaginative. I was not disappointed. The people I saw, Mary Adams in particular, were truly interested and added only that it would help decisively if I could organize my own film unit.

I had already thought a great deal about a film unit and had two major possibilities in mind. Friends of mine had long been urging me to take on one of my expeditions a young Scandinavian film producer, of whom they expected great things. Then there was another, a continental free-lance film producer called Eugene Spode. I knew him personally because a South African friend of mine had introduced us some five years before, asking me to write some lines for a short and impressive war film he had made. Since then I had met Spode quite often in London. He seemed to me an unusual and gifted person: not only painter, musician and scenario writer, but also composer, producer, and cameraman. He hardly spoke a word of English, and conversation with him was either in French, of which he had some knowledge, or through my friend as interpreter. My friend, who knew him extremely well, was certain he needed only a fair chance to prove himself a film-maker of note. But, more important to me, I liked Spode and my imagination was touched by all I was told of him. It is true that he struck me as a profoundly unhappy person and perhaps I should have been warned by that. I don't believe that a truly creative person can be permanently as unhappy as Spode appeared to be. But my friend had told me of his suffering under Nazis, Communists, Fascists and other lesser tyrannies of the modern world and society, which adequately explained this. I was told also of the intensely heroic role he had played in the resistance movement of his country. More, I was told he loved Africa, had been there several times and had even made a documentary film of it. His record in the war and his reputed knowledge of Africa decided me. I chose Eugene Spode. I wrote to my friend in Africa for his address and again got an immediate response, ending with the sentence: "I have always known you and Eugene would do great things together in Africa."

My sense of the "togetherness of things," already flattered, now became proud of yet another positive response to my planning. I sent Spode a telegram and he came at once to meet me in London. I had never seen him so charming, happy and confident. He was like a person renewed. I told him all I could about the conditions under which I expected he would have to work. I told him also about Vyan and Hatherall and the qualities that made them so important to me and the expedition, and about the black people I hoped to take with us. I stressed how decisive personal relationships would be on the journey. I told him, with irony deferred, of the lesson commended to me when I was very young by a great hunter and gentleman: "Little old cousin, if you want to go into the blue in Africa, always pick your companions only from among men you have known for at least five years. And the chances are, even then, that you will pick the wrong one." I found myself talking to him as I do to all people who are drawn to my native land. I described Africa as a great, exacting and often shattering personality. I told him of the extremes of heat, the glare and the glitter that attacked one's senses, the parasites, spiders, ants, snakes and scorpions, and the incessant sapping of one's physical endurance and drag on one's watchfulness. Later, I remember becoming lyrical and saying something to the effect that Africa was a great and unfulfilled

barbaric woman still seeking a worthy lover and testing all
newcomers by every caprice, extreme and strategem of her
unfathomable nature, but that those who were not discouraged from loving her, would, in the stillness of an unbelievable night, find themselves suddenly rewarded with a tenderness, delicacy and absence of reserve that passed European
comprehensions.

Spode smiled sweetly at this and reminded me gently that,
after all, he had been to Africa and knew all this. He was certain that, as always, he would love Africa and was prepared
to take over from me the entire responsibility of organizing
the film side of the expedition. At this, I said I would have to
insist on only one thing: I must be responsible for the story
and the words of the film, though how it was translated into
its film idiom of course would be his entire concern.

For some days we talked over all this until we both felt we
had nothing more to say. Our agreement was complete. Even
questions of money had been clearly and simply decided. I
would finance the expedition. If there was a profit we would
share it equally. If there was a loss I would bear it alone. More,
I hoped to get contracts to write for newspapers all over the
world, and I said I would get them to agree to buy his photo-
graphs to illustrate my reports. The income from the photo-
graphs, I insisted, would be entirely his.

That settled, we went together to the B.B.C. and came to a
final agreement. They arranged for Spode to study their own
film methods in their studios and consult their most experienced film people. Meanwhile I had to leave for Africa almost at once. I warned him that for three months or more I
would be unable to have any but brief, business-like exchanges with him. Was he able to arrange for the film and the
technical requirements? He said he was not only able but
moved by "the generous opportunity" put in his way. I arranged for him and his cameras and film material to be flown

out to Africa. We confidently fixed a place for our next meeting in a hotel in Bulawayo in Southern Rhodesia on August
21. One of the last things I said to him was: "Please bring
your violin with you. It's a wonderful thing to have music
round the fire in camp, and you'll help us more than I can say
if you'll play for the lions at night!"

Chapter 5

THE SHADOW IN BETWEEN

I LEFT for Africa with my wife and my personal Land-Rover in May, which gave me three months to prepare for the expedition. Even that was barely enough. I had a great deal of Bushman research to do in libraries and museums. I had thousands of miles to travel from the Cape to the Zambezi, looking at old Bushman caves, sites and paintings and refreshing my memory of the heart of the immense country of the vanished little men. Happily unaware of the fate awaiting them I made plans and selected locations to re-enact certain key scenes from the Bushman's story for background material for the film. I saw scores of officials to get the many permits, introductions and vouchers necessary if the journey was to succeed. I organized supply and refuelling points in and around the vast Kalahari, knowing that in order to get fuel to some of the more remote points in time I would have to see it on its way by sea, rail, truck, at least three months before I needed it. I engaged the rest of our personnel. I ordered all the complicated supplies from mosquito nets, snake-bite serum, dehydrated foods, camp-beds, field-chairs and work-tables to the latest drugs for malaria and dysentery as well as aureomycin and morphia in case of serious accident. I had hoped to see something of my own family, but I found the time for such contacts rapidly devoured by increasingly urgent demands. On top of all this, there was always the inevitable intrusion of the "unpredictable" in Africa to take greedy bites out of such time as was left. Then a shipping strike in England delayed the dispatch of the Land-Rovers and cut down the leisurely six weeks we had planned for their assembly.

Also, I began to be vaguely troubled about Eugene Spode. I met many people who had known him in Africa, and though everybody acknowledged his gifts, yet there was an odd reservation in their manner, a suggestion that he might not be tough enough for the journey. Also, I found myself in dispute with authorities in territories where he had worked because they seemed reluctant, since he was not British, to grant him a working permit on the same terms as the rest of the company. It all ended in making me apprehensive for a time. But more than anything else I worried increasingly over the mechanics of making the film.

I had been aware from the start that in undertaking the making of a film I was stepping outside my own experience. I had learned by bitter precept how gravely one can expose oneself to accident and disaster in this process, and especially in Africa. The original idea had been that Spode, as well as being photographer to the expedition in his minor capacity, would make a separate documentary film of his own. The more I thought of this, the madder it seemed to me. We had taken on too much. I wrote to Spode suggesting that we should make only the television film, using it as a pilot scheme for a greater documentary in colour later. I added that, even so, I considered the work would be too much for one person and begged him to engage a first-class technical assistant. I left the choice of individual to him, insisting only that the person should be British since I wanted no more trouble with the authorities. If he failed, I offered to engage an assistant for him in South Africa.

Spode wrote back saying he had already come to the same conclusion and was prepared to bring an assistant at his own expense if necessary, only he would prefer to engage one himself in Britain. The practical good sense and generosity of his response was a complete antidote to any misgiving I had picked up on arrival in Africa.

I left it all gratefully behind me and hastened on for I had a growing mass of intractable detail to deal with. Fortunately I have many friends in Africa and there is a strong instinct in all pioneering countries to come to the help of a pioneer. I was helped everywhere generously, and the idea which ultimately rescued the expedition from near disaster came not from me but from friends. The Mines in South Africa, in order to get the necessary labour, have built up a vast recruiting organization all over the country. It maintains its own roads and refuelling stations deep in the remotest bush and in the most primitive parts of Africa. A friend in the Chamber of Mines said to me one day, "You ought to have letters from us to our people in the blue just in case of need. One never knows . . ." So a letter was written commending me and my needs to the care of their recruiting officers, directors of air services and pilots. Without it, my expedition would almost certainly have failed.

In early August, hard-pressed, but still within our prescribed schedule, my wife and I came to the Victoria Falls on the Zambezi to complete the last link in the chain of ground organization. From there, my wife was to return to England because I had no intention of exposing to the hazards of the journey anyone who had not been conditioned to Africa or born with the immunities of Africa within her. The wisdom of this decision was demonstrated almost as soon as we arrived at the Falls. My wife quickly developed a mysterious and dangerously high fever. The doctor summoned from fifteen miles away declared himself unable to diagnose it, so for a fortnight the fever swayed violently up and down. It has sometimes appeared to me that fever is designed, in part, to magnify reality, so that the imponderable contribution of the spirit to the malaise which produces fever, can become visible. There seems to be deep within it a rounding-up process of time which brings past, present and future all lucidly together in the focus of a single symbol. As I sat, frightened, by my wife's bed day after day, listening to her quick breathing, with the shock of the great Zambezi waters falling a mile away shaking the windows and rattling the doors without cease, I saw how deeply anxious she was, not about herself but the journey. Her anxiety expressed itself in the single entreaty, constantly reiterated, "Buy your own gun, the best there is, and take it on the expedition with you."

Since the war I had lost all taste for shooting and on previous expeditions had left it to those of my companions who enjoyed it. Vyan and Ben, I knew, were counting on shooting the game that would be our main diet, and it would deprive them of one of their great joys if someone else took a hand. My wife knew this. But now she kept on imploring me to buy a gun of my own—"the best in the world." And when she came out of her fever she held me to my promise.

As far as the expedition was concerned, she came out of it just in time. We were already well in the third week of August when I saw my wife into a plane on her journey back to England, and I left the same day by road for Bulawayo. I drove my Land-Rover through the hundreds of miles of shimmering and singing bush as fast as I could and did so because

Spode had arrived in Bulawayo earlier than at first planned in order to study and adapt his arrangements.

Too late for effective advice, I had received two letters from him about his assistant saying that because of the expense he had decided not to engage a professional assistant but to bring out a South African studying at a university in Britain, "a friend of his" with a "useful knowledge" of filming and prepared to pay his own way. Both my wife and I had been alarmed by this because it was not what we had agreed to do at all. Still, filming was Spode's department and I could hardly protest, except to write back saying I hoped he had chosen the right man, begging him not to let expense stand in his way and repeating my offer to find a local professional.

Now, on my way to my first meeting with Spode in Africa, I called in at the garage which was our agent in Bulawayo. I found Spode's equipment and films neatly stored in the cool of the office. I was somewhat taken aback by the space they occupied because I had had no idea what 80,000 feet of film, night flares, cameras, stands and screens in bulk would look like. But I was completely staggered by a bill from the Rhodesian customs for close on a thousand pounds duty! The agent told me he had pleaded in vain that the material was "in transit" but the customs had been unyielding. He said, and I agreed, that the matter could only be settled with the Ministry in Salisbury. I had hoped for at least a day with Spode in Bulawayo before returning to Johannesburg to receive the Land-Rovers still plodding their way out from England. Instead now, I would have, to use that day for a journey to Salisbury. I went straight to book a seat in the morning plane to Salisbury, put my own Land-Rover into the garage for a thorough overhaul, and went to meet Spode.

By this time it was evening and dark. I found Spode waiting for me in the hotel. My friend who had first introduced us was with him, having decided with characteristic generosity to launch him safely on his way. I was delighted to see them, they both appeared glad to see me, and we talked well into the night. I told Spode frankly about my misgivings regarding his choice of an assistant, who, incidentally, had not yet left England.

He used, in French, an opening phrase with which I was soon to become familiar: "You don't understand, Laurens. I don't want another cameraman. I need only someone who knows me and understands me, an intelligent friend who will do as I say, lift and carry for me and help me with all the complicated adjustments of focus, angles and screens. Don't worry! He is just right for me."

I protested no more. It was not what I had wished, but there was no other reason to conclude that he could not do the job.

Spode then told me of his ideas for the film and the background filming he wanted to do around Bulawayo. I told him I had to go to Salisbury the following day and begged him not to begin work until I joined him, saying it was important that I, who was responsible for the story, and he for translating it into film should work closely together from the start. I assured him that the moment I rejoined him I could give him whatever time he needed. We parted affably and I had no inkling whatsoever that in what I had said I had committed an offence for which I was never to be forgiven.

I left for Salisbury at dawn the next day, saw the head of the customs who, with the capacity of quick informal decision that is so refreshing in his country, picked up his telephone and instantly ordered his subordinates in Bulawayo to cancel the monstrous duty of one thousand pounds. At noon the next day I was in Johannesburg. The Land-Rovers were still aboard a ship in Algoa Bay harbour, but Land-Rover agents and all my friends joined forces to speed their arrival. I do not think a goods truck has ever travelled faster from the coast to the interior than the one containing my remaining three Land-Rovers. Four days later they were in Johannesburg and were at once unloaded and assembled. The two short-wheelbase Land-Rovers already had their extra fuel tanks and water containers built in; the third, a long-wheelbase vehicle like my own, still needed its extra tanks to be fitted locally because it had been ordered later. The Land-Rover mechanics turned to the task with such a will that two days later it was complete with four additional tanks, and emerged like its smaller companions with the Union Jack and South African flags and a neat label, KALAHARI EXPEDITION, painted, unbidden but bright for luck, on its flanks.

We loaded our supplies and spares that afternoon. All radio equipment I had had finally to reject in view of what I had seen of the bulk of the film equipment in Bulawayo. As always in Africa, when there is the rumour of a journey a crowd of people quickly gathered, silent with inarticulate longing, to watch us tightly tying down the heavy loads and tucking in the canvas covers round them. At last the Land-Rovers stood there ready in the clear light of a late August afternoon on the high veld, like three little ships battened down before a storm on a remote ocean. Now I had only to complete my promise to my wife and to collect a case for "the best gun in the world," which I had already bought in Rhodesia—my favourite all-round weapon for Africa, a .375 Magnum express. That done I went tired but content early to bed.

We left Johannesburg at sunrise with the smoke tumbling down purple among the tops of the gaunt skyscrapers, and the light of morning pink and gold on the battleship-grey dumps of the mines. At the head of the small convoy travelled Charles, our expert Land-Rover mechanic. He was tall, slender, dark, with wide, hurt brown eyes, sensitive, soft-spoken and rather highly strung. With his long hands he had gone at the task of assembling the Land-Rovers like a swimmer in a race diving into water. He had worked fast and accurately, with a mind for nothing else. I had, I must admit, hesitated for a moment before engaging him because I thought he might be too complex and sensitive a character for the occasion. But I have always had a predisposition for people of quickened spirit and this young man had plenty of it. Though too young, he had volunteered for service in the war and disguised his age so effectively that he became the youngest soldier on active service with the South African forces. He had fought in the Western Desert and Italy, and the moment he heard of my expedition implored his employers for leave of absence to accompany us. In neat, well-pressed khaki clothes, shining boots and wearing his wartime South African desert bowler, he climbed into the first Land-Rover and deftly led the way out of the awakening city. I came last because I've learned from experience that convoys are best led from behind, where trouble, like the dust, invariably collects. We could not travel as fast as I would have liked, for our Land-Rovers were new, so at the prescribed maximum of twenty-five miles an hour we drove the three hundred miles west to Lobatsi where Ben Hatherall was already awaiting us.

The sun was beginning to decline when we crossed the Transvaal border into Bechuanaland. I noticed that since last I had crossed the frontier the fences had been repaired, gates mended and painted, the stones at the side whitewashed and a new flag hoisted, bright in the blue, to the head of a shining pole. The post, too, was manned again, and a policeman in smart uniform and polished boots raised his hand in a precise salute as we went by. Then in the distance a cloud of red dust rose like an explosion over the pass and a roar of urgent traffic rolled toward us. Charles drew on one side, wisely stopped the engine and we all drew in behind him.

Charles got out and came back to me, saying, "Looks as if we are being met! A reception committee?"

I shook my head. "No! I suspect an old Lobatsi custom: a wedding with an escort of every car in the village to speed the bridal couple safely over the frontier for a honeymoon in Johannesburg!"

I had hardly finished speaking when the dust and a long line of cars swept past us. The first had a score or more of old boots and shoes tied to the trunk. In the last car, despite the red, stinging sand, a pair of broad shoulders and a fine massive head with iron-grey hair, a deeply tanned and lined face and shrewd grey eyes glowing with recognition suddenly were pushed far out of the window and a surprisingly young voice called: "Colonel! Colonel! I'll be with you in a second." Still shouting, man and car vanished in a dark stain of dust.

"Who on earth is that?" Charles asked.

"Ben Hatherall," I answered, laughing. "You'll be seeing a lot of him from now on. I'm glad to see he's lost none of his zest for life! Like him not to miss a wedding!"

Lobatsi, little more than an administrative and shopping hamlet among the last of the Waterberg foothills on the brink of the desert, was almost empty as a result of the wedding. I went first to the Government Offices to call on a friend and was talking to another old friend, the head of the police, when a distressing little incident occurred. As it reveals the exposed state of mind I was in at the time and something of the oppressive and electric atmosphere everywhere in Africa, I tell it briefly here.

I was laughing with the police lieutenant over some reminiscence when suddenly for no obvious reason at all desire to laugh went from me. More, I felt all confidence and zest drain swiftly out of me. I had no idea what caused it. Alarmed, I turned round. Immediately behind me, shackled between two policemen, on his way to judgement went a young man of

Bushman blood. Our eyes met briefly and I knew then that the black invasion of my being came from him. I looked in those eyes filled with neither hope nor despair and recognized the black hand that puts out that candle in the heart when it knows its gods have failed it.

"What's happened to him! What's he done?" I asked the lieutenant in distress.

"Ritual murder," he answered grimly. "Murdered his own little sister to make medicine for the clan. His people, too, were suspected of the murder of some airmen who crashed in the bush up north some years ago."

The coincidence was almost too much for me. I remembered that some years before I had spent a night at the scene of that murder. I had met his people and used a kinsman of this very man as a tracker.

"Poor devil!" I said. And immediately felt sad that here, at the physical beginning of the journey, I was confronted with the overwhelming question that assails one at every step of the way these days in Africa. "What am I to him, and he to me? And what am I to do about it?" For this question has haunted me ever since I was a child in Africa.

I have never seen justice in treating "ritual murder" as murder. We have a share in it too, for the increasing revival of ritual murder is an expression, in part, of the sense of insecurity that we have inflicted on the indigenous spirit of my native land and a desperate attempt, by natural children, to appease an insupportable fear. It is also a product of our denial of what is naturally creative in Africa, and we, too, who arrest and judge the murderer are accessories before and after the fact. After the trial, the law-officers, judges and accusers and I talked the matter over. I thought I had rarely seen nicer faces or met fairer minds. I think they would have liked to agree that life and the situation in Africa needs more than justice to carry it out of certain disaster. But law and order came first and had to be maintained with mercy if possible, without it if not.

I spent the evening and night with the Resident and his wife, who were old friends of mine, in the ample Residency, comfortable and serene behind a tight green hedge and surrounded by an impeccable lawn and budding trees. I went over every detail of my plans with the Resident and made many an adjustment on his experienced advice. Between tea and dinner he took me to call on my old safari cook, Simon, who was now totally blind as a result of an accident on my previous expedition. But he was well cared-for and I thought I had never seen so fulfilled an expression on Simon's wrinkled old face as he sat in the setting sun outside his neat hut with his children around him and a wife beside him.

"May you go slowly, master," he entreated me in farewell, for in my part of Africa to "go slowly" is to go wisely and peacefully.

"Indeed, I will go slowly, Simon," I said. "And I'll come back to see you on my return and bring you and your children your Christmas presents."

From there my friend took me to meet Simon's successors, a cook and a camp assistant he had engaged for me. The cook, like Simon, was a Northern Rhodesian from Barotseland. His European name was Jeremiah, his surname Muwenda. He was a tall, straight man who held himself with obvious self-respect and a certain reserve in his manner. He wore horn-rimmed glasses, and when he talked he sounded, perhaps, just a trifle pedantic. I asked him only three questions.

"Can you bake bread in ant-heaps?"

"Yes, *Moren*," he answered and smiled. "Yes, Master. But I prefer baking it in pots."

"Can you cook in thunder-storms?"

"Yes! I can cook in thunder-storms." At that he laughed and his whole face and eyes joined in the laughter.

"Would you like to come on this journey? I'll look after you well but it will be long and not easy."

"I am here to come," he answered simply.

His companion was taller, broader, looser-limbed and a different type. He was a man of the Bamangkwetsi, John Raouthagall, of few homely words, great inner composure and with a pair of large black eyes that looked steadily into mine without concealment or evasion. He was a close friend of Jeremiah's and when I asked him if he was certain he wanted to come said gravely he was there precisely in order to come.

I slept badly that night. I kept on waking up and seeing again the face of the condemned Bushman. As a result I got up when it was still dark on that Sunday morning and climbed the hill at the back of the Residency. I got to the top as the dawn broke and to the west the Kalahari showed up like a coil of a wine-dark sea. Barely fifty feet from me five rheebuck got up from their warm beds behind a ledge of rock and shook the dew from their slender yellow flanks. Some bush pigeons came streaking by on whistling wings like messengers of fate, provoking the feeling of great urgency which had been with me so much ever since I decided on the journey. I went fast down the hill, jumping from stone to stone and feeling all the better for it.

Charles, Ben, Jeremiah, John were already packing the last of their new gear into the Land-Rovers as I arrived. With his gun beside him, Ben drove off first; Charles and John followed; Jeremiah and I came last. We passed the "cliffs where the elephants once fell over" and travelled all day on the red road of history that runs north from Mafeking in a straight line right into the interior with the foothills of the Transvaal on one side and the wide-open threshold of the Kalahari on the other. Toward noon we achieved the first five hundred miles on our speedometers and were able to travel a little faster. At noon the next day we were in Francistown, the little village on the railway where a rough road cuts into the Kalahari. I stopped there to call on "Masai" Murrell, the chief representative in the area of the recruiting organization for the Mines. I discussed fully my plans and possible emergencies with him and was greatly heartened by the ready promise of help he and his staff gave me. We lunched with two of my oldest friends, Molly and Cyril Challis, and drove into Bulawayo after dark on Monday evening. Neither Spode nor my friend was in the hotel. I left a note for them to say I had arrived very late and gone to bed. Before sleeping, I was given a local newspaper by the receptionist who "thought I would be interested to see" an account of the expedition "Eugene Spode, the distinguished continental film producer" had outlined in interviews with local journalists.

At breakfast I saw no sign of Spode and my friend, but after a while I was handed a note saying they were both waiting for me in the lounge. I finished my breakfast and went up the stairs to meet them. They were both sitting side by side on a couch at the far end of the vast room. I waved to them but they hardly acknowledged the greeting and remained seated. For the first time I began to feel something must be very wrong.

As I came up to them I was handed a typed document.

"I think," my friend said coolly, "you had better read this first before we say anything."

I could hardly believe my ears and eyes. I read through two pages in single-spaced type of reproaches too varied for repetition. The main point was that Spode had been deeply shocked to hear at our last meeting that I had ideas for the story for the film. If that was so, why had they not been conveyed to him months ago? He could then have started converting them into their proper film idiom, an exacting task, of which I clearly was lamentably ignorant, and so on and on. The document from there continued for another closely typed page to demand, among other things, a guarantee in writing that Spode would be in sole command of the story, filming, sound, music, editing and production. The whole thing ended with the afterthought: "You, Laurens, with your knowledge of the country no doubt could be of great assistance to me," and a threat that, if the guarantee was not forthcoming, Spode would withdraw from the expedition there and then.

I looked up from reading this unexpected epistle, not into the large friendly grey eyes I had last seen, but into a face clouded with resentment and injury. Even the square shoulders of Spode's squat figure seemed suddenly set at a fighting angle.

My heart shrank with dismay not because of this situation, but because I realized that perhaps I was seeing the whole Spode for the first time in my life. The scales fell from my eyes and I was aware in a moment of sudden though complex illumination that I was looking at a person whom denial of chance and opportunity had filled with conflict great enough to defeat both himself and others. I realized I had been content to see him through the eyes of a devoted friend rather than make the troublesome assessment of character out of my own not inconsiderable experience of the world and men that the occasion had demanded. But what to do now?

I tried to reason with them.

My friend quickly warned me, "I'm not in on this, Laurens. I'm the interpreter. I can only pass your messages on to Eugene."

For two precious hours or more I went patiently through each reproach, and all the others, too, that sprang up like giants from dragon's teeth sown innocently in the wake of each explanation. Near the end of the talk a tall young man with close-cropped hair, soft voice and a pleasant, open face, whom I was told was Stonehouse, Spode's assistant, came and joined us.

Finally I told Spode that if he still persisted in such an attitude and insisted on such a guarantee he had better go back to Europe at once. That instantly changed the atmosphere. Spode declared himself happy with my explanations and ready to go on as before.

"He'll be all right once he is at work," my friend said to me, *sotto voce.* "You both have such a love of Africa, and that will see you through."

The popular, pink marsh-mallow conception of "love," which considers it a lush force that does for human beings the things they are too lazy or greedy to do for themselves, instead of the call to battle that it is, always irritates me. I nearly gave an angry retort. Yet I bit it back. The immediate tussle with Spode was over, but the campaign, I knew, would go on. Sick in the pit of my stomach, I felt all the joy of the journey vanish. Obviously it was going to be a difficult task keeping Spode in a state of mind to do the work we had contracted to do. I would not for a single moment be able to take him for granted. More, I was not at all certain I had done right to reason either with him or myself. Now that it's all over I think that Spode's renewed contact with Africa had made him realize that he had undertaken greater responsibilities than he could fulfil, in physical conditions for which his metropolitan nature was unsuited. Ten days in a luxury hotel, watching the summer beginning to flare up fast around the little Africa-beleaguered city, had driven the point deeper home. In making such a scene on such trivial pretexts, I suspect his inmost nature was imploring me to send him back to Europe before it was too late. In not doing so, I failed both him and the expedition. Yet the reasons I had for making the wrong decision were excellent. Spode had been trained and specially briefed by the B.B.C. for the task. He was the film unit accepted by them as a basic part of my contract. Sixteen miles of film material was designed, rolled and made up for his special cameras and magazines. Besides, where and when was I to get a substitute? Motionless, the expedition cost fifty pounds a day to maintain. Also, there was a limit to the time Ben and Vyan could stay with me. Nonetheless, I believe now that I should have had the courage of my instincts, cancelled the old plan and started again from scratch.

Instead, we went on with resumed amiability to film rock paintings, caves and graves around Bulawayo. But I soon got some more shocks. Simon Stonehouse, I discovered, could hardly be called a friend of Spode's because he barely knew him. Before the proposal that he should join us, they had met only twice. He knew nothing about making films and had been attracted to the expedition solely because he was studying anthropology and accordingly was interested in the Bushman. In fact, he had come with a case full of specially printed forms of a census he wanted to make of Bushmen! More, he was a relation of my friend's. There was, of course, no harm in that. It would have acted as a recommendation with me. But it was odd I had never been told. However, while we did our little background filming outside Bulawayo, he and Spode appeared to be on the best of terms so I accepted the situation with all the grace I could.

Only once did I come near to an open quarrel with Spode and my friend. We were loading Spode's gear and film material in the Land-Rovers. I was doing the stacking when suddenly a case of tinned cheeses was handed up to me.

"What's this?" I called out, amazed, because I had ordered nothing so luxurious for the journey.

There was no answer. Spode and Stonehouse looked uneasily around them.

"Here! Chuck it out," I said, handing it back to Ben.
Then followed cases of peanut butter in jars, Marmite, glucose, vegetable protein extracts, sweets and other solids. As I had already brought the basic foods we would need and, except for sugar, salt and meal, most of these were in dehydrated forms in order to save weight and space, I rejected all these extra, unordered foods because we needed every ounce of carrying capacity we could spare for fuel and water.

I had hardly got back to the hotel when Stonehouse came to my room.

"I suppose," he stammered, most distressed, "you don't realize I'm a vegetarian?"

"A what!" I exclaimed.

"I'm a vegetarian. I explained it all to them in London because I thought it might be a complication, but they assured me it wouldn't matter a bit!"

"So I've chucked out all your patent foods?" I said touched by the boy's evident conflict.

"Of course, I thought you knew," he replied. "Will it make things much more difficult for you?"

My impulse was at once to go to Spode and my friend and ask for an explanation. But it seemed to me that the situation was already beyond help from post-mortems. "Look!" I said. "If I'd known this before, I wouldn't have let you come. Our main diet must be meat. We've no extra carrying space. One man has come all the way from East Africa to do nothing else but hunt game all day for us to live on. However, since you are here, Simon, we'll do our best for you. But I can't promise you much more than porridge and dried milk for days on end. So what about it?"

"I won't mind a bit," he said, obviously relieved. "And I promise you I'll do all I can to make up for it."

That evening my friend flew on home to Johannesburg. Spode returned from the aerodrome darkly silent and went straight to his room, sending me a message through Simon that he didn't feel like eating and wouldn't be at dinner.

Early the next day we left for the Falls. I asked Spode to travel with me because I was the only one who could talk French and because I was determined to do all I could to restore our relationship. I tried to interest him in the country, the types of bush, trees, birds, elephant spoor, the fragments of history and personal reminiscences evoked by the journey. But the work was hard and the response leaden. We arrived late that afternoon at the Falls Hotel. Spode went straight to his room, from which in due course he issued a statement that he was not coming down for dinner.

Meanwhile I had gone to look for Wyndham Vyan. This hotel in the bush on the edge of one of the great rivers of the world has been like a second home to me. I've known it since boyhood and seen it grow into one of the most remarkable establishments in Africa. Before many a long expedition, I have spent the night there and enjoyed celebrating the successful end of many another with a hot bath, dinner jacket and civilized dinner. The manager, staff, servants and waiters were well known to me. It took me some time to get over all the necessary greetings before I was free to find Vyan, whom I had arranged to meet at this hotel. He was sitting where I knew he would be, under his favourite flamboyant tree, smoking his pipe and watching the mist from the vast falls spinning the light of the setting sun into a rainbow bridge over the deep, fiery gorge of the Zambezi below him. The expression on his face was utterly resolved, as if life had long ceased to present any problem to him. With his glasses and his sensitive English features he looked, not like a hardy pioneer of Africa who had just travelled two thousand difficult miles by truck to meet me, but more like a scholar dedicated to reading the hour of the day like the script of some ancient document whose illumination had suddenly begun to fade.

I cannot describe the relief of seeing him there after these long sullen hours with the unhappy Spode. Before we'd uttered a word, something of quiet and strength immediately came from him to me.

After our first greeting he asked in his brief way, "Ben here? Shall I fetch him to join us?"

"No! Not for a moment, Wyndham. Let's hear your news first and have a bit of a talk," I answered quickly.

So healing did I find it just to be with someone who was obviously glad to see me and to whom it was not necessary to justify myself.

Chapter 6

NORTHERN APPROACHES

———————

W<small>E SPENT</small> two days at the Falls organizing ourselves on a fully operational basis, Spode meanwhile filming fastidiously what he found of interest in our great surroundings. We broke down our bulk supplies and re-allotted them according to the role each vehicle and its occupants would have to perform. As far as possible each Land-Rover was rendered self-contained in fuel, water and spares even to such detail as a snake-bite outfit and serum beside the seat of the four drivers. Though it was not fully justified on a weight and space measure, I thought it best to give Spode, for his sole use, one of the largest Land-Rovers, which like my own had been intended originally to absorb our overlap. I took in what slack there was in my own and the other vehicles. While Vyan and Hatherall supervised the reloading, I went to Livingstone to deal with small things omitted in the initial order. At the end of two days I was confident nothing of importance had been forgotten, and in the evening, while

Charles and the others went to fill up the vehicles with fuel
and water, I drove out into the bush to have an hour or two
to myself to reconsider everything for the last time.

Some miles from the Falls I found a track to take me down
to an open space by the flashing river. I had not been there
long when a noise like a bubbling witches' cauldron rose up
around me. I looked out of the side of the Land-Rover. A
herd of elephant, ebony-black at that hour, was emerging
from the bush and filling the golden clearing behind me. It
was compact, with cows and calves in the centre, but the
bulls, with long gleaming tusks and trunks nervously curling,
were well out patrolling their marble perimeter. As I looked,
one great bull stepped clear of the rest and, his trunk
stretched out between long shining tusks, came swiftly and
delicately toward me. Quickly I closed the plastic windows
of the Land-Rover and watched his resilient approach in the
driving mirror. He halted within a few feet of the Land-
Rover and pushed his trunk out until it nearly touched the
exhaust. Then it flicked back suddenly, and such an expression of distaste at the internal-combustion smell appeared on
his corrugated face that I nearly laughed aloud. For a moment he stood there working his ears like the fins of a fabulous fish and swishing his trunk with indecision, before he
turned to lead the herd sideways past me deep into the bush.

I relate the incident, however, not for the delight it caused
me, but for the encouragement it gave me. It was proof that
our timing had been right. It was evidence that the great
withdrawal of beast and man from the desert, on which so
much of our calculation was based, had started.

On the way back I met a pilot, who daily flies visitors up
and down the river, coming back from his landing strip in
the bush and told him what I had seen.

"Ag! Man!" he exclaimed with a pronounced South African accent. "That's nothing! You should see from above!

The bush from here for seventy miles west is alive with them—zebra, buffalo, giraffe, wildebeest and heaven knows what not—all falling back on the river now the summer's coming."

I sped back happy with the news to the others, but before I could speak I was told by Charles with a gloomy face, "Bad news, Colonel. Some of these tanks we had to fit in such a hurry in Johannesburg are leaking at the seams!"

The next day was a Sunday and like so many Sundays on this journey a day-elect for climax and crisis. The garage in Livingstone was shut, but again a friend came to the rescue. We broke in on his fishing, and all day long Charles, I and two mechanics dismantled the tanks and worked on them. By nightfall they were ready, tested and passed fit for desert travel. The tanks were refitted the next day, the vehicle refuelled and reloaded, and by two o'clock on the afternoon of September 3, only two days after a zero hour fixed months before, we began the main journey. Someone suggested, vaguely, that we could spend another night in the comfort of the hotel, but Ben silenced it with a quiet: "Look! There is only one time to start on this sort of a journey, not when you feel like it but when you're ready for it."

With Ben leading, we drove west along a deep sandy track in the black-bush parallel to the river. We camped early, for the first camp is always the most difficult and I wanted to allow enough daylight for the inevitable confusion and complications that would arise. Ben, Vyan and Cheruyiot (the Knipsigis servant and tracker Vyan had brought with him from East Africa) needed no prompting. Some of the others, however, wanted their tea before pitching camp. I stuck firmly to a rule I had learned from my own pioneering kinsmen: organize camp first against the night before pausing for rest and refreshment; otherwise it is never done so well or so quickly.

There is nothing like one's first, or one's last, camp. Others may be more beautiful, hold more delight and produce greater drama, but those at the beginning and end have a unique quality all their own given them, not by the people who build them, so much as by some abiding symbolism of life. They are Alpha and Omega, and they give, rather than take, from one. I don't know what the others were feeling on that still, transparent evening, deep in the red Kalahari sand in the black-bush which crowds the catchments of the rivers of northern Bechuanaland. I know only that it would be impossible to exaggerate my content in being there at last. For the moment I forgot even my disquiet about Spode and watched, not without a quick glow of satisfaction, the detail of the plan, so long and affectionately held in mind, come alive in its native setting. I had chosen African blankets of vivid colour and different tribal design for each one of us, and I was heartened to see the colour and pattern of Africa in the nine separate coverings lighting up the long evening shadows among the trees.

From the vehicle I was unloading I watched Cheruyiot, tall, lithe and fine-boned as are so many East Africans, moving with the long elastic step of a born plainsman between the Land-Ropers and the kitchen that John and Jeremiah were making near by. Although he did not speak a word of their language the three of them appeared old friends. As he put down a can of water Jeremiah looked up with a smile and said precisely, in English, "Thank you, Jambo," using the nickname they had given him after the Swahili greeting he had used on their first meeting. I watched him and John go off into the bush and come back dragging branches of dead wood until a pile high enough for a pagan king's pyre was stacked handy for Jeremiah.

"Thank you, John! Thank you, Jambo!" Jeremiah said again, the laugh that went with it quickly giving way to that dedicated look which comes upon a man's face when he makes a fire in a natural place. For one brief instant between the striking of the match and the quick leap of the first flame upward on a pig's tail of startled smoke, Jeremiah's bowed head might have been that of the first man lighting his first fire. Miraculously, just at that moment a little bird appeared on the branch of a tree behind him, flapping its wings and delivering with a silver clarity the urgent message my Bushman nurses had decoded for me as a child: "Quick! Quick! Honey! Quick!"

At once Jeremiah stood up from his fire in amazement, and then a laugh straight from the pit of his stomach and round with content broke from him.

"Look! Master!" he called, the marvel deep in his voice. "Look, John! Look, Jambo! The honey-diviner."

He took a step forward as if prepared to drop everything and follow the bird to the store of wild honey it was so ardently advertising. The little bird saw his step and fluttered hopefully on to a tree deeper in the bush.

I smiled at Jeremiah, shook my head and said, "It's too late!"

Soon the unfollowed bird was back again on its perch by the fire and stayed there beseeching Jeremiah with the hysteria of despair, until the sun red and tired sank into the leaves of the dense trees.

"That, John, that, Jambo," I heard Jeremiah lecturing them in his pedantic way as he busied himself about his pots, "is the honey-diviner of my country, which, I'll have you know, lies just on the other side of that river which goes like a great wind through these trees. . . . Follow the bird and it will lead you to sweet brown honey, but always be careful to share the honey with it. If you do not, it will punish you heavily. . . . I once knew a man whose stomach was too big for his eyes—no, not a man of my own people but of the stupid Bapedi. He cheated the bird out of its share and the very next day it called on him again and led him straight to a hole where there was no honey but an angry female puff-adder who bit him on his greedy hand and killed him. Another bird who had been cheated once led a man into the mouth of a lion. . . . I tell you that bird is too clever for a man to cheat."

"Clever" was Jeremiah's favourite adjective of praise.

"Auck!" exclaimed John, who had understood it all and laughed out of politeness as well as wonder. But Cheruyiot, who caught only the gist of the meaning from the onomatopoeic words and expressive gestures, just showed his white teeth and pointed with his finger appreciatively at the bird.

"Look, Jambo!" Jeremiah told him, demonstrating his meaning on his own thumb. "If you must point in that direction, please be so good as to refrain from doing it so rudely with your finger straight out like that, but instead, politely, only with the knuckle of your thumb, the tip turned down toward your hand thus. Otherwise you'll send away the rain we'll be needing soon."

Meanwhile Vyan had taken out his gun and mine to give them the attention a good rifle needs each night in Africa.

Hatherall set a bottle of brandy and some tumblers on the table that he and Charles had just put up. This was an old, established ritual of ours, conscientiously observed each day as the sun went down. While the others drank brandy and water I had a large jug of coffee. "Look, Ben," I said, "Wyndham's brought it with him again."

Vyan, pipe in mouth, was looking up the barrel of his favourite gun, his 6.5 Schönhauer Mannlicher. The stock was worn bare with long use like a constantly washed kitchen draining-board. It was Vyan's first gun in Africa and it would probably be his last. It was, I suspect, more than a gun to him, but rather a proved instrument of his accurate and unwaver-

ing spirit. I would not have been surprised if he had given it a
name as Arthur's knights named their swords in order to
express their symbolic character. But I had listened to many
arguments in the past between Vyan and Ben about that gun.
To the hunter a gun is what a pen is to a writer. One must
have one's own pen for writing—and one's own gun for
shooting. Ben was convinced that Vyan's gun was too light
for the big game of Africa. Vyan was determined that other
guns were too heavy, less precise and not quick enough.

"But he'll never have another gun," Ben had said to me,
frowning. "You know, Colonel, it's the one thing I can't
understand about Wyndham. He knows Africa so well, and
yet is content with so puny a gun. If he weren't such a good
shot he'd have been dead long since. But he'll never change.
Strange that he should be so obstinate about it."

Looking at Ben's own gun, a nine millimetre Mauser of as
ancient a make as Vyan's, tenderly laid out for its evening
cleaning on a fiery pile of blankets, I laughed to myself.

When all the work was done and the party complete
around the table, I was delighted to find Spode well under the
influence of his first camp. He was once more the person I
had seen in London, both charming and thoughtful. He
joined in the conversation so freely that I was unable to take
part in it but had to concentrate on interpreting between
him and the others! After the first drink he went to his Land-
Rover and came back with a box of expensive cigars which
he pressed on us all. After the second he went and fetched his
violin.

Walking away from us to the jagged edge of the light
thrown by our fires on the darkness, he stood with his back
to the camp and began to play as if somewhere in the bush
there was a great and expert audience. Everyone stopped
talking. Even John, Jeremiah and Cheruyiot went silent by
the kitchen fire. For about half an hour Spode stood there

playing with increasing concentration and power. It seemed to us, watching his short, square figure, head bowed over his violin and the bow itself flashing in the fire-light, that there was far more than fiddling to it. I myself had a feeling that he was trying to exorcize some obstructive spirit, or defying some judgement of fate. I found myself strangely moved by the sight. Then he suddenly stopped, swung round abruptly and came stumbling back out of his border zone toward the light.

I jumped up, feeling it was urgent to go forward and thank him.

He was in tears. He put his arms round my shoulders and said, "Laurens, for a moment I forgot myself and just thought of the music to play to the forest! It was wonderful! I completely forgot myself, and I do not know when I have last done that— Oh! Why does life do such terrible things to one?"

All that evening I reproached myself for having been too critical of Spode. I told myself, What you have seen tonight is central. You must never forget it; you must keep it at the core of your attitude.

Even Vyan and Ben, though they knew nothing of my difficulty with Spode, for I had not spoken a word of my misgivings to them, were aware of the change in Spode. They responded so warmly that when we went to bed soon after, I felt once more we had a chance of all being united on the journey.

I did my last round of the camp with a lighter heart. The bush was more silent than I had ever known it. Not a bird called, no jackal barked, no leopard coughed nor lion roared. Only faintly to the north the air of night like a wind of summer brought up the sound of the great river hastening out of the west toward the sun in the far Indian sea. I crept into my blankets and lay on my back watching the stars swinging above me, like the masthead lights of a great concourse of shipping, and feeling the earth, black sails filled with the trade wind of time, hastening over the swell of the dark to keep in station with them.

"This," I thought, before sleeping, "is Alpha Plus."

As always in the bush I woke many times, listening only long enough to decipher the signs of the night. But even the river had gone inaudible and the stillness was unbroken, if one can speak of stillness on a clear night under the stars in Africa. Night silence in Africa always holds the far sea-sound of urgent stars. This first night was no exception. When I woke for the last time, it was as if to the surf of a starry breaker hissing in my ear. My favourite constellation, the belted hunter Orion, was about to enter a forest beyond the foreshore of a new world. My watch showed the day was about to break. I rolled out of my blankets. I like to be up first in my own camp, to wake the cook myself, to shave while he boils the kettle and then to call the rest of the company with a warm cup of coffee. Jeremiah, I was pleased to see, rose easily from his bed. Before the sun rose, breakfast was on the fire and the camp on foot.

The moment it was light enough, Vyan, Ben and I went to examine the record of the night scribbled on the sand around the camp. This, too, has been a rule of my life ever since I first went into the bush, and the three of us never fail to find the early-morning reading of the hieroglyphic spoor in the earth of Africa full of meaning. We learned, this day, that our arrival had not passed unnoticed. We had been roy-ally observed. Not fifty yards from our fire a great lion had made a circuit of our camp. Ben thought the spoor only an hour old because the sand along the ridge of the broad *pug*-marks had not yet settled and still rolled inward when touched lightly with a stem of grass. There was much other spoor as well, but all old. Only this imprint of an imperial paw was new and deep in the blood-red earth like a seal on the warrant for our journey.

By eight o'clock we were once more on the move. On this occasion Spode travelled with me at the head of the line so that we should be the first to see the game and, if possible, film it. But I was dismayed to find the old look of conflict back on his face. It was not improved by the heat. Although we were only in the first days of spring in subtropical Africa, by European standards it was already hot before ten. Yet the journey was of unending interest and I tried to get Spode to feel it too.

We had not gone far when a volume of sub-human scream-ing and sobbing broke out in the long grass of the clearing between us and the bush along the river. A troop of about two hundred baboons came fleeing across our tracks in the hysteria of overwhelming fear. Some baboon mothers had tiny babies with rose-pink faces and eyes wide with terror sobbing on their backs, their long little fingers and prehensile toes clutching at the auburn hair on lean maternal flanks. Others had babies slung underneath their stomachs. All with long, loping bounds fled across the clearing toward the tall trees beyond and the promise of safety in their branches. The sight of us merely opened up another prospect of terror al-ready too great to bear, and some old male baboons, who were trying manfully to keep silent as they feverishly brought up the rear, immediately added their booming bark to the high-pitched shrieks and cries of their women and children. So fast did they travel that in a moment they were out of sight and the bush as still as ever. Were it not for some vultures in the blue air spinning over the place from which the baboons had fled, there would have been no sign to re-mind us of the desperate retreat from tragedy. Close to the wheels of my Land-Rover I found the fresh spoor of a lion warm in the still crumbling sand.

We had stopped to give Spode a chance to film the incident, but it was over so quickly that he could not do much about it. It was certainly no fault of his. Yet the lack of success weighed on him out of all proportion and seemed to fit only too well into some gloomy preconception of his about the journey. It also seemed to make him want to get away from me. He asked to be allowed to join Simon Stonehouse in his Land-Rover.

I fell back into my old place at the rear and put Ben in front, with Spode's Land-Rover immediately behind, and instructed Ben to do all he could to help with any filming Spode might want to do. We pressed on hard in this formation all morning. By noon we were close to the junction of the Chobe and Zambezi rivers and could begin to swing away to the south-west. We stopped briefly at the frontier post of Kasane. An efficient young officer welcomed us and insisted only that we should take on with us one of his African policemen who already had done several patrols deep into the country ahead. I was about to refuse, because taking another new personality into our small group before it had found its own coherence seemed to me a complication, when I saw the man he proposed should accompany us. He stood there as if about to go on ceremonial parade, looking at me out of shrewd, steady Bantu eyes. He, too, was an old soldier who had served abroad in the war, spoke good English and to my amazement had a smattering of French. When I asked him his name, he came to attention and said crisply, "Trooper Khgometsu." *Khgometsu* is the Sechuana for "comfort," and a comfort he proved indeed.

I had him next to me in my Land-Rover for the rest of the day. We moved up again to the head of the line since I had been warned that the next fifty miles were extremely dangerous because great herds of elephant were wandering between the waterless bush and river. As always, the responsibility of young calves had set on edge the nerves of cows and bulls. Comfort told me of several recent, exceedingly uncomfortable meetings with herds. One old bull, already so notorious that he had been christened "Old Sway Back" because of the violent manner in which he came out on any scent that perturbed him, some days before had forced the police jeep to retreat precipitately in reverse for close on a mile. The track for nearly fifty miles was a continuous series of elephant spoor deep in the sand. Elephant dung everywhere lay still warm and steaming in the grass. The going was made rough and difficult for the leading vehicle by elephant pot-holes. But just before sundown, when we climbed out of the sandy depression in the river basin to camp on a rise overlooking the Chobe, the heavy spoor diminished suddenly and fell away abruptly behind us. We thought we were clear of that particular hazard, but we thought too soon.

At two o'clock in the morning in my deepest sleep an alarming noise reached me. It was already over when I awoke but it lingered in my memory like the echo of a gunshot. I listened and looked. The fire had died down to a great coal pinned like a crimson rose to the dark earth. Everyone was fast asleep. Had I been mistaken? No! There was something moving with a heavy, sagging stealth just beyond the fire. I threw my mosquito net aside and leapt to the fire, calling on Jeremiah to wake up as I threw fresh wood on it. Jeremiah huffed and puffed air into the coals like Aeolus blowing up a gale, and the fire flared up quickly. The bush immediately began to heave and crackle and the regiment of elephant which encircled us quickly retreated into the night. At sunrise we found one elephant spoor satin in the sand only ten yards from the fire, and close by was the broken branch of dead wood on which he had trodden and awakened me from my sleep.

The day, however, brought shocks of a different and more

lasting kind. We were entering great baobab-tree country. These fantastic trees had already stirred Spode's imagination in a manner which looked as if it might really become productive. One of my favourite Bushman stories declared that these trees were planted upside down by a mischievous member of "the persons of the early race." Livingstone, who could be as prosaic in words as he was imaginative in deed, said they looked like carrots put in the earth the wrong end up. They are unlike any other tree, looking more like a product of fever and sunstroke than a normal botanical concept. Even the bark of the baobab is flushed and hot. Its varicose veins, full of permanganate sap, show up on the surface swollen and clotted with the malaise of its birth. For all its immense girth and appearance of strength, it is hollow inside. On this hot morning, stripped of leaves and tartar fruit, they stood out beside our route, with their swollen apoplectic columns like the arms of a brood of Titans buried alive, with wide-open hands protruding from the grave, vainly appealing to the stark blue sky now filled with vultures. The botanist, too, has caught the image of these contorted fingers and called the species *Adansonia digitata*.

Spode took eagerly to the suggestion of filming these trees, and I, determined to follow to the end any hint of the creative in him, set everyone to help. For some hours we filmed baobabs both singly and in flushed battalions, from afar and from close up, finishing with a great grandfather of a tree by the edge of the Chobe River at a place where both Livingstone and Frederick Selous, the hunter of Africa, are said to have camped.

It was there that I realized suddenly that all was not well between Spode and Stonehouse. Stonehouse had worked hard. He had driven a vehicle for the whole of two difficult days and not shirked a duty in camp. But already I had the impression that he was unduly tired for one so young and strong. I noticed that the night had not really rested him. He was slower than usual in his responses. Spode, who had done little except his camera work, seemed to take Stonehouse's fatigue as a personal offence. He became so irritable that in the end I asked Vyan to drive his Land-Rover for him and took Stonehouse in with me and Comfort for rest. I feared now that it was not just physical exertion but mental conflict that had helped to exhaust Stonehouse.

The second shock came just beyond a small African outpost on the edge of the sleeping-sickness country of northern Bechuanaland. My plan had been, first, to see if there were any remnants left of the fabulous River branch of the Bushman race. That was the main reason why I had begun the journey on the northern frontier of the Kalahari. If there were one place left in Africa with enough water and isolation to have enabled the River Bushman to maintain himself intact, I felt it could only be deep in the land which lay behind the dense sleeping-sickness barrier and the waters of this vast swamp, made by the rivers flowing down from their source in the highlands of Angola to spread out and vanish in the sand and sun of the northern Kalahari. While the growing heat of summer was purifying the central desert of foreign invaders, I thought I could, without loss of time, explore those enigmatic northern marshes. My intention was to begin the task by cutting in between the Chobe River and the great Okovango Swamp and to probe all along the edges of the marshes for signs of the River Bushman.

But here, just beyond the discreet huts of reeds and grass where I had proposed swinging away to the north-west, we found our route blocked by vast sheets of flood water. I knew that the flood in the swamps had been abnormal. An old friend who had helped me to plan this part of the journey, the valiant Harry Riley, of Maun, had been drowned in them some months before. I had expected, however, that the worst of the flood water would have subsided by now. Yet here the floods were, decisively blocking our route.

We had no option but to feel our way far round the water to the east and to climb out of the lapping basin onto the high bush-covered dunes that flanked it. It was hot, tough and in many ways nerve-racking driving. We had to use our Land-Rovers like tanks and crash our way blindly through bush and undergrowth of tangled, spurred and spiked thorn-trees. The sand beneath us was deep and fine enough for an hour-glass. We had continually to use the four-wheel drive of the Land-Rovers in the lowest gears. Time after time the wind-screen and windows of my own Land-Rover were so deep in leaves and branches, brushing like angry sea-green water over them, that I could not see what lay beyond. The vehicle shook and was submerged like a vessel shipping wave after wave of tumultuous ocean to its funnel tops. Twisting and turning to avoid only the trunks of adult trees, we crashed our way through, like this, for hours. I thought it dramatic enough to justify a picture, but Spode when I suggested it said, "I'm sorry I have not the strength . . . later."

The sun was low when at last we came down the side of the dunes onto a level plain covered with *mopane* trees. They are always a brave sight. I know of no tree which partakes so deeply of the nature of Africa and is so identified with its in-domitable spirit of renewal. All the year round they are green, red and gold, and though the bark of the long slender trunks is twisted with the struggle to break out of tortured earth, they mount undismayed, in an upright spiral, into the rainless blue. There the dying leaf, the new-born bud and the green, expanding butterfly-wing of the adolescent hang side by side to give great, silent and forgotten plains the look of early autumn. Now when we camped among them, the last of the sunlight was dripping like honey from their leaves and barley-sugar stems. The night, however, was not silent. From sunset to dawn the croaking of frogs to the west warned us that the waters from the overflowing marshes were still near.

As a result, the next day we held on south until we came to the first of the blue Shinamba Hills. I have always longed to climb them. No white person, I believe, has yet done so. But regretfully I felt compelled to swerve smartly round them and leave them like a puff of smoke above the flickering flame of the burning, northern, waterless plains.

Just beyond the hills, the plain levelled. Three amazed giraffes in harlequin silk watched us go by, and suddenly far below we saw vast herds of game grazing up to their chins in the grass between the sparkling mopane forests and the pink and mauve mists drawn up, steaming, from the molten marshes. The animals shone and glittered as if their colours were newly painted, and every now and then a group of youngsters broke from the herd to dance a provocative ballet of sheer fire above the yellow grass.

Vyan and Hatherall climbed onto the roof of their vehicle to watch. Jeremiah, John, Cheruyiot and Stonehouse excitedly followed their example. Only Spode, tired and depressed, leaned against the door of his vehicle.

"By Jove, Ben," I heard Vyan say, "it's unbelievable! They're there in thousands! Zebra, wildebeest, roan, sable, giraffe, tsessebe and hartebeest!"

Some twelve miles further on, just within the outskirts of another colourful mopane forest, we found two round pans side by side and full to the brim with water. It was only eleven in the morning but the look of strain on the faces of Spode and Stonehouse decided me. Perhaps I had been going too fast and too hard for them. Perhaps the fault lay there. I must give them time to get acclimatized.

"We'll camp here for a day or two and scout around at leisure to see what this part of the country can produce," I told them all.

The relief on their faces seemed to prove the wisdom of the decision, and even Vyan and Hatherall seemed pleased.

We unloaded our vehicles so that we could repack with the benefit of the experience gained. We built an ideal camp. Vyan and Hatherall went out to hunt for food and came back in the early afternoon with a purple hartebeest slung over the bonnet of a Land-Rover, saying, "There's enough to feed an army out there."

Part of the hartebeest we stacked in the fork of a tree near by as bait for lion or leopard in the hope, after dark, of filming them and recording their table-talk. I myself went out later, taking Stonehouse with me. The mopane forest and clearings were scribbled bright with the colour of zebra, roan and kudu. I came back in the evening to see Spode preparing flares and microphones for work in the dark around the camp. Already the rest seemed to have done him good and we sat down to a cheerful dinner of pot-roasted steak and liver of hartebeest. We went early to bed with crickets, owls, and frogs singing us to sleep. Only the lion, no doubt too easily fed with so much game about, did not come to try our bait. Instead, at midnight a fearful hyena crept into camp to taste it. The sight of the coals of our fire, however, sent him howling with dismay back into the night.

Early the next morning we tried another probe into the country to the west. We made straight for the great depression which lies between the marshes of the Chobe and Okovango. Ben was leading, and had just broken out of the mopane forest to enter the yellow grass and black-thorn tree veld at the beginning of the long declivity, when he suddenly stopped. Our Land-Rovers were already black with the tsetse fly, bearers of sleeping sickness, pricking whatever was bare flesh with quick rapier thrusts. Ben himself, slapping his arms and neck continuously, was kneeling in the grass and pointing. Almost against the front wheels of his vehicle was the

gleam of a line of jet-black water advancing slyly through the
tangled turf and thorn. The day was hot and cloudless. For
months the days had been bright and dry, yet, uncannily it
seemed, there was water rising inexorably at his feet.

"September and the flood waters still rising!" he exclaimed.
"I bet it's centuries since it got as far as this. Nor would I
have believed that tsetse fly would come out so deeply into
the plain."

We were forced to turn round and soon were back at our
camp by the waters among the mopane trees for another easy
day and early night.

The following day we made a further determined attempt
to outflank the rising water by a wide turning movement, first
east, then south and finally, toward evening, west. We did
long miles of driving through deep sand the colour and texture of powdered Parisian rouge. The work of breaking
through both it and the bush, simultaneously, was so hard
that I constantly changed the leading vehicle. We broke
through in the end without delay or mishap, but the hard
labour of the engines, the heat and dust of the day, the constant bumping and rocking up and down, added much to the
strain of another long lap in the journey. When once more
at sundown we found our way blocked by impassive waters,
the sense of frustration was more than some of us could bear.

I had gone ahead to pick a site for a camp on ground as high
as possible above the water. It was a lovely situation in the
open between immense black-thorn trees, with water for
cooking and wood for fire near at hand. Only it was over-
populated with tsetse fly. The first outcry came when the fly
started stinging us immediately we began pitching camp. I
pointed out that the fly would go the moment the sun went
down and the complaining ceased. At that moment, however,
Spode and Stonehouse, who had taken my place at the tail,
drove into the clearing. The Land-Rover had hardly stopped

when Spode flung himself out of it and came running toward me with a canvas water-bag in his hand.

"What's the meaning of this?" he shouted, shaking the bag. "What d'you mean by giving me such filthy water to drink?"

"What's the matter with it?" I asked, keeping my voice low, but aware that everyone had stopped to listen, though no one except Comfort understood French. "It was boiled last night. I saw to it myself."

"It's foul to taste and I'll not put up with it any longer!"

"I'm afraid you'll have to drink worse before we're through," I told him.

"Stop speaking to me as if I'm a child," he cried out, more angry than ever. "I'll have you know I'm not a child."

"Sometimes, Eugene, I'm not so sure of that," I said, saying, I believe, the only sharp thing I ever did on the journey.

Taken aback for one moment, he glared silently at me. For a moment I thought he would hit me. Instead he shook a clenched fist and demanded to be sent back to Europe at once.

"You've contracted to do a film with me," I told him firmly. "And I'll release you from your pledge when you've done it. We've done little enough work so far. I think you're just tired out. You'll feel better after tea. Ask Jeremiah for a lemon and squeeze that into your water if you don't like the taste."

"A lemon, bah!" He made a mouth of disgust at what, for the rest of us, was a luxury and stumped off irately to his vehicle.

After drinks at sundown, however, he drew me on one side and apologized handsomely. The real trouble, he explained, was that he could not get on with Simon Stonehouse. He was really no use to him and he would rather go on alone, doing all the work himself, than have an unwilling helper. I told Spode I thought they were both tired and not yet acclimatized. I asked him to try out the situation a bit longer. I didn't labour the obvious point: that we were nearly a week's hard travelling from the nearest railway and couldn't possibly exchange personnel. He seemed content with that and assured me he was more determined than ever to make our film. In the meanwhile, I had heard another version of the situation from Stonehouse, who was making me increasingly anxious. I had never known a more willing person and as I watched his drawn face closely in the fire-light that evening, I told myself that if it were purely a question of physical strain he could learn in time to endure it. But I was not so certain that he could support as well the strain of working under someone so different as Spode. His open young face looked to me almost tragic with two kinds of fatigue.

For once the charm of hot food, a night of stars and the prospect of sleep in the singing bush failed to cheer me. The doubts which had been in my own mind since Bulawayo had been emphasized by Spode's scene in the afternoon. It seemed to me that everyone round me—Vyan, Hatherall and Charles, Cheruyiot and Jeremiah—was now busy reinterpreting our situation with new insight. Comfort, who had understood more than most, was particularly uneasy that evening. He kept on getting up from the fire and standing and listening intently on the edge of the fire-light.

"What's the matter, Comfort?" I asked at last, joining him there.

"Don't know, sir," he said, turning round, the fire-light warm in his shrewd, disciplined eyes. "Don't know. There's plenty of lion about, I think, and strange people out there and . . . But I don't really know, sir."

It was certainly odd that we had gone hundreds of miles without hearing a lion. As Vyan remarked later, "The silent ones are the dangerous ones. I certainly like mine to roar at night." But there was more to it than that, as Comfort knew.

Before it was fully light Comfort left camp with a gun in

the crook of his arm. He was back at sunrise leading an old man armed with one of the carbines that had caused the Indian Mutiny and accompanied by a little boy. The old man trembled with fever; his cheeks were hollow, his eyes dull with the drowsiness that precedes the final sleep of the sickness carried by the fly. Yet he was hungry and we fed both well.

While eating, the old man told us that neither lion nor water had ever been so plentiful. Everywhere the water between the Chobe and Okovango stood in one continuous and expanding sheet. There was, he assured us, no hope of getting through to the west, and no Bushman on our side of the swamps. In fact, he had not seen one for many years. His own hut was the only one in a distance of four days' walking, and he lived there alone with his ancient gun to feed his women and children.

It was by then eight o'clock on Sunday morning and immediately after filming, which Spode did willingly and well, I called them all together and said, "I'm afraid it's no use going on trying to get through the floods on this side. We'll call it off and see if we can't take the water in the rear. We'll make for Harry Riley's old track to Maun, and go the six hundred miles round the marshes to Old Muhembo on the Okovango, at the sluice-way to the swamps. We'll leave our Land-Rovers there, get a boat, or dug-outs if necessary, and break into the swamp that way. If the water is still high enough, we might even go through the centre on the current for the whole of the four hundred miles back to Maun. If there are any River Bushmen left that's where we'll find them."

After breakfast we picked up the rut that Harry Riley, many years before, had opened up between the Zambezi and Maun. Our Land-Rovers sped along it, once more making that musical sound I love so well when they travel fast. The only real discomfort was caused by the tsetse fly. They settled on our vehicles in such dense masses that the metal bonnets looked as if covered with calico and I could hardly see through the wind-screen. We had to keep our windows firmly shut and that of course made it very hot. I stopped only once to try and get Spode to film the tsetse fly.

He asked, "Will there be another occasion later on?"

"There may be," I said. "Though I doubt if so impressive a one."

"Later!" He muttered firmly, quickly shutting the window of his car against the hungry fly.

Soon we struck the first of the Batawana settlements that crowd the edges of the streams and swamps round the small administrative settlement of Maun. Just before we reached the rough home-made causeway of mopane timbers and stone thrown across the water to the village, a tall European came running out from behind a near Batawana hut to stand beside a pile of kit and a pair of guns on the edge of the track. When he saw us it was clear we were not what he was expecting, for listlessly he waved us on. But there was time enough on that Sunday, between the swamp and the desert, for us to catch the glimpse of night in his eyes.

"Good God, Laurens!" Vyan exclaimed involuntarily as we drove by. "What was the matter with that fellow? Did you see the look on his face?"

"Yes," I answered, thinking it was exactly the look I had seen on the condemned Bushman's face at the other end of the journey. Suddenly the darkness seemed to link all together. "Shall we stop?"

"No!" Vyan said, looking out. "It's no good. He's waving the others on as well."

I thought no more of it for the moment because we were approaching Maun and I was wishing, for the sake of the others, that they could have seen the place as I first saw it years before, after days of weary travelling across the long miles of empty waterless country between it and the Great North Road. Then, the wide river of water, the lily-covered creeks, banks of green grass and spreading acacia, flamboyant and other trees took on in one's travel-stained senses the wonder of a dream oasis fulfilled. I remembered the welcome Harry Riley had given me in his remarkable little hotel, which he had founded for the odd, intrepid traveller who had been determined enough to cross the desert, as well as for the score or so of Europeans patient and courageous enough to make Maun the unique outpost of life that it is today. The settlement lay there in the overwhelming sun of noonday, a fortress of green with a moat of blue Okovango water round it keeping out the great grey Kalahari wasteland.

"You know, Wyndham," I told him, "the first night I ever spent in Maun, Harry and his friends gave a dance. We danced barefoot on the deep grass to the music of concertina, banjo and guitar, our feet wet with dew and the lions roaring back at us down-river."

"I can't imagine the place without Harry," Vyan said quietly, for he too had known him.

We made directly for the little hotel, where Harry's nephew and widow prepared lunch for us. While the others waited to eat, I went to confirm that the petrol and stores, ordered many months before, were there. Then I called on the District Commissioner and his wife, both old friends. He was about to go fishing with his family, but they delayed their departure to organize baths for us and allot us a camping site under a tree at the bottom of his garden by the river. I visited the representative of the Mines I have mentioned, also a friend. He was listening to a gramophone record of Tchaikovsky's "Nutcracker" music when I arrived. We sat on the veranda of his house in the cool, discussing my plan at length.

"Of course we can help," he said simply, and got up instantly to send a colleague in Muhembo a request by radio telephone (the only means of immediate communication between Maun and it) to organize a boat, or dug-outs and paddlers, for a journey into the swamp.

I got back to the hotel just as the others were finishing a lunch of yellow Okovango Bream, duck and lager beer. At that moment, also, the door on the mosquito-proof veranda opened and slammed sharply. The tall European we had seen on the road walked in, sat down silently in a wicker chair, giving us again just one dark, unseeing look. For the moment I had the impulse to ask him to join us in a drink, but I was in a hurry and felt already somewhat overburdened. The impulse passed. Without bothering about food I took the others to pitch camp. While we were doing so, Simon Stonehouse suddenly began swaying on his feet. I ran to him and led him away, making him lie down in the shade of the tree. One moment he was white, then deeply flushed in the face. His pulse was racing. As soon as the camp was made, I took him to the hotel and asked for a spare bed for him. In the evening when all was finally organized I went and sat by him and we had a long talk.

I explained that what we had been through was child's play compared to what was to come. For some days already I had been afraid that without a long period of conditioning the kind of journey we were making would be too much for him. The temperature and collapse that afternoon showed how justified those fears had been. I wanted him to know, therefore, that I was not going to take him with us, but was arranging for him to be flown out to the railway at Francistown by one of the aeroplanes of the Mines as soon as he was better.

I did not tell him Spode had already suggested his going,

nor did I say I could imagine nothing more unfair to an impressionable boy than being made to endure in conditions of severe physical strain a conflict of loyalties between Spode, who had invited him, and the leader of the expedition, who engaged him. I told him also, because I thought uncertainty was bad for him, that the decision was final.

I then went and told Spode what I had done, saying I proposed asking the head of police if Comfort, who was supposed to turn back at Maun, could continue with us. I suggested that as he spoke French he should be attached to Spode as his full-time assistant. Spode appeared delighted with the arrangement. In camp that night he was once again his charming continental self.

I was hardly asleep when the noise of someone running toward the camp woke me. It was Stonehouse in pyjamas and boots. He seized me by the shoulders, saying wildly, "What am I doing in the hotel? Why am I not here? How did I get there?"

"I took you there this afternoon. Don't you remember?" I answered.

"No, I don't— What's happening to me?"

"I'll tell you in the morning."

With great difficulty I persuaded him to go back to bed. I was about to sleep again when the sound of a truck, approaching at high speed, startled me. Its lights flashed wildly above the bush and water. Brakes screaming, it stopped abruptly at the D.C's house. In a few minutes it was off again and vanished, travelling fast. Somehow it brought an element of hysterical alarm into the atmosphere of the night and became quickly associated in my mind with the more negative forces which seemed to beset us. I had done all I could to beat off shadows, yet a sense of subtle disintegration, working against the purposeful composition of our party, persisted. I have had many difficulties on other expeditions in Africa and the East. I had expected difficulty and disappointment on this journey too, but nothing so elusive as this. I lay there for a long time, watching our fire die down, and the darkness beyond seemed to me as charged with negation as one of those fire-light pictures Goya crowded with nightmare shapes.

In the morning when I met the D.C. on my way to his bathroom, he seemed abnormally tired. "Sorry," he yawned. "Had a bad night. Fellow committed suicide."

Instantly I remembered the truck in the night. And as instantly I knew who was the victim. To an amazed D.C. I described the tall European we had passed on the way.

"That's the man," he nodded. "Poor fellow, he had put a black woman in the family way. We thought it was best to send a police truck for him yesterday to get him to go back to his own people. But he didn't want to go."

When I told the others about it at breakfast Vyan became immensely angry. "There's a pretty comment," he said, "on your European civilization. A man has to commit suicide because he's done the most natural thing in the world. And what could be more natural than that a young man in his loneliness—and, my God, how lonely it can be for them in places like this!—should go with one of these black women? But the end has to be suicide. I believe 'suicide' is written in capital letters over all your European culture, in Africa and everywhere else."

"What worries me," I told him, "is my end of it. I've a feeling we might have prevented it."

I told him of my impulse to ask the man to join us in a drink, and my belief that such a gesture, slight as it was, might have turned the tide in him, breaking the sense of isolation imposed upon him by his official excommunication from European society and his own civilized conscience.

"Perhaps," Vyan answered. "But, dammit, Laurens, one'd go mad if one carried one's sense of responsibility to such lengths!"

"When one's aware of these things perhaps one's mad not to," I replied. And to this day the question persists. All I suspect is that the fear that drove the Bushman to ritual murder and this poor lonely boy, caught between the swamp and the desert, to suicide, together with the forces of the law and order that condemn them both, is all part of the rejection and subsequent inhumanity of the slanted modern mind. And on this particular occasion I feared, beyond explanation, that the coincidence of these events with our own movements could not have been so precise unless we were, unwittingly, off the beat of some mean of time in our own spirits.

"What are you all saying?" Spode now asked in French, his voice still gruff with sleep.

I told him at length. He listened without comment, his eyes sombre and without surprise of any kind.

When we went to the small radio station which daily linked Maun to the outside world for one hour, I sent a telegram, among others, to Molly and Cyril Challis in Francistown asking them to meet Stonehouse on his arrival and help him on his way home to Johannesburg. Jeremiah sent an expensive telegram to his wife and son, reading: "I greet my son and you. We have arrived with God in health and safety at Maun and with God we go on today." Ben telegraphed to his home for a forecast of rain. Vyan inquired after the health of his humpbacked cattle. Spode, though I knew it only months later, sent a telegram to our mutual friend to the effect: "I commit my child to your care stop fear I shall not come out of it alive." Simon Stonehouse did not want to send a telegram and lay in bed so disappointed that he barely said good-bye to me. Charles, too, had no message to send. Like a long-distance runner with mind and breath only for the race, he spent the morning refuelling, oiling, greasing and otherwise tending his beloved engines with such effect that soon after noon our Land-Rovers were humming along the track like bees with syrup hastening back to their hive.

Chapter 7

THE SWAMP OF DESPOND

Now that the routine of camping was clearly established, we spent two whole days travelling until sundown. For the first day the new arrangement of Comfort helping Spode seemed to work miracles. But on the second there was a regression. Comfort came drifting back to my side and I had to give him the orders I imagined Spode would like, instead of Spode himself taking control. Charles, however, to my delight distinguished himself by spotting long before any of the veterans a twenty-foot python, looking like a stocking filled for Christmas, dragging itself ponderously through the bush. Armed only with a stick, he tried gallantly to head it off and turn it back toward Spode to film, but the serpent was not willing.

Soon after sunrise on the second day out from Maun I was startled to hear an outburst of rapid gunfire ahead of me. I came to Ben's Land-Rover abandoned in the track with three dead wild dogs lying close by it. Some moments later

Ben and John reappeared dragging two more dead dogs after
them. It was an extraordinary demonstration of Ben's quick
reactions and accuracy as a rifleman: five shots at five of the
swiftest animals in Africa and all five fatal. Ben's sun-lined
face had a benign expression on it. I believe of all natural
things he hated only the wild dogs for their ruthless ways
with weaker animals. He climbed back into his vehicle like a
horseman swinging back into his saddle, and we were off
again.

Toward evening of the same day we reached a small rest
camp, used by the recruiting organization of the Mines, called
Sepopa, "the place of the eddies." It was on the edge of the
swamp, about ninety miles by water below the entrance to
the Okovango delta, and the terminal of a small ferry service
run by the Mines between the south and north banks of the
marshes. I knew that close by there lived the remnants of a
race of dug-out, or *makorro*, men. Since there was still an
hour or two of daylight, I went on alone to see if I could
contact their headman, a veteran renowned for his travels by
makorro and with the musical-sounding name of Karuso, as
well as honorary title among Africans of "King of Paddlers."
I did not find him. Instead I met a man, a home-made axe
upon his shoulders, walking out of the bush into a long savan-
nah of buffalo grass restless under the tuneful air of evening.
He reminded me of a city-dweller, umbrella in hand, out for
a stroll in the park after a day in the office. To my amazement he knew me at once, said that the "big master from
Muhembo" had been there the day before to see Karuso, and
that already dug-outs and paddlers, of whom he was going to
be one, were standing by down-river.

I slept the better for the axe-man's news and had, that
night, an especially vivid dream. I was in the centre of a great
swamp. The sun was setting. Between me and the red of evening rose an enormous tree with a smooth, straight trunk ris-

ing some hundreds of feet and with its branches and leaves filling much of the sky. In the dream I recognized it as the final object of my search.

Next morning I rose early to tell the others I was leaving them to rest at Sepopa and going on alone to Muhembo. I asked Spode to select only what films he would need in the swamp and took the rest to store in Muhembo. Though there were only two European couples and three bachelors in Muhembo, it was a transit depot of great importance to the Mines. From all over the roadless country beyond in northern south-west Africa and Angola, year in, year out, sturdy black men made their way toward Muhembo on foot through bush and swamp to apply for work in the Mines. I had known it years before, when the men were taken in trucks nine hundred miles or so over the wasteland to the railway of Francistown. But now, whenever their numbers justified it, they were collected by aircraft and flown in a few hours over a distance that had previously taken weeks.

Both the two lone Europeans who administered the depot were at the airstrip when I arrived. Most of the African population of the village was there too. As always there were many women and children because the able-bodied men were away earning money to pay taxes and buy food. They were an attractive people. They had smooth, shining black skins with a gleam of raven's wing in the sun on their broad shoulders, and long supple legs. The short, peppercorn hair of the women was made longer by plaits of fine, black fibre, skilfully woven into it and falling in straight strands to their smooth shoulders. They were naked to the waist and their firm breasts fully exposed. Round their stomachs they wore a kilt made of plaited fibre and beads drawn into patterns of shining black and white. Their faces were illuminated with the feeling that accompanied their animated talk. Their voices were low, and when one caught a dark eye it looked at one instantly, not as a stranger but as a woman, before the frankness of its own gaze made it shy and a head was quickly turned away. They looked, indeed, more like one of the Libyan tribes vivid in the gossip of Herodotus than a crowd assembled to greet an aeroplane. Yet there they were, hemming in the airstrip, and their numbers growing as eager new arrivals emerged from the end of a red footpath on the edge of the flaming bush. In the centre of the crowd were two lone European topees like lobster pots adrift on a dark sea. Their owners however, I found, were anchored and at home, ready in exchange of wit and good humour with the crowd.

"They love this moment," the senior of the two told me. "They even know something about flying that we don't! It's humiliating but true. They stand there and can tell from the way the plane approaches which pilot is flying it! You'll hear them say, 'Oh, that's the bald-headed one coming today,' or 'That's the one with the fire on his head,' 'Hippo-belly,' 'Red-nose,' 'Shining-face,' 'a new one' and heaven knows what! But you can be sure they'll be right."

When the aircraft had come and gone we went to this official's house on the river, where we sat on the veranda among a vast though oddly ordered chaos of books, magazines, fishing-rods, spoons and flies and all the paraphernalia that had helped him travel the long years, alone, without injury to his spirit. Almost at our feet, the great Okovango River broke into splinters on the pointed papyrus mat at the door of the swamps. Beyond the green of the marshes the bush of the northern Kalahari sandveld burned like coal in the fire of the day, which we saw as though through a sheet of Venetian glass, glowing because of the essence of silver water feverishly extracted by the sun.

"It's beginning to get hot early this year," my host said with a suspicion of foreboding in his voice, all the more alarming considering the many seasons he had seen coming and going in that place. "But, first, let me tell you what I've done for you."

He had been to see Karuso and provisionally engaged dug-outs and paddlers. They were standing by at a place called Ikwagga just below Sepopa. He had left me to settle the terms, but they would take me where I wanted to go if the state of water permitted. But the funny thing was, already they had seemed to know where I was going. They were convinced I was looking for the unknown tree in the swamps. "Good heavens!" I exclaimed, remembering my dream of the night before. "Why a tree?"

He explained that deep in the swamps there was an enormous tree, unlike any other tree in the rest of the country. It had as yet no name, nor was it known to what species it belonged, but it was called "the unknown tree" by all.

"Well, I've not come for that!" I laughed.

He nodded and said I could work that one out with Karuso. What really concerned him was my intention to travel so far by dug-out at that time of the year. He begged me not to do so. The swamp was alive with crocodile and hippo. Every year the hippo were more and more aggressive because they had been hunted constantly and badly. Man was taken, on sight, as an enemy. Only three weeks before, just where the river bent like a cutlass of stainless steel, a hippo had upset a makorro and bitten a man in half. A week before a boy had lost a leg in the same way. So it went on. He asked, why not compromise? He had a launch built with timbers stout enough to resist any attack by hippo. It had a small ferry service to run once a week, but he was willing to let me have it at cost price, working between schedules. He suggested I should take it as far as the water allowed and then use makorros. "In the shallows you'll have a chance," he concluded, "but in the deeper channels I wouldn't put a penny of my money on you."

He then called in his colleague, and for some hours the two of them told me all they could about the swamp. I owe much to what they told me of their unique experience. When I left "the place of the eddies" I carried written instructions to the ferryman to place himself under my orders.

The next day we sailed in the launch soon after sunrise. John and Cheruyiot, whom we had left behind with our Land-Rovers and main baggage, waved to us sadly because they longed to come too. Soon the main stream carried us away from the bushveld banks and into long, deep channels between tall papyrus growths. The smooth, cool, effortless passage over even water after days of hot dusty bumping and bucking eased our troubled senses. Everyone was in a good humour and instantly nicknamed the solemn skipper and his lively engineman "Grumpy" and "Shorty" respectively. Every now and then, away to the south, some high thrust of green over the roof of river forest rose like an explosion of cumulus, uncurling in the dynamic blue. Occasionally the dead stump of a gigantic tree stood out, bare, above the papyrus and reeds bent double with birds, like some bone of pre-Okovango history, and inevitably it wore a gleaming fish-eagle on its top. Giant herons, crested water birds, hammer-heads, kingfishers, crimson bee-eaters, the royal Barotse egrets and sometimes even sky-blue African rollers rose every-where out of the resounding reeds. Each bay cut in a cliff of green was ardent with white and blue lilies' hearts, open with abandon to bumble and sun. From one lily leaf to an-other, lying flat on the surface, raced long-legged trotter birds, a silver dust of water at the heels, to cut off translucent insects from refuge in the papyrus shadows. All the time, above the chug-chug of our small engine, the air was loud with the nostalgic call of birds and waterfowl. The sandy spits in the deeper bays were compact with stream-lined croc-odile. They lay on the sands, eyes shut with delight, mouths wide open, while adroit little birds picked their ivory teeth clean of meat. Shorty, who clearly hated them, begged us to shoot. But we refused. All we shot for dinner were some duck when they rose like stars from some exclusive water.

Spode without prompting got out his film camera. As I watched him I found my heart beating somewhat faster. It was no longer any use glossing over our present lack of progress with hopes for the future. This journey into the swamp was the final test in an increasingly grave situation for both him and me. As yet we had done scarcely any filming. If he now found nothing worth-while to film, it would be a crisis without imaginable end.

I had hardly posed the question to myself when I saw Spode putting away his camera.

"I can't work. The engine vibrates too much," he said turning to me.

"Whenever you want to film we'll stop the engine and drift. Just give me the sign," I offered.

"Tomorrow," he answered curtly. "There's nothing much anyway to film here."

About eleven the channel brought us once more to the edge of the bush on the southern bank of the swamp. The makorro people, who had heard the launch an hour before it appeared, were assembled, sitting silently in the shade of a great tree on the tiny cape of earth forming the little bay called Ikwagga. There was no hut or kraal to be seen through the bush or grass—only this group of men gravely observing the launch manoeuvring closer and making no sign of greeting or offer of help. It made an odd impression. Most people I know in that part of the world are friendly and demonstrative. These men were neither, not hostile, just withheld and profoundly reserved. Their faces, too, were strangely uneven, as if each one belonged to a different race from which he had been torn by a violent fate to be arbitrarily attached to this patchwork assembly before us. Later I understood they had all come together in the swamps not by choice but when escaping destruction by the Matabele in the time of Africa's great troubles in the past. All I knew at that moment, however, was that I did not really like the look of them. There were several faces that interested me, for instance, that of the axe-man of my previous meeting. When I caught his eye he did smile and lift a hand to point me out to someone beside him. That person immediately rose. He was tall and finely made. Leaning on a punting pole he looked at me intently out of keen brown eyes, a look of great experience. He was in rags put on out of respect for us, but he wore them with unragged elegance if not a certain innate swagger. On his head was a Boer War scout's khaki hat, with remodelled brim and a string of beads around the crown. As the launch grounded he doffed it, to show a head of grey hair. Obviously he stood ready to speak for them all.

He was of course Karuso; and he forthwith began to bargain for the assembly with eloquence and great pertinacity. It was an affair that could not be hurried. The wage itself was a pretext, but the bargaining was important. Had I agreed immediately to the little money he demanded, all would have felt cheated and the poorer for it. The whole process was essentially a provision of wisdom and an affair of primitive honour that should not be minimized. It was a drama designed also to bring out the human factors to which Karuso was committing them all. I knew they would stop bargaining, not only when the wage seemed fair, but also when they felt they knew what kind of people we were. Well aware that their future conduct would depend a great deal on how I managed this exchange with Karuso I put all I could of time and imagination into it. Soon the others started joining in. Before long I was getting to know them as they slowly unravelled. Again I did not like my knowledge much. Yet I felt they must do, because I had no other immediate choice.

After two hours I decided the time had come to end it. I made a final and generous offer, climbed into the launch and started writing a letter while I waited for their answer. For a while longer they talked among themselves and then accepted my offer: twenty-eight men to man thirteen makorros and to join me early the next day.

While the negotiations were going on, a slight man with a thin, ascetic face and grey hair sat silent and apart from the rest. He did not speak once though I was aware that his eyes hardly ever left my face. When all was decided he suddenly got up.

"Please," he said, turning to me. "I would like to come with you." He told me his name was Samutchoso. It meant "He who was left after the reaping." I had no idea what forces were set in motion when I agreed without hesitation that he could come.

There remained only one more thing to explain.

"You know, of course," I told Karuso, "that I'm not looking for the unknown tree."

For the first time he looked upset. "But what else could you be looking for in the swamp, Moren?" he asked in a voice now pitched high like a woman's with surprise.

I told him, and asked him what chances we had of finding River Bushmen? He was squatting on the ground and I remember still how he scooped up some earth in his long paddler's hand, began crumbling it and then, with a faraway look, said we might succeed but there were not many left.

"What's become of them, then?" I asked.

"I don't know, Moren," he said, shaking his grey head. "They're just gone." And he let the crumbled earth in his hands trickle through his fingers into the water at his feet.

We spent the night about forty miles on by water, at the last African outpost on the northern edge of the swamps between us and Maun. Below it lay the great unknown swamp district. When we arrived, there were only a few hours of daylight left. Quickly I extracted all the information I could from an African headman who was clearly fearful of what I proposed to do. He did his best to dissuade me by reciting the disasters inflicted by hippo and crocodile on those who still travelled by makorro the three hundred miles to Maun. When that failed, however, he produced for me as guide a great, simple man who knew the deep interior of the swamps because he made his living trapping and hunting there.

By this time the news of our arrival had spread and a tragic procession of sick and ailing started coming into our camp. A doctor visited this place on the far side of the swamp only once every two or three years. An African dispenser on a vast round called in twice a year. That was all. The need for even the simplest medicines was overwhelming. I treated twenty-seven children for infections of the eye which would probably leave their vision permanently impaired. Many of the little faces already had deep scars at the temples and cheeks where the witch-doctors had cut into the flesh to let out the evil spirit that caused the infection. When I asked the mothers how they could allow that to happen to their children, they each exclaimed, indignant in defence of their maternal honour: "But what was I to do? Night and day my child cried with pain. Was I to do nothing?"

After the children, came persons of all ages with festering sores and unhealed wounds, the inevitable cases of chronic malaria and a few far gone with sleeping sickness. There were also the cheerful lovers of castor oil trying to maintain a tortured look on their healthy faces so that I should be moved to satisfy their strange addiction for so odd a lubrication! Finally I was taken to a hut where a little wasted boy was stretched out shivering on a mat of reeds in the last rays of the sun. When he saw my white face close to his, he let out a sob of fear and turned his head to his mother beside him. I thought he had had pneumonia for overlong and could not live, but nonetheless I dosed him with a sulpha drug. In the morning when I saw him again he was shivering no longer, nor was he afraid of me but held firmly to one of my fingers, reluctant to let me go.

I was more than ever glad that I had carried more medicines with me than I could possibly need. This kind of occasion and the quickening look in the eyes of those treated seemed great reward. All the time I longed for Spode to film the scene. I felt the camera could catch its import more immediately and vividly than words, and would help to convey its implications to the many who think of Africa's greatest needs in terms of politics of an alien pattern. However, Spode appeared not only disinterested but deeply involved in the emotions of a private world of his own.

When at last I had finished my amateur nursing the sun was touching the tall papyrus tops. On the far side of the stream, clearly outlined against the bleeding west, a lone paddler was about to turn a makorro into a channel leading into the heart of the impersonal universe of water, darkness and reeds. Already in the channel a swell had risen full of evening fire to rock his craft over a pool where a hippo had just dived out of sight. Unconcerned, he paddled on with long, slow, easy strokes as if before him was not the evening twilight but the dawn of a new day. His silhouette was slighter than that of any African man and had something oddly Chinese about it.

"There he is, Moren!" the headman beside me said, a strangely urgent note in his voice. "There he goes."

"Who?" I asked.

"The River Bushman," he answered.

I wanted to send someone hastening to bring him back, but I was told it would be useless because he was deaf and dumb. For a generation or more he had been living alone on a small

island about fifteen miles on into the swamp. There he lived
by trapping fish and birds, from time to time coming out to
exchange them for tobacco. His lean-to shelter of grass and
reeds on his island, they said, was surrounded with mounds of
the bones of fish he had consumed over the years. No one
knew where he came from or who his people had been.
Whether he knew himself, no one could tell. I stood there
stirred to the heart, watching him progress across the burning
water deeper into the papyrus standing so erect before the
night. In that mythological light of the dying day he seemed
to me the complete symbol of the silent fate of his race.

At about ten the next morning Karuso and his men burst
out of an obscure channel through the reeds, shouting and
singing with triumph and relief. Two to each makorro, except
in two of the biggest which took a crew of three. They
stood upright in the long, narrow hulls, swinging rhythmically from the shoulder and hips as they drove the black dug-
outs forward across the bright water, racing one another for
the harbour below our camp.

"It looks easy," Ben told Vyan and Charles as we watched
them coming. "But make no mistake about it, it's very difficult. Years ago I had to train in one of those for a race at Maun
and it was harder than learning to ride a bicycle! You can't
just sit or stand still in them. If you do, you upset at once,
and then you're lost. They're made of wood heavier than
water and go like lead to the bottom. You have continually to
keep them balanced from the hips, even as a passenger. It's
really a skilled job, and the first time I did it, I was stiff for
days! But look at them! Don't they make a lovely picture?"

He turned to look over his shoulder at Spode sitting silent
and unhappy on a pile of baggage and then turned question-
ingly to me. I pretended not to see. Spode had already dis-
missed an earlier suggestion for filming with a cross "You
don't understand, Laurens. One can't film in this way . . ." In

what way one could film he had not stayed to say. Besides, his cameras were locked away in their cases. In London I'd imagined that we would make a film to catch reality on the wing; now, it seemed, we'd be lucky to shoot it sitting.

Karuso, already leaping out of his makorro like a young boy, shouted, "Moren, if it were not for God I would not be here now! Four times I was attacked by hippo bulls!"

"And I three times," someone else interrupted, jumping ashore.

"I, five times," another yelled.

So each pair of paddlers had their own story of early-morning attack, particularly two boasters whose faces I had disliked the day before and who now claimed to have survived the maximum of eight furious onslaughts. Only "He who was left after reaping" and his companion, a tall young man with narrow hips, broad shoulders, an open unclouded face and a name signifying "Long-axe," volunteered no information about their journey. When I asked Samutchoso if they too had been attacked, he looked surprised and shook his head in emphatic denial.

Nonetheless, exaggerated as were some of the paddlers' tales, there was enough truth in them to confirm the wise advice given us: namely, not to use makorros until absolutely necessary. Meanwhile, we ourselves had gone one better than our advisers. The launch seemed to us big enough both to hold our paddlers and to take their makorros in tow. That way the journey, we felt, would be safer and faster for all.

When we told Karuso of the plan his relief and delight were intense. It took him and his men only a short while to transship their baggage and food, which, since they looked to us to feed them on the meat we would shoot, was little. In the heat of the day we were once more afloat and driving east as fast as the launch would go. The huts and the shouts of the un-comprehending people who crowded the banks below our camp soon fell away behind the dense papyrus screens. For long, however, we heard the great drum outside the headman's hut, the most melancholy drum I have ever heard, tapping out a call of farewell in a curious sobbing and inverted sound which translated itself unbidden in my imagination as:

Go! Go! Going Gone!
Go! Go! Going Gone!

We held on throughout the brilliant afternoon, twisting and turning with the stream as it pushed its way backwards and forwards through dense swamp growths. Sometimes the sun shone full in our faces; at others it burnt the back of our necks. From time to time I climbed up in the prow to look over the cliffs of reeds, rushes and papyrus growing along the water's edge. The bushveld vanished. There was nothing solid left in sight, only this world of grass, uneasily stirring in the draught drawn by the furnace of the surrounding desert, and all along the smarting horizon was the glow of transubstantiated sulphur where the great fire was ceaselessly tended. After the first rush of excited chatter even the paddlers were driven to silence, or if they spoke they spoke in whispers.

In the evening we moored ourselves to an island. It was barely an inch or two above the prevailing water, about fifty yards by fifty, made of sodden black clay and frail trees so entangled that one could barely see the sky through their branches and leaves. So isolated was it that several of the water birds had made their nests only a foot or two above the surface. Two of the nests were filled with fluffy yellow chicks all screaming for food, and we looked straight down into their pink throats as we clambered out of the launch to go ashore. All the while their frightened mothers flew in circles round us moaning with despair.

Once ashore we lit enormous fires to cook our food and smoke out the mosquitoes. We crept early under our nets, all night long hearing the mosquitoes singing their wild pagan hymn. Often the sound of their tense song was drowned by crashes of impatient hippos cutting through difficult papyrus knots, or the noise of great bulls diving for refreshment in the starlit water and huffing and puffing with delight whenever they broke to the surface. Some of their more violent splashes drove the water lapping over the edges of the thin sheet of clay on which we slept and sent a tremor through the foundations of our precarious earth. I lay, as was my habit, apart from the others, in order to be free to make the rounds of the camp when necessary without disturbing my companions. From where I was I could not hear the sleepers. There was no human sound to come between me and the audible life of the great swamp. At the core of that ancient prenatal music my heart made its bed and rested beyond all disquiet of man and uncertainty of future days.

Just before the sun rose we sailed on again. The stream, which falls barely a foot in over a hundred miles, seemed still more unsure of its direction east. We twisted and turned with it to all points of the compass, but no matter to which extreme it took us no firm land or bushveld tree-top could be seen from my post in the prow. The hippo, warned by the noise of our engines and in any case accustomed to forsake the streams in the heat of day, left us only a silky swell to remind us of them, or a dripping, muddied tunnel deep in the reeds where they had gone, heaving, to their rest. Judging by these and other signs, I was sure there must be thousands of hippos in the vicinity. Could we but silence the siren-song of birds and shut off our engines, we would hear a tidal surge of snoring blurring the clarity of the day around us.

As we went deeper into the interior the crocodile seemed to grow bigger, sleeker and less alert. They were sleeping in the sun on every spit of earth that protruded beyond the cool papyrus shadows. We would be upon them before they were aware of us and then, instantly, they took straight to the water like bronze swords to their sheaths. One, surprised on a sandy shallow, gave the ground a resounding smack with his tail, hurled himself high in the air and looped a gleaming prehistoric loop straight into the deepest water. Round another bend we sailed into the midst of a feud between two desperate males. They rose half out of the water, their small fore-feet sparring like dachshund puppies', but their long jaws snapping and grappling with incredible rapidity. They went under still wrestling, the tips of their tails agitating the water just beneath the surface like a shoal of eels. Where they vanished, a scarlet bee-eater swooped low from the bank and I saw its reflection scatter confetti on the broken water.

Soon after sunrise the first column of smoke stood upright, a palm purple with distance, on the eastern horizon. My pulse quickened. No smoke without fire; no fire without man! Could it, by some miracle, be a sign of River Bushmen? I signalled to Karuso and our guide to join me. A long and earnest consultation took place between us. They agreed on the possibility of my interpretation, but they thought it more likely that the water in the swamps now was getting low enough for odd hunters from the few African posts around to move in after buffalo and other game. They said there were a few hardy hunters who, each year before the rains, burned certain favourite areas of the swamp in order to bring out the shy antelope that lived there, and to attract them and their spring progeny to snares set cunningly among the succulent young shoots that would soon arise out of the ashes of their fires.

"But surely this stuff is too green and wet to burn?" I exclaimed, waving my hand at the hundreds of miles of vivid swamp around us.

Nonetheless, they assured me gravely, without a smile at

my innocence, I would soon be able to see for myself that it
not only burned but burned well if one had patience to kindle
it. Before long I spotted two more columns of smoke north
and south of us. As the morning went on they grew streadily
in size and spread fan-wise in the higher atmosphere until the
smoke of all three was joined and the air astringent with tran-
spired resin and burning fibre. We saw more and more palms
and, finally, dense clumps of great trees standing up with
sombre determination in the flat green under an arch of blue
through which the smoke of remote uncontrolled fires now
drifted densely. Like so many trees in love with water, great
and straight as were their stems, their leaves tended to be frail,
tender and pointed and to curl shyly about the intricate
branches not unlike another kind of smoke or mist. Yet all
were clear signs that the swamp was forming more and
greater islands. At that distance, to me one clump of trees and
feather of palm was very much like another. To our guide,
however, each group was different and he proceeded to read
them like separate words forming a sentence in a well-
thumbed book.

At noon the stream brought us alongside an island where
our guide said we could safely land. At first glance it looked
like a junction for the main nocturnal traffic of hippo, for
the clay was broken with their spoor, and the paths they had
trodden ran in all directions into the reeds. But scarcely had
we landed when Vyan called me. He, Ben and the guide were
on their knees in the clay studying some of the largest buffalo
spoor I had ever seen. The spoor was fresh, and our guide
looked up, his eyes shining with excitement, smacked his lips
loudly and said with a deep laugh, "Soon plenty of meat."

Though the buffalo spoor and the steadily narrowing
stream convinced our ferrymen that the launch was near the
end of its journey, we had to hold on in this way for another

four hours. It was the hottest time of the day and even the natural life of the swamp had withdrawn to rest. The birds and crocodile vanished. There was so little to distract the eye that most of our company dozed, their heads deep on their chests. However, I could not take my eyes off the swamp. The columns of smoke, the buffalo spoor, all had stirred me deeply. I had a hunch that despite the blank look of the papyrus grass, people, perhaps Bushmen, were near, and I feared that if I allowed my concentration to lessen for one single instant I might miss some sign or clue vital to our purpose.

Then, about two hours out from our last port of call, I thought I was rewarded. Between me and the sun, almost down to the glassy water-level, the papyrus was shyly parted by small yellow hands and a young woman's face peered carefully through the stems. A pair of odd Mongolian eyes, bright even in the shadows, looked up straight into mine.

I took the sleepy Comfort roughly by the arm to waken him but in that moment the face disappeared.

"No, Moren!" Comfort said, peering deep into the green. "No, I see nothing at all. It must have been the play of the water and shadow on the reeds."

"Why, then, are those fine papyrus tops trembling so?" I asked, pointing to where gilded tips vibrated like a nerve with fever above the place where I had seen the face.

"Oh, that! It's the wind coming to turn the day," he answered and went back to his sleep.

I climbed up into the prow. There was no island near. If it had, indeed, been a human face, how could it have got there? What feet could have carried it over the papyrus water, and where could it have come from? There was no apparent channel through the reeds even for a makorro. On reflection, it all seemed so unlikely, and had passed so swiftly and obscurely, that I could not even be certain I had not imagined the incident. Yet two hours later when we came to the end of the journey by launch, I still saw the face vivid in the shadows above the bland water.

The island on which we disembarked was the biggest we had yet seen, and the first of a kind of marsh archipelago. It was crowned in the centre with a copse of magnificent trees in full leaf, and instead of being merely an inch or two above the water, was raised a foot at the edges and slightly higher in the centre. The grass and clay were criss-crossed with hippo tracks and crocodile slithers but unlike our last resort it rang solid underfoot. A mile and a half below the island the main Okovango channel ran into a triumphant papyrus barrier, then broke up and vanished into obscure runnels between the roots and plaited growth of the deep centre of the swamp. East of the island lay a broad lagoon which, our guide assured us, was linked to other lagoons forming a gleaming chain of water which, in the right season, would lead a makorro through to the river that flows a further hundred and fifty miles past Maun. Both he and Karuso, however, believed we would now find the water-level too low, though both were prepared to try to make passage. One thing alone was certain. We could not go on by launch. On the other hand, if the water ahead was too slow for makorros, it would be too low also for a return to Muhembo by any other route except the main channel.

From what I had seen on our journey I realized I could not expose my companions, particularly Spode, to the dangers of a slow journey by makorro against the current on the main stream. Therefore I arranged with the ferrymen (who had to leave almost immediately if they were to be in time for their scheduled ferry service at "the place of the eddies") to return to the island as soon as their run was accomplished. Either we would be there to meet them; or else I would leave written instructions for them buried in a tin in an agreed place. As we had come no more than two hundred miles by water from the entrance to the swamps, I reckoned they could do the round-trip journey in five or six days.

I settled all this as quickly as possible because all the time I was aware of the potential forces of disassociation among the paddlers. They had behind them a far easier journey than they had bargained for. Yet, judging by their faces, the long hours of idleness in the launch had only increased their latent capacity for dissatisfaction. Also, they were very hungry for the meat of which the average African gets too little and needs so much. I reckoned that before long they would come in a disgruntled body to demand more food; and I did not want that to happen. Believing that what one gives unasked is worth a hundred of that conceded on demand, I was determined to use what daylight was left in an effort to get meat for our evening meal. At that moment it seemed to me our whole future might depend upon the issue of the hunt. I organized three shooting parties and sent one under Vyan, and another under Ben, into the areas which the guide thought most likely to have game. Karuso and two of his best hunters went with Ben; the guide and two others with Vyan. Since I was less in practice and had a new gun, I took the least likely and the wettest area across the main stream. Samut-choso, Long-axe and two others came with me. The look of revived interest on even the most sullen of faces as we all set out with our guns on our arms was most encouraging.

My own party crossed the channel in two makorros. It was my first experience of this craft. I sat in the middle with my .375 across my knees, because it was the hour when the hippos began to re-emerge from their beds of reeds and pools of sleep. Indeed, before we left the bank Long-axe, paddle in hand and erect in the prow, first looked carefully up and down stream. Then, satisfied the channel was clear, he called softly on Samutchoso to shove off, and in a second they were paddling with long sweeps as fast as they could for the cliff of papyrus opposite. Where I sat, the sides of the makorro were barely three inches clear of the water and I realized at once what Ben had meant about the difficulty of keeping balanced so temperamental a craft. I found myself moving continually from the hips like someone riding a tight-rope and had to discipline myself not to extend my arms also. Yet my companions, upright on the footboard, rode the waters with a confident rhythm that instantly rebuked my uncertain waist. The other makorro followed serenely in our wake and once we had both reached the shadows of the papyrus turned to slide into the shelter of the green.

All the while we spoke only in the lowest of whispers. It was astonishing how sound travelled in the quiet evening air. For a long time we heard the normal talk of the camp behind us, and however silently the polished crocodile or larded hippo took to the creamy water round us, the ripples resounded like flute-song among the reeds. Only when the noise of the camp had died did we make an effort to land on a raft of uprooted papyrus caught among the trunks of some young trees. Long-axe, in one supple stride, stepped straight over the prow, took the grass mooring ropes of both makorros in hand and tied them to a trunk. When he had done so, he turned to beg us, with a finger on his curved lip, for silence.

Leaving two men with the makorros, he, Samutchoso and I, barefoot, waded carefully through a broad channel of water between our raft and an ancient termite mound of immense size which had a great tree planted in the middle of its crown. To my amazement, beneath the water my feet trod not in mud or clay but on firm Kalahari sand. There, as everywhere in the swamp, earth and clay existed only in islands; all else was water and pure drift sand. Without a word having been spoken, I was grateful to see Long-axe and Samutchoso behaving like veteran hunters: Long-axe keeping his eyes focused on what might lie ahead, Samutchoso ignoring the distance and concentrating on what was around our feet. After that I felt less apprehensive of crocodile. Soon we were creeping up the shadow side of the mound, and when at last we looked furtively over the summit I thought I had never seen anything more beautiful.

The sun was low and already beginning to redden. Above us the sky was intensely blue and without a bird or cloud, but round the sun was formed a wide band of emerald-green with an inner ring of gold. The island trees and the tender curls of slim young palms on tiptoe in the water rose like the smoke of hunters' fires from vast fields of papyrus, reeds and grass, all tasselled and so lit with light that they might have been corn ripening for a newly forged sickle of the eager moon. Wherever the shadows lay, the swamp was purple, and within the purple, like cut-glass buttons on young velvet was a sparkle of round water. All had the look of things made pure for sleep in devout ablution. Yet even more impressive than the colour, the crystal clarity of the immense scene, and the perfection of the curve of the horizon going toward the night smoothly as a ripple left by a round pebble in a round pond, was the quality of silence rising from this evening world. It was not so much an absence of sound as a delicate music plucked by the long fingers of the light from that finely strung hour to send to sleep a world that had suffered much under the sun. I looked at Samutchoso, and with apparent irrelevance the expression on his ascetic old face reminded me that it was Sunday and that I had overlooked it.

At that moment Long-axe, tense as a bowstring, whispered in my ear: "Look! Moren, look! Lechwe!"

Some distance away a luminous sprinkle of water was thrown up against the dark reeds. I could just distinguish the outline of a shy and graceful antelope picking its way carefully through the water between two mounds. So still was it that a faint tinkle of the spangle of water on its evening shoes just reached my ear. But it was too indistinct and too far for a shot, though we all thought I might have a chance from the farthest of the two mounds. We made for it as fast and as silently as we could, only to find that the lechwe had changed direction and we had not bettered our position. We tried again to get nearer but with the same disappointing results, until at last the sun stood in scarlet on the blue horizon. There was no time left now for more manoeuvring. The lechwe, uneasy, stood between us and the light, up to its pointed chin in reeds, and looking hard in our direction. It was my last chance to shoot, but so forlorn a chance that it was barely worth taking. I reckoned the distance was 150 yards, the visible target an elegant head and a bit of smooth, slim throat, the direction almost straight into a sun level with the eye. If I had not been so convinced of the absolute necessity of getting meat for the camp, I would not have attempted it for fear of wounding the lechwe. But I had heard no shots from the other hunters. If they had shot, in that silence I would have heard them. I looked at my companions. Both faces were solemn with resignation to a vain issue of the hunt and offered neither advice nor encouragement. In my hand was the new gun which I had bought because of my wife's insistence. I had not yet fired at a live target, though, of course, I had zeroed it at a marked one. I said a wordless prayer to the unknown gods of the world around me and aimed at the living target. As soon as I had the lechwe within my sights, I shot quickly without deliberation and as much from instinct as from observation. As the harp-like silence fled swiftly from the day, the lechwe vanished instantly in the long reeds. I was certain I had missed, but my two companions were shouting: "Oh! Our master. Oh! Our father. You've hit it. Lo! The lechwe is dead!"

A young Bushman woman

The author, Charles and Samutchau on a ledge underneath a painting that carries imprints of the vanished artists' hands

Following an old Bushman spoor through the Desert Bush

The first of the Slippery Hills rising out of the Kalahari Plain

In camp near the Slippery Hills

One of the last of the River Bushmen at his traps in the Okovango Swamp

Bauxhau at the Sipwells sucking water out of the sand and squirting it into an empty ostrich egg shell

Nxou hunting a spring hare in its hole

Two women with their grubbing sticks digging for roots in central desert

A young wife

A mother and child with Bauxhau at the Sipwells

A young hunter climbs a tree to look out for game

Women on a walk: their faces are oddly Mongolian and, despite the sun, their complexion is pale

Women playing their favorite game
with a Zamma melon as ball

Women in camp listening to Nxou making music
on his beloved one-string instrument

Bushman making fire outside his shelter

Hunter watching as fresh poison is spread on his arrows before the hunt

Dauxhai, "Spoor of Gazelle"

The author with children in camp

Nxou with a "cupid's bow" he has made

Dancing the magic circle as the sun goes down

Dabe, a Bushman interpreter

Ben with two dwarf Bushmen: the smaller, with dancing rattles around his neck, is about fifty; the other, a father of two children

Women singing and beating the rhythm for the fire dance

The fire dance

"No," I told them, "it was an impossible shot. I think I've only frightened it and it's off round that mound."

Yet, when we waded through the water now red with the sacrifice of day, we found the lechwe shot through the middle of its long throat, the bone of the neck so cleanly broken that there was no look of pain on its delicate face. Its coat was golden with warmth and its long magnetic toes were still coming trembling together. Yet I had no regret at so needful a killing. Indeed I felt a profound gratitude to the animal and life that I had been allowed to provide food for so many hungry men.

If only Ben and Vyan could now have the same luck, I thought, we'll be safe for a few days.

However they had had no such luck. I could tell that instantly from the tense, silent way in which they and the entire camp lined the island bank when we grounded on it in the dark. All had heard the shot and because of the late hour had been afraid to trust the sound. I was greatly rewarded by the look in Ben and Vyan's eyes and the shouts of welcome and praise that went up from the others when they saw the sleek lechwe carried ashore into the leaping fire-light of our camp.

Under my net that night, listening to an indignant hippo bull snorting and stamping around our camp because we had stolen his favourite moonlight walk, I thought long about the nature of the link between the kill and my wife's strange insistence, so many weeks before, that I should buy for myself the "best gun in the world."

Early the next morning the paddlers, singing lustily, lifted their makorros out of the main stream and carried them high on their shoulders to the lagoon on the far side of the island. Spode, too, was there filming the scene. When the makorros were launched again on the far water, he came with us, camera in hand, in a craft of his own to film the probing first lap of our journey deeper into the swamp. He worked hard and well until we ran into difficulties in the channel connecting one lagoon with the next. It was clearly too shallow for any but the lightest of crafts to get through and I thought it useless to waste the energies of the whole party forcing a way through until it was established that we could go on beyond. Therefore, I suggested to Spode that he and I should go on in two of the lightest makorros to explore the swamp ahead. He refused at once, saying the sun would soon be too high for effective filming. As he had already given us a long day's work I accepted his refusal gracefully, though I could easily have countered that where we went in the afternoon the light would again be right for filming. So I sent them all back to camp, asked Vyan and Ben to cross over to the area where I had shot the lechwe and try to shoot more food for us, and decided to push through the swamps alone. Ben, however, was reluctant for me to do this. He pleaded that either he or Vyan should go on with me. The swamp, he said, was full of the worst-tempered buffalo in Africa. There was hardly a bull in it that hadn't a slug or two in his hide and black hatred in his heart, because the moment the herds tried to leave the swamp they were hunted and hurt by the worst shots armed with the worst guns in the world. Ben argued with unusual vehemence that one should never hunt buffalo except in pairs, and nowhere was that truer than in the long grasses and dense reeds of the central swamp.

I tried to reassure him, saying I was not setting out to hunt buffalo but merely to examine the water-way and islands for signs of Bushmen. Besides I would not be alone since Samutchoso, Long-ace, Long-axe's cousin, a man with greying hair and a steady brown eye, Comfort and our guide were coming with me.

Ben interrupted almost impatiently, saying the point was

I might run into buffalo unexpectedly and then paddlers armed only with spears would be unable effectively to help.

Touched as I was by his concern, I reminded him that, much as I would like to have one of them with me, we could not afford the waste in manpower. It was imperative, if we were to get on with our search the next morning, that we get more meat that day. The lechwe was almost finished and I hoped he and Vyan would set about replacing it as swiftly as possible.

At this Vyan took his pipe out of his mouth and said, "He's right, Ben. But keep a watch out, Laurens, won't you? If you do run into buffalo, try and keep a tree or two between you and them!"

I set out across the still waters of the home lagoon, alone then with my black companions. I travelled ahead with our guide in the prow and Long-axe in the stern, Comfort and the other two following behind in another makorro. The lagoon was flashing like a mirror with light. Near the edges the blue and white lilies shone like stars and a giant-crested heron curtsied repeatedly to his own mauve and gold reflection. But in the centre the water was vacant and deeply amber. Ahead a crocodile slipped neatly, almost without a ripple, into the lagoon. Then two hippo nostrils and a pair of pointed ears rose hard by, as if swinging the periscope of their submarine being upon us.

"If his ears start fluttering like a bird's wing and then lie back like a cheetah's," our guide whispered urgently, "please shoot, Moren!"

However, ears and nostrils, like two toads on the water, remained still long enough for us to reach the channel between the home lagoon and the next. The channel was just wide enough to take our makorros. My companions laid down their paddles and produced their long, forked punting poles. To my relief they managed to push our slender craft with little loss of speed through the reeds and sedges. These rose to a height of about ten feet all around us. I could not see through them at all, and their spurred tops waved rhythmically over the bowed heads of my tall companions. The sky itself was reduced to another blue-black channel as if it were a narrowed reflection of the water below in a mirror above. Suddenly the blue vanished, the channel became a tunnel through columns and branches of interwoven trees. The startled eyes of a baboon looked into mine from a perch fifteen feet above. It let out a booming bark of warning and immediately the silence was broken by the crashes and screams of an invisible multitude of baboons leaping wildly from branch to branch out of our way.

"Oh! You thing of evil," Long-axe exclaimed aggrieved. "What is the use of us keeping so silent when you cry 'Beware!' so loudly to the world, and that not even to a world of your friends?"

For a hundred yards or more we poled our way with difficulty through the intricate tunnel to emerge once more into an open channel between tall reeds. A quarter of a mile on we reached a great open lagoon where we looked on many miles of islands set in silver water. We took once more to the paddle. Our guide seemed to have no hesitations about the way and set his course like a homing pigeon. The wind of our increased speed was cool in our hair and on our faces. As always, for fear of attack by hippo in deep water, the paddlers never slackened until they were near shelter of some kind. On the far side we entered another channel and so it went on for some hours, lagoon, channel, and once more lagoon. Only the channels became narrower and the lagoons broader and shallower. About one o'clock, perhaps sixteen miles from the home lagoon, we found the passage east shut against us.

Our guide put his punting pole down firmly and said, "If we cannot enter here, Moren, we'll have to lift and carry the

makorros for two days before we find water deep enough
again to go on."

We had clearly come to the highest and most solid part of
the swamp. Much as I would have liked to go on to Maun by
water, I was not over-disappointed. We were through the
outer defences, across the last moat, and within the inmost
keep of this formidable stronghold of ancient life. If there
were River Bushmen still to be found in organized entities it
would be here among the sparkling islands rising now everywhere out of the burning water. Behind screens of elegant
reeds and sedges and fringes of palms, their dense bush and
gleaming crown of lofty wood stood out resolutely in the
blue.

"Do you think there could be any people there?" I asked
our guide. I did not mention Bushmen specifically, because I
had become daily more superstitious about too direct an approach in so indirect a world.

"Sometimes, perhaps two, perhaps three," he said, gravely
dubious, knowing what I meant.

"Where do you think would be the best shade to rest for
a while then and perhaps find a buck or two to shoot before
we go home?" I went on, pressing him no further.

At that a look of new life came into his eyes and a low
laugh broke from him. He jumped into the water, swung the
makorro round so fast without warning that Long-axe was
nearly thrown off his balance, climbed quickly in and raced us
across to the north where a long slope of yellow winter grass
went slowly up from green reeds to clumps of dense, black,
high wood. So slight were all gradients in the swamp that we
had to disembark a hundred yards from the edge of the lagoon and wade ankle-deep ashore, leaving the makorros
caught in the reeds. Instinctively no one spoke but conveyed
their meaning by signs. The water was so hot it almost burned
my cooler ankles and at the first touch of the fiery island

earth I put on my boots. How still the island was! And yet I had an odd feeling that some kind of vibration was running there through the shining air, as if somewhere within these black woods a powerful dynamo was running to charge the lonely place with electricity. My companions seemed aware of it too, for as I took my gun from Comfort to move off toward the clumps of wood, the paddlers, each with a long throwing spear in hand, began hotly disputing with one another as to who should lead the way.

"What's the matter?" I whispered to Comfort.

"They're afraid of buffalo, Moren," he said. "No one likes being in the lead when there might be buffalo about."

Tired of the dispute, Long-axe turned his broad shoulders disdainfully on the others and with a superb look of scorn on his broad, open young face walked to the front. But I held him back and called the guide.

"This is your place," I commanded him in a whisper. "You are the guide. You go ahead and I'll follow immediately behind you."

He looked as if he would still demur but he was at heart a fair person and the justice as much as the note of command compelled him. Perhaps I should have paused a moment then to let the turmoil of the dispute subside within him. However, I let him walk straight on, his long spear in hand but not looking about him as attentively as he should have done. I followed, with Comfort next and the paddlers in single file behind him.

We walked thus for about a quarter of a mile. All the while I felt increasingly uneasy and aware of the odd vibration and crackle of electricity charging the shining element of the high noonday air. As carefully as I looked around me, I saw no fresh spoor of any kind, and I am certain none of the others did or they would have warned me. Nonetheless I was about to halt our small procession because of my growing uneasiness when it happened.

We were in a round, hollow depression up to our chins in yellow grass and approaching the centre of the island. All around us were dense copses of black trees sealed with shadow and invariably wearing a feather of palm in their peaked caps. Suddenly the guide slapped his neck loudly with the flat of his hand. I myself felt the unmistakable stab of a tsetse fly on my own and neck and thought, If there's fly here, buffalo can't be far away.

At that precise moment the copses all around us burst apart and buffalo,* who had been within, sleeping, came hurtling through their crackling sides with arched necks, thundering hooves and flying tails, all with the ease and speed of massed acrobats breaking hoops of paper to tumble into the arena for the finale of some great circus.

The guide dropped his spear, instantly fell flat on his stomach and wriggled away into the grass. So did the paddlers. Comfort stood his ground only long enough to call out to me hoarsely, "Master, throw your gun away. Let's crawl on our hands and knees and pretend to be animals nibbling the grass. It's our only chance."

However, I stood my ground because, in some strange

* The African buffalo is not to be confused with the American bison. It is a species all its own, is far more powerful and dangerous than the bison. In fact, wherever hunters in Africa meet, a fierce controversy invariably rages as to which of the three African animals is the most dangerous: the elephant, the lion or the buffalo. I myself have no doubt that the buffalo is the most unpredictable and, when wounded, the most dangerous of all. It is as fast as it is powerful and normally charges with its great head up and its eyes wide open, but on this island in the swamp they broke out of their thorny copses with their heads down and lifted them high into the air only when they were clear of the thorns and going down the slope toward the water.

way, now that my uneasiness was explained I was not afraid. Perhaps I knew, too, it would be useless to run. But whatever the reason I remember only a kind of exaltation at witnessing so truly wild and privileged a sight. Automatically I slammed a cartridge into the breech of my gun and held it ready on my arm while the copses all round me went on exploding and the ground began to shake and tremble under my feet. For one minute it looked as if some buffalo, coming up from behind me, were going to run me down. But at the last minute they divided and passed not ten yards on either side of me. From all points and at every moment their number was added to until the yellow grass and the glade far beyond ran black with buffalo, as if a bottle of India ink had been spilt over it. They took to the channel ahead in a solid black lump, like a ship being launched, throwing up a mighty splash of white water over the reeds before they vanished round a curve of the main wood. I thought with strange regret, They have gone, and stood turning over in my exalted senses the tumultuous impression of their black hooves slinging clay at the blue; bowed Mithraic heads and purple horns cleaving grass and reeds and sprays of thorn, like the prows of dark ships of the Odyssey on the sea of a long Homeric summer; deep eyes so intent with the inner vision driving them that they went by me unseeingly.

Suddenly there was another crackle of paper wood behind me. A smaller copse burst open and the greatest bull I've ever seen came charging straight at me.

The paddlers and Comfort, who were all miraculously reappearing, formed a kind of Greek chorus round me shouting over and over again, "Shoot, Master! Shoot, Father! Shoot, Chief of chiefs! It's the lone one! It's the lone bull!"

Yet again I held my fire, though for a different reason, and such a fantastic one that I must apologize for it in advance. When my paddlers shouted "Shoot!" I knew they were right. Here, even if safety did not seem to command it, was a chance to ensure our supply of food for days to come. But all my life I have dreamed about one particular buffalo. Much as I love the lion, elephant, kudu and eland, the animal closest to the earth and with most of the quintessence of Africa in its being is for me the buffalo of the serene marble brow. Ever since I have been a small boy I have dreamed of one particular buffalo above all buffaloes. I will not enlarge on all the fantastic situations in which my dreaming mind has encountered him, and the great and little-known stretches of the continent in which my eyes have, for years, sought him with a growing hunger. All that matters is that unless absolutely forced to, I could not shoot on this occasion because here, at last, was the buffalo of my dreams. He took shape as a lone bull charging at me, the purple noonday light billowing like silk around him. He came straight at me, so close that at last, reluctantly, I was about to put my gun to my shoulder and shoot.

For the second time my companions vanished. Then the buffalo abruptly pulled up short, swerved aside, and charged by me so close that his smell, the lost smell of the devout animal age before man, went acid in my nose.

I stood there watching him vanish like a man seeing his manhood in the field die down before him, thinking: "Only one thing saved me. I was not afraid. Because of that I belonged to them and the over-all purpose of the day and in their magnetic deeps they knew it. But afraid, no gun or friend on earth could have saved me."

I came to, trembling all over with the fear of what would have happened if I had been afraid, to hear the guide, sufficiently relieved to find himself alive to be mockingly reproachful of me, saying, "There was meat there you know, Master, for many days." His voice sounded as if he were far away and not rising out of the grass near me. I gave no answer but walked over to where the others were uttering cries of astonishment over the spoor of the lone bull.

"Look!" Comfort exclaimed, pointing to the puncture in the clay behind each of the rear hoof-prints: "Look how deep his after-claws have pierced the clay!"

The buffalo, once he has stunned his enemies with head and horn, likes to give them the *coup de grâce* with the pointed dagger he carries in a leather sheath at the heels of his hind legs. But none of us had ever seen after-claws so long as these.

"Auck!" Long-axe said, shaking his head and his voice gentle as a woman's with wonder. "He must be the Chief of their chiefs!"

But Samutchoso was looking more at me, not the spoor. In the same tone of awe that he had used in the evening before when I shot the lechwe, he said quietly, certain of his meaning, "He knew you, Master. He recognized you, and knowing you, turned aside."

After that we tried to rest in the nearest shadows but the shade-loving tsetse fly soon drove us out to seek relief in the hot sun. I made no attempt to hunt because I was certain the alarm raised by the buffalo would have stampeded the game for many miles around. In fact, we were hardly back in the open when a baboon, now thoroughly on the alert, spotted us and broadcast a loud warning to the bush below him. Instead we did a complete circuit of the island to look for signs of human occupation. We found none except, well above flood-water level, the remains of three ancient makorros, unlike our paddlers', of flat-bottomed design, slowly rotted and rotting in the grass.

"*Massarwa!* Bushmen!" Samutchoso, who seemed more aware of my main purpose than the others, explained unbidden as he came to stand sharing my absorption beside me.

All this time I noticed that the nerves of my companions

had been sorely tried by the encounter with the buffalo. Whenever a baboon frantically rattled a palm in the silence, or a foraging party of indefatigable termites dropped a dry limb from a dead tree to crash in the bush below, they started violently and appeared ready to run. They followed me into the dark main wood with reluctance and sought the daylight beyond with the eagerness of a vivid apprehension. Their relief when we rounded the circle where we had left the makorros among the motionless rushes, and started back for camp, made them chant as they bent down to take up their paddles. However, I lay on my back in the bottom of the craft looking deeply up into the blue channel of the sky framed between the trembling reed tips above me, with my heart and mind still so much in the scene with the buffalo that I had no room even for the negative answer implicit in the rotting Bushman dug-outs on the island. I felt that the encounter had for a moment made me immediate, and had, all too briefly, closed a dark time-gap in myself. With our twentieth-century selves we have forgotten the importance of being truly and openly primitive. We have forgotten the art of our legitimate beginnings. We no longer know how to close the gap between the far past and the immediate present in ourselves. We need primitive nature, the first man in ourselves, it seems, as the lungs need air and the body food and water; yet we can only achieve it by a slinking, often shameful, back-door entrance. I thought finally that of all the nostalgias that haunt the human heart the greatest of them all, for me, is an everlasting longing to bring what is youngest home to what is oldest, in us all.

I was lifted out of this mood by the sight of an aeroplane coming down the centre of the blue channel above me like a translucent insect about to be burned in the yellow lamp of the sun. I was told by the pilot later that it was full of primitive black people on their way from Muhembo to the distant gold mines. Far down on the swamp we moved in the slow, ancient way; but above, with the blazing afternoon water hurling long spears of copper and bronze light at their eyes, the black travellers sang incessantly for reassurance the one hymn, "Abide with me," which the missionary priests, the medicine men of the peoples who built the magic plane, had taught them. They sang it so loudly that the pilot heard it above the noise in his cockpit. But from where I lay I heard only the engines droning discordantly among sounds dedicated to a world before and beyond us all.

So we came home in the evening, the smoke of our camp-fires blue among the lofty tree-tops. Since morning two vultures had taken up their position on the summits of two of the highest of them. They were starkly outlined against the rest of the sunset and made an ominous impression. The moment we walked into the camp I knew it was more than an impression. Coming back content and still somewhat exalted by all that had happened in a long and exacting day, I did not know at first what had happened. The paddlers, with few exceptions, were huddled round their fires cooking the remains of my lechwe, and when they saw we brought no meat looked up to give us no greeting but only a long sullen look. Both Charles and Spode were already in bed under their mosquito nets and Ben and Vyan, coming to greet me, looked very tired and thoroughly downhearted.

"We've been all over the country," Vyan said wearily. "And found nothing to shoot at. The paddlers are pretty fed up and poor old Charles has had to go to bed with a bad attack of lumbago."

"And he?" I asked, pointing to Spode's net.

"Oh! He, poor fellow," answered Ben, who slept near him, "says he was kept awake all night by wild beasts prowling round his bed and went to rest soon after we returned to camp this morning."

I went at once to doctor Charles, who was lying uncomplaining but in great pain from an affliction he had not had before. I then woke Spode and persuaded him to join the others for an evening drink inside a large mosquito net, fifteen feet long, twelve feet wide and twelve feet high that I had designed for just such an occasion. We sat there safe from mosquito attack, and soon the drink, the smell of Jeremiah's dinner on the fire and our exchanges of the day's news brought into being a mellow objectivity. After Spode's first laugh I went out to hold my nightly sick parade among the paddlers. Samutchoso and the rest of my party appeared to be remonstrating with unusual vehemence to those who had stayed at home. However, when they saw me they fell silent and began, half embarrassed, to come forward with their slight ailments.

When I had finished I thought the atmosphere seemed lighter, and Karuso felt free to ask, "Please get us more meat. We're not getting enough food."

"First thing in the morning," I promised him and walked back to our communal net white in the darkness.

Tired, we all crept into our nets immediately after eating, and whenever I woke I heard the hippo bull of the night before stamping and huffing and puffing with rising resentment around our beds. Once when he sounded almost on top of me I flashed my torch in his direction. The moon was rising. Though reeds and trees were too dense to reveal his shape, his eyes showed up long, slanted and emerald-green. Toward morning he seemed to accept us and withdrew to the moonlit waters with resignation. Thereafter, I believe, he learned even to enjoy our company and the change in routine that our presence provided. He visited us nightly, announcing his arrival with a loud crash through the wing of reeds, a fat boy trying to make our flesh creep with fierce puffs of breath. For a while he would study us from all angles and then return, full of simple wonder to his soft water, where he made solemn and reverential noises at the moon. Because he appeared alone and celibate and was full of devout utterance I called him Augustine, after one of my favourite saints, who, I am certain, would have been the first to understand since he, too, had been a bishop of Hippo. Unfortunately Spode found no joy in our hippo. He kept Spode awake for hours and in all his larded innocence added greatly to our problems.

At first light, when I took my companions their coffee with the intention of asking Vyan and Ben to go out hunting before breakfast, I found Vyan with his feet so afflicted by protracted immersion in the swamp waters that I could not think of suggesting it to him. Ben, too, looked out of his net with a flushed face, a hand shaking with fever and a look of tightly withheld suffering on his sun-lined face. He had a high temperature and told me he had been bitten by a poisonous spider that had crept between his blankets. It lay in the earth beside his bed so crushed that it was not recognizable, but its bite clearly was dangerous. I had antidotes effective for any snake or serpent bite but knew of nothing for this kind of spider. I could only insist on his keeping quiet and drugging his pain. Charles was paralyzed in the grip of lumbago. That left only Spode and me among the Europeans, and Spode arose dark with yet another enigmatic variation of humour. With so much real suffering around, his mood did strike me as a gratuitous complication and for the last time I insisted on his carrying out the programme we had agreed upon. I gave the paddlers for breakfast such meat as we had left, hurried through our own so as not to miss the light for filming and, with Comfort to help me, I acted as assistant to Spode while he made some individual studies of the paddlers in camp. That was soon over. Then I asked Spode to accompany me with his camera for the rest of the day.

"What for?" he asked.

"For whatever we can find," I told him. "You would have had some wonderful stuff to film if you'd been with me yesterday."

He looked hard at me for a long moment and then said, "I have not the strength. I am not well. My back is troubling me."

The day was riding high, wide and handsome into the deeps of the incredible blue sky. I could not argue with Spode to any good effect before the brittle company watching us so keenly; nor indeed could I force him to work when he felt he didn't want to. Above all, I had no time to waste if I were to find food for the forty odd mouths I had to feed before nightfall. So I just left Spode, the camp and all in it to the great-hearted Vyan, and with the proved company of the day before took to the main stream. One extra makorro and crew of two brought up the rear. Vyan, apologetic to the last, stood on the island bank watching us out of sight.

This time we struck out up-stream. We travelled in the shelter of the papyrus on the far side of the stream for some miles until we came to a channel between two green cliffs. We turned into it and crept along it for about half a mile to emerge into a big and lovely lagoon. It was blue with light and Chinese with reeds and clumps of wild bamboo. Straight ahead of us rose a gentle yellow island mound with a great, glittering lechwe male surrounded by seven does coming like a dream of Joseph out of Pentateuch water. They were as yet totally unaware of our presence. Our guide motioned the other two makorros back into the reeds. In order to make his craft lighter he signalled to Long-axe to transfer himself to them and then with one long sweep of his paddle he took the two of us, alone, into a jungle of tall sedges at the side. There he put his paddles away, lay down in the prow with his chin over the edge and with his hands began to pull us by the shorter reeds, foot by foot, slowly toward the lechwe. He did it so well and patiently that a mauve heron came floating low over my head without even looking down at us.

Once, when he paused to rest, the sweat running like water between his shoulders, I looked over the side and saw we were going down a line of baby crocodiles all drawn up, a yard apart, lips curling over white teeth at the corners, just below the surface of the still water. I tapped his shoulder to warn him, for they were old enough to bite off his fingers. He grinned endearingly and pointed at the opposite bank where another row of white-toothed infants was facing us. It all looked very official, as if we were witnessing a dress rehearsal for some trooping of crocodile colours.

I don't know how long our journey lasted, but when finally the guide motioned to me to shoot and I rose carefully to my full height in the unstable craft to look over the tops of the sedges, the lechwe and his brilliant women were standing half-way up the slope of the island staring hard at the place where we had first broken into the lagoon. I shot quickly and he dropped where he stood. That was one anxiety resolved. We handed over the lechwe to the crew of the extra makorro to take back to camp, and then prepared to search the backwaters to the north of the main stream for signs of people.

As I stood there once more at one with myself, my surroundings and my companions, I saw a new column of smoke rising purple in the midst of the papyrus, approximately, I judged, at the place where I thought I had seen the young woman's face in the papyrus. Comfort confirmed my reckoning and when I teased him, saying, "D'you think that smoke is perhaps just another play of water and shadow over the reeds?" he laughed, though he said nothing.

"Well," I went on, "we'll go and have a closer look at that particular smoke the first clear day we get."

His reply was prevented by the flutter of a bird which appeared on the branch of a tree on the crown of the island, crying, "Quick! Quick! Honey! Quick!"

They all wanted me to accept the bird's invitation at once. However, I refused, explaining carefully that I wanted to come back and film the whole honey-bird episode. Comfort, self-disciplined as ever, set the obedient example with grace. Only he could not resist whispering to me, in English, that in his view it was futile to wait, because "the foreign master" (as he called Spode) would never come. Not as pessimistic, or as clear-sighted, perhaps, in this regard as Comfort, I took the reappearance of the little bird as a good omen and went on happily to search island after island in the swamp.

Again we found no signs of recent occupation by human beings, only some more antique makorros rotting in the sun and damp. That, of course, was disappointing, and yet as the day opened out like a coral sea before us I felt increasingly uplifted by the tranquil lagoons filled and overflowing with light; and the island, contemplative with trees and graced with palms, succeeded one another so regularly that they still dangle like a necklace of diamonds and emeralds on a thread of gold in my memory. Each one of them seemed to have its own privileged view of the intimate life of bird, reptile and animal to deploy for us. For instance, about midday when a wind rose to blow rose-pink through the silver air and carried the sound of our feet, like dead leaves, away over the waters behind us, we arrived at a green island meadow sunk in a round shelter of high woods. There, as still as if they were stitched petit point by point into olive-green tapestry, lay an apricot lechwe male with a harem of five, all fast asleep around him. I watched them, barely thirty yards away, for twenty minutes as they continued to breathe deeply without opening an eye behind their long black lashes. My companions begged me to shoot but I couldn't do it. Since we already had our daily food I felt it would be a betrayal of natural trust, and such treachery to the deep feeling of at-oneness that had grown up in me since leaving camp that I feared some terrible retribution would follow the superfluous deed. So I led my companions carefully away like someone withdrawing from the bedroom of a beloved sleeper he did not wish to wake. The last I saw of the male was his long lips ceaselessly moving, as if some dream had brought him to the pastures reserved only for his translation and his gods.

Also, I cannot stress sufficiently what a growing relief it was not to be solicited by the noise and importuned by the colour of my own metropolitan time. Our senses were totally immersed in sounds and colours that had nothing to do with man. I can only say that I found a new freedom for my senses in the swamp that day, so concrete, for all its imponderable expression, that it was as if a great physical burden had been lifted from me. That freedom had a voice of its own, too, for we all spoke instinctively in tones that we did not normally use and which came from us as naturally as the sound of the wind from the trees.

So it went on until we were all resting, not in the shadows of the tsetse-fly-ridden copse, but well away in the shade of a lone quiverfull of palms. Samutchoso was carefully rolling up the discarded skin of a chrome-yellow cobra we had found, hung out, like some dandy's washed cummerbund, to dry on a screen of white thorns. The guide, I had noticed, when he found it had instantly handed it over to Samutchoso as though it were his right.

Suddenly Samutchoso looked up intently at me and said, "You know, Master, you won't find many Bushmen here!"

"Why not?" I asked.

He explained at length that the tsetse fly had become so bad in the swamp that, even in his lifetime, it had forced his own people to withdraw from parts of the swamp they had occupied and cultivated before the Matabele first drove them out of the north. The Bushmen had either done likewise or had died of sleeping sickness in the swamp.

When I asked where the surviving Bushmen had gone, he motioned vaguely with his hands, but stressed again that very many had died. Then he paused for quite a while, weighing some issue carefully in his mind before he announced that he knew a place where Bushmen annually met. No, he could not say whether they were River Bushmen or not, only that they were true "naked Bushmen" and that the place was not in the swamp.

Where was it? I asked eagerly.

Pleased with the startling effect of his announcement, he paused dramatically; but then it all came out in spate, though as he spoke his voice was like a stealthy footfall for awe of what he said. Some days' journey from the place where he lived in the swamp, he informed me, straight out into the desert there were some solitary hills. The Bushmen called them the Tsodilo Hills, "the Slippery Hills," and they were the home of very old and very great spirits. He had heard that European huts were divided into many rooms, and so, he would have me know, was the interior of the Slippery Hills. In each compartment dwelt the master spirit of each animal, bird, insect and plant that had ever been created. At night the spirits left their rooms in the hills to do their business among the creatures made after their fashion, and the spoor, the hoof-marks left by their nocturnal traffic, could be seen distinct and deep in the rocks of the Slippery Hills. In a place in the central hill lived the master spirit of all the spirits. There below it was a deep pool of water that never dried up. Beside the pool grew a tree with the fruit of knowledge

on it, and hard by the tree was the rock on which the greatest spirit of all had knelt to pray the day he made the world.
The dent in the rock, where his vessel with sacred water had
stood so that he could rinse his mouth and hands before
prayer, and the marks made by his knees as he knelt to pray
over his creation, could be seen to this day. All around on
the smooth rock surfaces there were paintings of the animals
the great spirit had made, and in all the deepest crevices
lived swarms of bees that drank at the pool of everlasting
water and tumbled the desert flowers to make the sweetest
of honey for the spirits. There, he said, among these hills,
once a year, for a short season, the Bushmen gathered.

Deeply impressed by his manner, as much as the substance
of what he told me, I asked how he knew all this.

He replied, "I have been there, Master. I have seen it all
with these old eyes of mine."

"But how did you get there? Why did you go?" I pressed
him.

"I went many years ago, Master," he answered with great
solemnity. "Because my own spirit was weak and weaken-
ing and I needed help to strengthen it if it were not to die.
I went to those hills to ask for help and I saw all the things I
have told you of, and I was helped."

Suddenly I began to understand, and wondered why I had
not done so before. First, there had been that glimpse of
special authority the day I hired the paddlers at Ikwagga.
And now this latest incident of the discarded cobra skin,
which I should have remembered was one of the great medicines and symbols of eternal renewal in Africa.

"So you—" I began.

For the first time he interrupted to say soberly, "Yes,
Master, I am a prophet and a healer."

However unlikely and superstitious it may sound in civilized surroundings, there on a far island in the unpredictable

swamp, as the wheel of the day's light, spokes flashing with the angle of the turn, went over the hump of blue to roll down toward the night, I was not inclined to be critical. Besides, I have always had a profound respect for aboriginal superstition, not as formulations of literal truth, but as a way of keeping the human spirit obedient to aspects of reality that are beyond rational articulation. Even Samutchoso's name—"He who was left after reaping"—took on an added meaning.

I put my hand on his stained old shoulder and asked, "Would you take me to these hills when we have done with all this?"

He looked long at me, while all the others stopped talking, before he answered steadily, "Yes! Master! I will take you, but on two conditions. There must be no dissension as there is now among those who come with you. You must compose your differences with one another before we set out; otherwise disaster will come. And there must be no shooting or killing of any kind on the way to the hills. No shooting, even for food, until the spirits have given permission for it. It is a law of the spirits that none must come into the hills with blood on his hand, or resentment in his heart. Even if a fly or a bee should annoy you, you must not kill it. I know of a Herero cattleman who went there with his herd in the rainy season. On the way he killed a lion which attacked a cow and that night the master spirit of the lions came from the hills and devoured him and his herd. . . . If you can promise me all that, Master, I'll take you to the hills, for I, too, feel a need to go back there again."

"Of course I'll promise," I said sincerely, not remembering that the words "of course" can be unduly provocative in a country still so truly of its own dark fate as is Africa.

I returned to camp with Samutchoso's story in the forefront of my mind. I was eager to tell the others such hopeful news, but the taste for it was soon driven from my tongue. Somehow, when I saw from afar three instead of two vultures outlined in the evening sky above the camp, I knew I was not going to have a chance. On arrival I found Ben was still far from well and Charles in great pain. Spode, after sweating under all his blankets in the heat of the day, was only just up and not yet prepared to speak to anyone. The paddlers, with meat enough on their fires, perversely had found something new to disturb their brittle spirit. Someone had started a rumour that the launch was not coming back for us and that they would have to run the gauntlet of hippo and crocodile for two hundred miles on the main stream in their vulnerable makorros with a cargo of broken-down white people.

Comfort and I on my medicinal rounds mocked them out of that particular rumour and, as the night before, the return of Samutchoso and the rest of my black hunting companions gave them something more constructive to think about. However, the odd thing was, I discovered later, that our launch at sundown that very evening did have a major engine breakdown 180 miles up-river!

"The trouble, Master," Comfort said to me when we had calmed them, "is that Karuso is king on water, but not king on land." He then asked as if ashamed of doing so, "But what will you do if the launch does not come?"

"Don't worry," I told him. "I've a good plan I'll talk over with you if it becomes necessary."

I spoke with more confidence than I felt because the night before the same grim possibility had occurred to me and I had been unable to sleep. I had decided that should the launch not come I would shoot enough meat to dry and so provision the camp for a month. I would leave Vyan in charge with Comfort to help him and take only Long-axe, the guide and one makorro with me. I had already been told by the guide that he knew a way across the swamp where, if I didn't mind abandoning the makorro after a while and wading up to my neck in crocodile waters, he could in two days bring me out on dry land fifty miles below "the place of the eddies."

I was certain I could walk the fifty miles to our Land-Rovers in little over a day, and so, within three days of leaving camp, I would be in a position to organize a rescue party for the rest. I thought it wiser, however, to say nothing of this to the others, for already there was a very negative atmosphere over the camp. So at dinner I tried to talk with a lively unconcern to my companions. However, the conversation soon dwindled to an exchange between myself and Vyan, who was at that hour always his steadfast best. We went early to bed and all night I was aware of Spode uneasy in his net, continually switching on his torch to shine at the places where Augustine was transported with fierce relish at the sight of our camp. Ben, too, was in great pain, and twice I got up to give him medicine. Still, I hoped that by morning our prospects would look brighter to all.

I was wrong. The paddlers were back in the mood of the night before, the sick were still sick, and when I asked Spode to come filming with me he said his back was hurting him too much for work. I offered to doctor him too as best I could, but he said only rest could put it right. I had to repeat the pattern of the day before, leave Vyan in charge, concentrate first on meat for the camp and then on the main purpose of my journey. Again my luck held. Before ten I had shot two superb buck: my first precaution in case the launch should not return. Neither was an easy shot and yet the animals dropped like stones in their tracks. I sent the extra makorro back to camp loaded to the water's brim with meat.

Relieved that the morning's housekeeping was so quickly done, I made for the new smoke uncurling over the place where I had had that tantalizing vision of a young woman's face among the reeds. Half a mile short of the smoke we found an obscure breach in the papyrus dyke against the main stream. We explored it apprehensively because the guide thought it might lead us straight into a hippo ambush. However, five minutes later we broke out of it into a characteristic Okovango backwater. Only, to the east of us lay a vast expanse of papyrus already burnt down to the water's edge by the fire, running with the noise and flame of an overland train, straight into the world of green. Past the black, ash-covered waste of water ran a broad open channel and at the far end of the channel was an island where smoke rose like the curl unwinding from a cigarette between a smoker's fingers.

"People! Master! People!" our guide exclaimed when he saw it, so excited that he breathed like a diver coming up for air.

Before I could stop him he let out a wild exultant yell and waved his paddle in the air. As a result when we reached the island it was as quiet and deserted as a churchyard at midnight. The fire, however, was still smouldering, and beyond it, tucked securely among the trees, were three substantial grass huts. The screens over their entrances were firmly held in place by bits of dead wood, but the grass was trodden down and littered with the waste products of a prolonged occupation. The guide gave the huts only the briefest of glances before he ran off deeper into the island calling out loudly in friendly tones in a tongue of his own.

"They are not far away," Samutchoso said, squatting by the fire. "No men, only women and children."

I did not ask how he could tell so much from so little but he was right. Half an hour later our guide reappeared leading two shy, almost frightened women by the hand, while behind came half a dozen children. They were dressed only in blankets of skin and wore no ornaments of any kind, and to my private disappointment neither of them owned the face I had seen above the water. It is true they had clear traces of Bushman blood, and some of the children, with light yellow skins, high cheekbones and slanted eyes, looked like pure models of their Bushman prototype. I had hardly time to make the women a present of tobacco and give the children a tin of old-fashioned "humbugs," before the elder of the two disappeared into one of the huts to come back with a large heap of sun-dried Okovango bream which she thrust upon us with both hands and shining eyes. The men, they told us, had gone away some moons before to trade skins somewhere on the perimeter of the swamps for tobacco. They had no idea when they would return and meanwhile the women manned the fishing traps and maintained themselves and their children alone and unarmed, without fear or complaint, in a world where I would not have liked to go without modern weapons. They had, they said, no neighbours and they knew of no Bushman communities. Since they could remember they had always been just themselves, their menfolk and their dead parents. They followed us down to the water, reluctant, now that their fears were at rest, to let us go.

I myself felt oddly cheated by such an end to our first encounter with human beings in the swamp. I had kept on looking over my shoulder for the true Bushman face I thought I had seen among the reeds. I did not realize how much I had counted on meeting it again, and was almost irritable with unbelief that now I had to leave without seeing it.

Then, at the last moment, a call clear and vibrant as a bell came from across the channel. The women and children all instantly replied and beckoned wildly with their hands, the youngest jumping up and down in excitement. A flat-bottomed makorro suddenly darted out of the reeds and made straight for us. In it, alone and naked to the waist, paddle in hand, came the young woman whose face I had first seen among the reeds. The makorro was loaded with tender shoots of all kinds, and the moment it grounded the children pounced on the cargo and began chewing white water roots like sugar-cane. A young woman of the purest classical Bushman colour and features stepped out and, paddle clasped to her firm breasts, looked with shy inquiry about her.

"Please tell her," I asked the guide, while Comfort's dark eyes went white with amazement, "that I greet her and that I have seen her before."

She turned her head sideways, smiled politely into her hand and said almost inaudibly to the guide, "I see him and know him too."

I would have liked to stay and question her, but for the moment the reward of having proved the reality of the vision seemed more than enough. Also, it was getting late. Thinking to come back with Spode to film this brave little group in their daily setting, I asked the guide to explain that we would return soon with real presents for them all. We said good-bye, and when we vanished down the breach in the papyrus dyke, we could still see the dark little group motionless where we had left them on the shining foreshore between fire and island hump.

"You are not thinking of coming to film these people as well as the honey-bird," Comfort called out half-mockingly in English from behind me. He was teasing me out of kindness, but touched me so accurately on the raw that I barely held back the retort he did not deserve. It was well I succeeded, for in fact I never saw the people or their island again.

That night I worked harder than ever to put our island camp at ease. I never had over-promising material in the paddlers, but I did not seek the explanation there. I was convinced that the responsibility lay first with me, and then in our European midst. The paddlers, with the vulnerability of primitive people to a more conscious human atmosphere, were merely picking up all that was negative in our situation, namely, the depression caused by the ailments inflicted on my white companions, and what I took to be Spode's failure to play his own constructive and contracted role. Charles, Ben and Vyan were all on the way to recovery, but the atmosphere round Spode was as disturbing as ever. Again he had lain inert under his blankets for much of that day. He did not speak unless spoken to, and his handsome face was so charged with resentment, hurt and disapproval, of such an unexplained and unfathomable kind, that it sent my own determined heart into my boots. What effect, then, must not his appearance and example have had on the primitive paddlers? I made one more supreme effort that evening, therefore, to talk and jolly Spode into something positive, only to wake up in the morning to find it had all been in vain. Indeed, from the start of that day everything seemed to go wrong.

Spode, when I talked to him about filming the group of women and the honey-bird, said irritably, "You don't ever understand, Laurens! I haven't the strength today. *Je n'ai pas de force.* . . . Perhaps tomorrow."

Hard upon this, Charles, whose nerves had been sorely tried by inactivity and pain, made his one and only scene with me because Vyan had used an enamel coffee mug as a shaving bowl! This was followed by Comfort drawing me aside and saying that the paddlers were more than ever convinced that the launch would not come for us. Further, the guide had warned him that a small group among them was saying that if that happened they would kill us at night, throw us to the crocodiles and take themselves out of the swamp the easiest way.

"Don't believe such nonsense," I said shortly. "And I order you not to repeat one word of such rubbish to anyone else."

"Of course I do not believe it," he answered, laughing without conviction. "I tell you merely to show you what sort of people they are here. But there is one thing I do not like, Moren. At first when I was among them they always spoke in Sechuana. Now they always speak the swamp dialect so that I cannot understand what they are saying."

I did not take Comfort's report of the paddlers' threat seriously. It was, I was convinced, only an extreme symptom of a general sense of frustration and negation in the island camp. Nonetheless, I took precautions. I decided to stay in camp myself all day and to keep with me the men with whom I had developed a bond during the past few days. Their presence I was certain would help to create a better atmosphere. For the rest, I proposed to break up in smaller groups the men who had idled longest round the campfires. Nothing more disconcerts the mass mind, particularly the negative mass mind, than to see its numbers reduced and its cohesion attenuated. I picked six of the most divergent characters and sent them off hunting with spears and an old shotgun. I asked Vyan and Charles also to take out parties, and gave Charles my gun. That done, I proposed to have a serious talk with Spode. But he had already gone back to bed and appeared asleep. Thinking I could leave that until he woke in the afternoon, I went and talked at some length to each of the men left in the camp. Spode was still asleep when I finished, and all chance of having a quiet hour with him to myself vanished when the parties of hunters started coming back in the early afternoon, all with the same total lack of success.

Up to that moment I had thought my plan was serving

its purpose well, but I was disconcerted to see how quickly the camp became despondent again. As a result I went out once more in the evening with my gun and the proved makorro crews. My luck continued to hold and at sundown I managed to bring off another extremely difficult shot. By my native Boer standards I have never regarded myself as anything except an average shot. Yet that evening I was shooting in an inspired Rider Haggard class, and to this day the way I shot, the manner wherein I acquired the gun, and the full extent to which it served the imperative mood of that part of the journey, for me holds something supernatural. I still do not like to think of what our plight might have been had I not had that gun and shot with it as I did. For days it was the only positive force in our midst, and the decisive factor in our fortunes. I do not know what the paddlers might not have done had it not enabled me to feed them so well. I shot with it nine times and killed eight buck. I shot twice at the same target only to put a fatally wounded animal out of pain. Once I used Vyan's shot-gun to kill, with unlikely duck-shot, a wart-hog, one of the toughest animals in Africa. Stranger still, I seemed the only person able to find game. All the others, black and white, failed though I kept them busy hunting as a matter of policy. Yet whenever I went out, even into areas just vacated by other disappointed hunters, I would find game enough and to spare. These factors in the sum of our sealed-off period in the swamp served to rally the random emotions on the fickle island. I knew without question that those who hunted with me, particularly Samutchoso, were overawed by my success, and when they held the gun their fingers curled reverently about it as if it were a living and magnetic object. And of course I too was endowed with something of the gun's "magic." The effect on my own spirit was considerable and gave me such confidence in belonging to the purpose of all around me that neither the intractable paddlers nor my utter failure with Spode could undermine it.

And so the long days went slowly by. Spode never filmed for us again and became more than ever silent. I never had my serious talk alone with him. I pressed him no more. I remembered all the hours which, at the end of a tiring day, I had devoted to building a bridge between himself, myself and the others, all the efforts I had made to amuse, interest, appease and stimulate him into becoming an active member of the expedition. I realized that perhaps I'd done too much of it, and that to try and carry him beyond his natural limits had made me neglect other duties. I had given priority to his moods and taken the others, even the paddlers, somewhat for granted. I had talked to Spode and thought about him when Ben, Charles, Karuso and his men could have done with more of my time and imagination. So now I left him alone to make his own terms with the trust that had been put in him, and to find his own unsolicited and natural level. What I had of spare time I now gave to the others. Henceforth I made a point of talking at some length to each person in the camp each day, and when it became clear to me, as it had long been clear to Comfort and the others, that Spode was not going to work on his own prompting I sent the guide with a special party to the little group of women we had discovered with presents to barter for more of their delicate bream. I sent another party to contact the honey-diviner. They came back at evening with the dark combs the bird had enabled them to find in a disused termite mound. I myself, sadly, gave up all the exploring I loved so deeply and concentrated on keeping the camp fed and in hand.

On the first day on which we could expect the launch, I took the precaution of telling everyone that I was not expecting it for another four days. I gave them all sundry tasks to do for distraction, yet I found myself, toward evening, continually listening for the sound of a diesel engine coming down the scarlet channel. It did not come that day nor the next, and on the third the atmosphere in the island was at its most ominous. I had the greatest difficulty in dispatching the hunters. Everyone, even Spode, who for once did not stay in bed, wanted to hang about, on the look-out, by the water-front. If it had not been for Vyan and Ben smoking, talking and imperturbably going about the tasks of the day, Comfort's disciplined presence, my hunter companions and Jeremiah tending his pots and pans as if he were truly at home, I would have felt utterly bleak. Jeremiah was, perhaps, the most impressive of all. Frequently I found him smiling to himself over his pots and pans, so often, indeed, that I had to ask him why he was always smiling.

"I was thinking of my son, Master," he said with a laugh of sheer contentment. "He is a very, very clever boy."

As the red sun sank close to the papyrus spikes standing rigidly between us and the west like green railings round a green park, the disconsolate watchers at the water-front began to drift back to their evening fires.

"The launch won't be here before tomorrow at the earliest," I mocked Comfort openly. To myself I thought, If it's not here in two days' time, I'll have to go out with the guide to see what's wrong.

Just then a great shout went up from the river-bank. In a second the camp was empty. The pulse of the launch's engine beat faintly though steadily in the evening air. I remained sitting underneath a tree upon which Comfort had carved my name some days before. A disgruntled paddler had asked him what he was doing, and with a cheerful laugh he'd replied, "Writing a history of the camp so that when we do not come back the people who come looking for us will know why!"

I looked up gratefully now to the tender blue sky far above the great branches and noticed that the number of vultures since our arrival had increased to five. The unaccustomed sound of the launch approaching, however, had made them stir uneasily. On tiptoe, with ruffled feathers and long scraggy necks stretched out, they appeared amazed and cheated. Just then one of the older paddlers whom before I had hardly noticed, left the others and came to stand shyly in front of me. He held out a walking stick carved out of yellow island wood and said, "Please, Master, I made this for you." I took it in both hands, humbled that someone in the midst of his own predicament had given thought also to me. Only at that moment did I realize what a strain the whole thing had been.

The next morning at dark we left our island. As I went round the camp for the last time to scatter sand on our dying fires, I thought Augustine's exhortations in the reeds were hoarse with protest at our going. At dawn we passed through miles of burnt-out papyrus water and I was amazed to see how confidently the shy Setatunga antelope of the inmost swamp walked across the parched surface. At one place Vyan shot a buck at the meatless ferrymen's request, and Samutchoso and Long-axe walked out on the pitted papyrus mat to get it in.

We caught up with the fire standing high in flame and smoke on the edge of the main channel. Opposite it burned another fire, as fierce and ruthless. I would not have thought it possible that green, water-fed fuel could burn with such abandon. The heat in midstream was intense. The water at one point was churning like porridge with mice, rats, snakes and reptiles cruising frantically backwards and forwards from bank to bank looking for shelter from the flames. Above the leaping heat the sky was flashing with the spark and glitter of a fire all its own, as crimson bee-eaters swiftly

dived around the roaring conflagration to pick off the insects taking to the air for safety on wings of shining glass.
We went slowly against the current through the narrow
gateway of fire like beings leaving a legendary world after a
fateful argosy. For a long time I stood high in my old position in the prow, watching the tallest flames fade until at
last a thick curtain of smoke came down between the central swamp and ourselves.

We travelled until after midnight before resting. Then we
set off again early the next morning to arrive at "the place
of the eddies" by evening. All the while Spode sat silent and
apart. He spoke to no one and seemed incapable even of
making his bed. I had to do it for him. He looked most unhappy and his grey eyes were filled with conflict. However, no sooner were we safe on firm, dry mainland than
some power of decision returned to him. I was helping Jeremiah to get hot tea and food because everyone was tired and
hungry, when Spode drew me aside.

"I regret, Laurens," he said, "but I cannot go on. You must
send me back to Europe. This life is too brutal—*un peu trop
brutale*—for me."

"Of course you realize what a terrible hole this puts me
in?" I couldn't help remarking.

"Please! Please!" he exclaimed at once, becoming deeply
agitated. "Can't you ever understand? *Je n'ai pas de force.*
I cannot go on."

"All right, Eugene," I told him, realizing that the situation was beyond reasoning and persuasion and wondering,
as often before in the stillness of the night, what I could do
to set it right for us. Spode might go, but I had to go on.
Somehow, if I were not to break faith with the people who
had trusted us and lose both them and myself thousands of
pounds, I had to produce the film we had contracted to
make. I would have to travel the odd thousand miles to the

nearest railway, and from there search South Africa for someone to take Spode's place. What was more I would have to hurry, because neither Vyan nor Ben could stay on with me indefinitely. In all the weeks already on the way we had barely done any filming. We had not even found our main quarry. I realized, sick at heart, I would be more than lucky if I finished the film quite apart from carrying out my own personal mission. Now at the fag-end of that long day when the curtain of smoke came down on the journey into the swamp, failure, which had for so long been peering over my shoulder, seemed to stare me full in the face. For a start, the technical difficulties appeared insurmountable. Even supposing I found a cameraman to take on the work, Spode had been using the latest German film-cameras, and all the film had been wound on spools and in laboratories in Britain to fit these special cameras. My chances of finding someone with such a camera in South Africa seemed infinitesimal, but, unless I did, all the film would have to be rewound painfully, foot by foot, in some improvised darkness in the heat and dust and glare of a desert journey. Would that be possible? And even if it were, would I find a technician patient enough to endure it? The journey behind us was child's play in comparison with what lay ahead. All this went through my mind in one brief moment as I faced the familiar tide of agitation in Spode and repeated, "All right, Eugene. I'll go to Muhembo first thing in the morning and ask them to fly you out when next they have a plane for the Mines. But I would be grateful if you'd leave your cameras behind. That would help a lot."

He did not let me finish, exclaiming at once, "Be reasonable, Laurens, what am I to do in Europe without my cameras?"

Without argument I left it at that, feeling it was best in the worst of circumstances to let the worst be the worst as quickly as possible. Often in my life I have found that the one thing that can save is the thing which appears most to threaten. In peace and war I have found that frequently, naked and unashamed, one has to go down into what one most fears and in that process, from somewhere beyond all conscious expectation, comes a saving flicker of light and energy that, even if it does not produce the courage of a hero, at any rate enables a trembling mortal to take one step further.

"All right, Eugene," I said again. "I'll leave at dawn and you all can follow at leisure later in the day."

He was calm again at once. Almost like a child he asked, "Would you please reserve a nice room in the hotel at Muhembo for me?"

If anything more was needed to illustrate to me how much Spode had lived in the midst of a world of his own feelings and rejected the formidable reality of Africa through which we had moved so laboriously for so long, it was that final request of his.

"There are no hotels in Muhembo," I said. "You'll have to camp out there, as here, until a plane turns up."

I took it as a good sign that, with illusion gone and faced with the worst, I slept better that night than any other on the journey. I slept so soundly that a leopard, judging by his spoor, passed close enough to my net to brush it with his tail on his way to kill some of the ferrymen's chickens in the tree next to me. At dawn I shaved, sluiced myself down with cold water by the river, put on clean clothes, ate quickly and set out for Muhembo. I must add that when I had gone Spode, for only the second time on the journey, produced his violin and played gaily, vigorously and at length to the camp.

Chapter 8

THE SPIRITS OF THE
SLIPPERY HILLS

B𝚈 CHANCE (to use the only phrase we have
for describing one of the most significant manifestations of
life) that very morning a plane with only half a load was
ordered to change its schedule at the last minute and to fly to
Muhembo to fill up with recruits for the Mines. I would
have missed it had I hesitated and stayed on at "the place of
the eddies" to try and over-persuade Spode, for I arrived
just as the two Europeans in charge of the depot were setting out for the airfield. Their generous and experienced
hearts at once sized up the extent of my predicament. There
was no filling in of forms in triplicate, no demanding of a
fortnight's notice in writing, no referring to some remote
impersonal authority for a decision, or any other of the
devices used by our timid collective age to eliminate the individual equation in life. The senior of the officials merely
said, "Come on, there's no time like the present." No plati-

tude, to me, has ever sounded more profound and original.

They raced me to the airfield where they introduced me to the pilot of the aircraft who turned out to be captain of their fleet. He wore a D.S.O. and D.F.C. on his neat tunic at the head of several rows of war ribbons, and like so many good fighter pilots had the gift of imagination stressed strongly in the lines of his face with an expression intimating that he was not yet reconciled to his undemanding peacetime role after such prolonged preoccupation with matters of life and death.

"Don't worry!" they called after me as I followed him aboard. "We'll see to Spode and do our best to entertain your chaps. Good luck to you."

Soon I was sitting behind the pilot in the cockpit peering far below where a haze of smoke and heat drifted over the waters of the swamp which glared back at me like polished brass. I spent the night in Francistown in the house of Cyril and Molly Challis. They promised to meet Spode when he came through and to help him on his way. I left them at dawn with the same pilot on his way to Northern Nyasaland, and was put down at Bulawayo for breakfast. I could barely believe my good fortune when I arrived in Johannesburg the same afternoon by regular mail plane only thirty-six hours after leaving "the place of the eddies" which had taken me so many long weeks to reach by land.

I went straight to my customary hotel and booked a room. I was just settling in when the telephone rang.

"A call from London," said the operator.

"For me?" I was dumbfounded, for I had been unable to keep regularly in touch with anyone for weeks.

In a moment I heard my wife's clear voice speaking from London, six thousand miles away.

"But how did you know I was here?" I asked, too amazed to listen to her questions.

"I had a feeling directly I woke up," she replied, "and booked a call through. What's happened?"

I told her. To my growing amazement she was not dismayed. "You'll really be able to get going now," she said. "I'm convinced of it. And I'm sure you'll find another cameraman— Sure of it! Everything'll be all right. Good luck, darling."

The three minutes were up.

This incident had a great effect for the good on a person like myself to whom coincidences have never seemed idle but always to hold something purposeful. I put down the receiver so profoundly reassured that I began at once to make a long series of calls on friends and acquaintances. One of them said, "I know a man who might help. I'll ask him to lunch with us tomorrow."

So from friend to friend of friend I began to track down a suitable substitute for Spode. On the third day, just when it seemed to me I would have to go to Europe in order to do so, the trail led me to Duncan Abraham. The son of a Scottish minister, born in Zululand with not a silver spoon but a Brownie in his mouth, as I once teased him, he had been obsessed by cameras all his life, and as soon as he was of age had set up as a commercial photographer. He had served as a cameraman with the film unit of the South African forces in the war and when peace came established himself as a freelance in Johannesburg, where he represented several international film news agencies and even from time to time made his own documentaries. He was so absorbed in his work that it rewarded him with the sense of a personal meaning in life. When he worked he had no mind for anything except his camera and his subject. Once when filming off the Natal coast Duncan had stepped backwards over the gunwale of his boat and fallen, camera and all, into the Indian Ocean. Duncan returned to the scene the next day with a professional diving unit. Guided by little more than love of his lost instrument, he selected a place in the heaving waters for diving and at last retrieved from the deep the camera which he still had in use when I met him. From the way his shrewd Scot's eye kindled at my proposition I knew his answer; but there were difficulties, he pointed out at once, which would be expensive to overcome. He was busy making an historical film of missionary effort in Africa, and also had important national events to cover for his news agencies. Everything turned on whether he could get permission to suspend the former and find substitutes to film the latter. In the end, for a steep consideration, we managed to do both. Unbelievable as it seems, Duncan's favourite working camera was of the same make as Spode's. At that moment in the whole of the vast city there was no other of that type!

I left Duncan to follow me within a few days and set out for Muhembo as fast as I could. I had complete confidence in Vyan and Ben, but I knew also how suspense and the general sense of failure and misfortune inflicted on us by Spode's disaffection would loom large in the heat, dust and isolation of such a remote little place. Also I could not fail to notice that already it was spring. When I first started out from Johannesburg with my Land-Rovers it had still been winter. Now the first delicate increase of the year, and young flowers wet with dew, were on sale in the streets. I had little time to spare, but just enough to allow me to stop at an open stall on the way to the airfield. I bought strawberries and young asparagus and wherever I landed on my way back left some with the people who had helped me and were still making do on their hard winter's rations. One marooned wife, who years before had confided in me a craving for English strawberries, burst into tears when I put a basket of the fruit in her hands.

I arrived back at Muhembo on an afternoon of increased

and searing heat just a week after leaving "the place of the eddies." I was fearful of what I might find but knowing Vyan and Ben as I did I should not have been anxious. In meticulous khaki they were all there with a shining Land-Rover to meet me. Only Comfort, whom I was to miss greatly, had been recalled to his far northern post. We drove back, all talking at once, to a model camp pitched in the shade of a great tree on the wide Okovango's bank, and so light, gay and natural was the atmosphere that I could hardly believe my senses.

Some days later Duncan Abraham joined us. He was in camp no longer than it took to eat a quick meal when he loaded the magazines of his camera and began filming: the birds coming out of the swamp like giant puffs of smoke; the noses, nostrils, ears and eyes of the hippo, hypnotic on the bright afternoon water; the Mambukush women going down to the river with jars shaped like Greek vases on their heads; and a hundred and one other colourful things. This eruption of activity in a department for so long dormant caught everyone's attention, and when Duncan suddenly clambered up a tree like a monkey to get a better angle on the river, my companions all exchanged astonished glances. Jeremiah, laughing so much that he could hardly find breath, exclaimed, "I tell you, Jambo, I tell you, John, that new man is a very, very clever person!"

When the normal light began to fail, Duncan was still filming the sunset colours. In the morning before I could give him coffee he was back on the river-bank waiting to film the dawn and sunrise over the smoking swamp. He was not a talkative person, for his thought, it seemed, was shaped not in words but in endless sequences of camera shots. I heard Vyan say jokingly to Ben at breakfast, "Our trouble has been reversed. Before, we couldn't get the filming to begin. Now it'll never stop!"

We stayed in Muhembo only long enough to repair something of the damage done by our failure to film more of the journey into the swamps. There was no time and no point in attempting to retrace our way back into the marshes. The evidence clearly showed that the River Bushman, as a coherent entity, had vanished from the Okovango delta. The tsetse fly and sleeping sickness, the invasion of more powerful and consciously assertive hordes of Bantu fugitives had caused him to disperse, and either to die or be absorbed into the taller peoples crowding his shrinking frontiers. What was left were merely pitiful fragments and one of our last tasks at Muhembo was to make an excursion into the swamp near by where Ben and Vyan in my absence had located a party of three River Bushmen, a man, his wife and a kinsman.

The woman was very beautiful but with a haunted face. She had an expression of total defeat in her eyes as if the end of her whole race was focused in her own person. I always felt it was no accident that she was childless. She camped with her husband under a tree on a mound by the side of a long, narrow backwater where her menfolk had built an intricate and beautifully woven trap of golden reeds and rushes across a sky-blue channel. The trap had two entrances against either bank, sealed with long, funnelled baskets, and on the five separate occasions during which they cleared them for Duncan to film, we noticed that the mob of barbel and mud-fish were always in the same basket and the aristocratic Okovango bream in the other, "preserving a nice class distinction to the rim of the frying pan," as Vyan put it.

I tried to get the three Bushmen to talk about their past, but I did not devote overmuch time to it, for I doubted if they had anything new to add. They had been so cut off from birth, and their spirit so deeply concussed by the headlong fall of their whole race into disaster, that I felt there was only an over-all ache to communicate. I did persuade

the woman to come into camp so that I could doctor a festering injury to her hand. Duncan took a photograph of her
then, her lovely ghost face warming at the gift of a coloured
kerchief. It was like the glow of some inherited memory, as
if she could still remember what such a present could have
meant to a woman like herself before life closed its doors on
her and her people at both ends of its narrow corridor.
However, we did film the little round of their circumscribed
living in the teeming swamp and extracted some conversation on the magnetic tape on our Ferrograph recording machine. The man, when he listened to a record of such talk
played back by Charles, instinctively spoke up again where
our original questions to him re-sounded on the tape, and
endeared himself to everyone by being the first to laugh at
himself when he quickly discovered his error. These, however, were the only glimpses we were allowed into their nature, for quickly the prevailing sadness would settle like a
mist on the blue of an autumn evening between them and us.
The husband, indeed, who was a good bit older than the
other two, steadfastly declined to leave the swamp. The last
I saw of him was at his fishing trap in his flat-bottomed
makorro, leaning heavily on his punting pole and looking,
not at our receding craft, but deeply into the water as if his
spirit had need of concentration on the one element that endured, unchanging, in his world into which angry men had
come so thick and fast upon one another's heels to cut down,
one by one, the branches of a race it had taken many thousands of years of secluded life to grow.

That evening we sent the woman and her kinsman home
to the swamp loaded with presents, and I told my companions to prepare to leave in the morning. Duncan pleaded for
two more days, saying there was still so much of interest to
film. But I remembered the warning Samutchoso had delivered solemnly in the swamp: I would have to hasten if I

wanted to see a gathering of Bushmen in the Slippery Hills. They would stay there only so long as the water in the crevices at the foot of the hills lasted, for they drew on the eternal sacred water at the top of the hills not as a routine but only in dire necessity. Already twelve days had passed since I promised to meet Samutchoso at "the place of the eddies" to guide us to the hills. Every day had added to the power and the glory of the sun. All around us the white waters were shrinking and even the great river falling fast, while my own spirit stamped like a horse kept overlong in the stable. Firmly I refused Duncan.

We sat under our great communal net in Muhembo for the last time because, once in the desert, though it had its own formidable insects, there would be no mosquitoes. We talked until late to the two Europeans to whom we owed so much, and during the pauses listened to the unique sounds of the swamp. Yet we were all up early, delayed only slightly because Duncan could not be torn from a last effort to film a dawn he declared to be the greatest of all. By noon we were back at "the place of the eddies." But Samutchoso was not there. After waiting patiently for us he had returned to his home in the swamps. While the others settled down to prepare lunch in the shade I borrowed a guide from the ferryman's family to conduct me to Samutchoso's home along the ridges of sand that were rising daily higher above the water. I found him some hours later surrounded by his women and children, all naked, except for tight loincloths round their stomachs, and fishing with long baskets in a fiery lagoon just below the reed walls of the courtyard round Samutchoso's neat thatched hut. The setting, the shining hour, the leisurely occupation, and the manner in which swamp, earth and the empty sky combined to make an impersonal law for all, reminded me vividly of the Old Testament. The impression was increased by Samutchoso's manner. The moment he saw me he waded out of the water to greet me as if I had not kept him waiting a fortnight. He asked no questions, but merely said that if I could please help him with one thing he would be ready to come with me at once. He led me into the courtyard of his home. There, full in the sun on a reed mat, lay a young emaciated boy shivering violently.

"Please make him well, Master!" Samutchoso pleaded.

I was back in a world before drugs and patent medicines existed and when healing was achieved by faith. I had no certain idea what the boy's illness was. I listened carefully to his breathing with my ear on his hot, trembling chest and instinctively chose aureomycin from my medicines, getting Samutchoso to explain to a wide-eyed family who had gathered around how to continue the treatment. I was to find later that the boy recovered. That incident over, Samutchoso went into a hut and emerged almost at once with a stick and a small bundle in hand. He spoke a few words to the women and children, and again there were no explanations, questions or protests. On the faces of all was an expression of the acceptance of people accustomed to converting chance and change into the currency of fate.

That evening for the first time after many weeks, we slept again in the bush and on the deep sand of the Kalahari. The flute-like sound of the swamps had gone and in its place arose a variety of voices: night plover, screech owl, jackal, hyena, and finally toward morning the greatest of them all, the solemn roar of a lion echoing between us and the hills.

We set off again on a cloudless morning. Ben and Vyan went ahead with two Land-Rovers to break a way through the bush; Charles, Duncan, Samutchoso and I followed at leisure in order to be free to stop and film undisturbed.

We were trying to stalk a dazzle of zebra which flashed in and out of a long strip of green and yellow fever trees, with

an ostrich, its feathers flared like a ballet skirt around its dancing legs, on their flank, when suddenly two shots, fired
quickly one after the other, snapped the tense silence ahead.

My blood went cold within me. Instinctively I looked at
Samutchoso. His face was without expression and yet I knew
he had heard and that a change accordingly had taken place
within him. With an acute sense of guilt, I realized I had forgotten to keep faith with him. My anxieties in the swamp, my
absorption with the problem of Spode, the long journey out
and back from Johannesburg and many other things had over-
laid the moment when he and I had first discussed the journey to the hills. I had completely overlooked the essential
condition of the promise extracted by him from me: that
there should be no killing on our way to the hills. I had forgotten to tell our companions of Samutchoso's account of the
spirits' law against killing on approach to their home.

I tried to console myself with the facile optimism of the
guilty, hoping that the shots might have missed, and said
nothing for the moment. We caught up with the advance
guard some miles further on in a place where bush and plain
had been burnt out by some hunter in preparation for the
summer's rain. For miles around it was black and scorched as
if a tongue of the fire which consumed Sodom and Gomorrah
had licked it bare.

John and Jeremiah were close by the Land-Rover disem-
bowelling a wart-hog. Vyan coming from afar toward us was
followed by Cheruyiot with a steenbuck across his shoulders. The expression on Samutchoso's face was almost more
than I could bear.

"I'm sorry," I said at once. "It's all my fault, not theirs. I
forgot to tell them. I had so much trouble I forgot my promise."

His face relaxed, and he said that he understood, but the
implication was that it was not for him either to understand

or absolve. With that, and a brief, belated explanation and warning to my hunter companions that nothing under any conditions was to be shot, I had to be content.

From there we pushed on faster because the passage over the blackened plain was easy. By eleven o'clock the highest of the hills rose above the blue of distance, and between us and them lay a bush of shimmering peacock leaves. After so many weeks in flat land and level swamp, the sudden lift of the remote hills produced an immediate emotion and one experienced forthwith that urge to devotion which once made hills and mountains sacred to man, who then believed that wherever the earth soared upwards to meet the sky one was in the presence of an act of the spirit as much as a feature of geology. I thought of the Psalmist's "I will lift up mine eyes unto the hills, from whence cometh my help," and marvelled that the same instinct had conducted Samutchoso to the hills to pray. The nearer we came the stronger this impression grew, and as the hills rose at last clear above the bush they seemed to communicate their own atmosphere to us all. The highest could not have been more than a thousand feet. But they rose sheer out of the flat plain and were from the base up made entirely of stone, and this alone, in a world of deep sand, gave them a sense of mystery. The others, too, felt it. We stopped, and Charles and I climbed onto the roof of my Land-Rover to observe them through field glasses. Jeremiah, who knew nothing of Samutchoso's story, stared hard at the hills. He had been for a short while to a mission school in Barotseland, and now he said suddenly in a small voice, "Master, they look like the rocks Moses struck in the desert to let out water for the Israelites!"

The rock on the highest of the hills certainly was imposing. Blue and shining like tempered steel, it covered the steep flanks in smooth slabs often a hundred feet or more high. On one of the highest faces there appeared to be rust-red markings of a curiously hieroglyphic design. Charles, for one moment, thought they were ancient Egyptian silhouettes painted on the rock, and my own heart beat faster for I had nursed a hope that here might be some isolated and secure place in the sandy desert with sufficient rock to enable the Bushman to practise his age-old art of painting. But long scrutiny through glasses disillusioned us both. The markings were of the terrible extremes of weather and time.

After that we studied the hills for signs of smoke, but not a wisp was to be seen. We consoled ourselves with the thought that it was not the hour for smoke. Also, according to Samutchoso, the Bushman camped in the hidden bush at the centre of the horseshoe swing of the hills. Slowly we moved closer, the sand getting deeper, the bush more dense and the blue hills higher. There was no wind, not even a heat-whorl to contort the terrible calm of the day on the face of the hills. The bushes in the crevices between the stony slabs looked more like objects petrified in stone than pliable leaves and branches. Nor was there a sound to be heard. At any moment I expected the inevitable baboon to challenge us, but it never did. I searched the blue-black sky arched over us like the span of a bridge drumming with the urgent traffic of darkness massing beyond the sun. But both it and the blue water below the arch were empty of the hawk, buzzard and vulture that normally man the lofty foretop of the desert day. Indeed, it was as if everything that might have distracted our senses from the Slippery Hills deliberately had been cancelled from the scene. The hills were in sole command and so dominated our impressions that the two Land-Rovers, their behinds wiggling and waggling over the rough, roadless plain as they searched for camping site and water, seemed like puppies fawning toward the feet of a stern master.

When we caught up again with the advance Land-Rovers some hours later, the vehicles were halted deep in the bush on the far side of the hills. The doors of both were flung wide open as if hastily abandoned. Ben, Vyan, Cheruyiot and John had all disappeared. The heat was overwhelming because the vast slabs of rock fired in the noonday sun added a gratuitous quota of degrees to the temperature. The silence was deeper than ever, and I was aware only of the sun flame hissing like a brood of yellow cobras in my ears. I thought of calling aloud to Vyan and Ben, but one look at the silent world of rocks and the tawny fringe of burning bush on the horseshoe crest above, forbade me. Any violence of sound I feared could be dangerously resented. I didn't want to risk worsening our situation, for already, in the crescent of the sullen rock, I felt rather like a mouse between the paws of a great cat.

I went and joined Samutchoso and the others underneath the tattered shade of a tree and said in a whisper, "No good fussing. The bush is thick here. I expect they've gone on foot to reconnoitre and will be back soon."

As I said it I had an idea Samutchoso did not take their absence so lightly. However, I put it down to guilty conscience over my broken promise and tried to think no more of it.

An hour later the others broke out of the bush almost on top of us. We had had no warning of their coming, for the air was so thin and stricken with heat that it had not life enough to carry sound. They were all four exhausted, eager to join us under our tree and to impart their news. They had seen no smoke and no traces of Bushmen old or new. They had found a good level place for a camp under trees that threw real shade, near a deep cut in overhanging rock where water still oozed through.

"It's lovely pure water," Ben said. "But, my word, it's plagued with bees! Never seen so many wild bees in my life! We had difficulty in getting a drink without being stung."

The sun was setting by the time we had made camp, collected wood for our fires and installed ourselves for a stay of several days. Still no sound or movement came from bush or hills. Even a stir of evening air would have been welcome to ease the immovable and shining heat hanging in the horseshoe bowl of rocks. Just before dark I took my gun and walked alone to the narrow gap between the highest of the hills in the hope that there I might meet some cooling air. But it was just as bad there, so I started back at a quickened pace because the light was fast beginning to fail, and the silent raised rock faces made me feel acutely uncomfortable. In that red afterglow of an immense Kalahari sunset they had a strange, living personality, as if their life had been only temporarily suspended in the sleep of motion that we call matter, and at any moment they might wake up, step down and walk the desert on some cataclysmic occasion of their own.

At this point I was deeply startled by a sound coming from the rocks on my right. I swung round, my gun ready and the hair slowly creeping at the back of my neck. A superb kudu bull with an immense spread of curved Viking horn above his long, pointed face was making his way from ledge to ledge down a crimson cleft in the rocks. He moved with utter confidence, free of fear or hurry, passed close by me without a sideways glance and made straight for the gap in the hills. Perhaps, I thought, he is one of the master spirits of which Samutchoso had spoken, who, now that night has come, is going from his dwelling in the rocks to do business among creatures in the world beyond? He vanished thus, leaving me to return to camp more subdued than ever.

It is significant that none of us was at ease during all that first night in the hills. At first light the camp came alive as though glad to be rid of such darkness, and everyone without urging from me began preparing vigorously for the day. Just before sunrise, however, we had an abrupt and odd interruption. Suddenly we were attacked by bees. From all directions through the trees they came winging sonorously at this unfamiliar hour. I have never witnessed anything like it. They came not in angry, militant swarms to sting, but in great, shapeless dark-brown hordes humming an esoteric tune of exhortation, crawling all over us and our belongings as if to sweep us, by sheer weight of numbers and volume of sound, out of their way. The smell and taste of our water could not have attracted them because they ignored it, as also the sugar set out for our breakfast coffee. They seemed interested only in beating their wings against our faces, crawling up our sleeves and trousers and from time to time driving the mysterious point of their visitation home with a perfectly timed sting in the most tender spots.

Perturbed by the thought of the retaliation the bees might provoke, I warned the camp, "Don't kill any of them whatever else you do."

If I had hoped to please Samutchoso by my admonition, it proved vain because his expression clearly implied that the warning would have served us better had it been delivered two days earlier. Everyone except myself was stung several times, and the camp was made to look foolish and ridiculously disordered by the evasive action, the involuntary jerks, sudden spasms, jumps, cries of protest and all other unnatural efforts at self-control upon which I insisted. Then the moment the first shaft of wild sunlight struck at the camp through the purple gap in the hills, without sip of water or taste of sugar to sweeten their throats, which must have been well-nigh hoarse with chanting, the bees withdrew suddenly as if on a signal from central command. Ben had been stung the most badly. He, too, had been the most sceptical of Samutchoso's story and the dictate against killing when we discussed it the night before round the fire, but I didn't carry that thought far. We ate our breakfast in unusual silence, with unexpectedly chastened expressions. However, hot food, coffee and tobacco soon restored the spirits of my companions and they followed me out of camp to start the day's work with a will.

Our plan was, first, to examine the places at the base of the hills where Samutchoso knew Bushmen occasionally gathered. We walked in extended single file because the bush of wide-spreading, bone-white acacia thorn was as tangled and plaited as it was dense. However, Samutchoso, who led the way, soon found an easier game track which at intervals opened out on small clearings from which the rock faces were visible, stark, bold and forbidding. The night did not appear to have improved the mood of the hills and I was not surprised when the bush itself came suddenly to a shuddering halt leaving a clear space between itself and the base of the central hill, as if centuries before it had learned the importance of keeping a respectful distance from such reserved and imperious beings. Beneath the hills the shadows were cool and heavy, but far above, the ragged, jagged shark's-tooth edges of the purple crags were lined with warm sunlight. However, below the bright hem of that still morning one saw other cuts, injuries, wounds and scars in the steep surfaces that from a distance looked so impervious. There was hardly a face that was not torn, pock-marked, pitted and wrinkled as if with incredible suffering and struggling. Everywhere great fragments had broken away to lie in massive splinters in the sand at the base, or to balance precariously on the edge of an abyss. Now one understood better the stern mood of the place, because one was looking on an entire world of rock, isolated and without allies of any kind, making a heroic stand against disintegration by terrrible forces of sand, sun and time. It was an awesome spectacle, because neither the rock nor the forces deployed against it would give or accept quarter. As I was looking sombrely into those stony faces, I heard an almost reproachful exclamation from Samutchoso at my side, "Master, but do you not see?"

Both his voice and pointing finger were trembling with emotion. Over the scorched leaves of the tops of the bush conforming to a contour nearby and about a hundred feet up was a ledge of honey-coloured stone grafted into the blue iron rock. Above the ledge rose a smooth surface of the same warm, soft stone curved like a sea-shell, as if rising into the blue to form a perfect dome. But it curved upwards thus for only about twenty feet and then was suddenly broken. I had no doubt I was looking at the wall and part of the ceiling of what had once been a great cave in the hill, safe above the night prowl of the bush and with an immense view into the activities of the flat Kalahari beyond. Some yellow stone from the dome of the cave was tipped precariously on the edges of the ledge; other fragments were toppled into the red sand at the base. But what held my attention still with the shock of discovery was the painting that looked down at us from the centre of what was left of the wall and dome of the cave. Heavy as were the shadows, and seeing it only darkly against the sharp morning light, it was yet so distinct and filled with fire of its own colour that every detail stood out with a burning clarity. In the focus of the painting, scarlet against the gold of the stone, was an enormous eland bull standing sideways, his massive body charged with masculine power and his noble head looking as if he had only that moment been disturbed in his grazing. He was painted as only a Bushman, who had a deep identification with the eland, could have painted him. Moreover, it seemed that he had been painted at a period before the Bushman's serenity was threatened, for the look of calm and trustful inquiry on the eland's face was complete. I was greatly moved because it seemed to me that this was the look with which not only the eland but the whole of the life of Africa must have regarded us when first we landed there. On the left of the bull, also deep in scarlet, was a tall female giraffe with an elegant Modigliani neck. With the tenderness of a solicitious mother she was looking past the eland toward a baby giraffe standing shyly in the right of the picture. In the same right-hand corner of the canvas below them, the artist had signed this painting on the high wall with a firm impress of the palms of both hands, fingers extended and upright. The signature was marked so gaily and spontaneously that it brought an instant smile to my face and looked so young and fresh that it mocked my recollection that rock paintings signed in this manner are among the oldest in the world.

"How old is it, Samutchoso?" I asked.

"I do not know, Master," he replied. "I only know it was like this when my grandfather found it as a boy, and from what he told me and what I have seen myself it never gets older."

"You mean the colours do not fade?"

"No! The colours do not fade, Master," he answered, and would, I think, have said more if our party, one by one, had not been forming round us. They, too, fell silent when they saw the painting of the bull and his two companions standing there so serenely in that quiet viaduct of time.

Duncan was the first to break the silence with an excited command to Cheruyiot: "Jambo, my tripod, quick!"

He set up his camera, trained a telescopic lens on the painting and began filming. The film ran for only a few seconds when the precise whirr of the mechanism became blurred and the camera suddenly stopped.

"That's odd," Duncan said, examining it; "the magazine's jammed and yet it's brand-new."

Samutchoso looked from him to me with the same expression I had observed on his face during the invasion of the bees in our camp, but said nothing. Duncan loaded the camera with another magazine and began filming again. A few seconds later exactly the same stoppage occurred.

"This is most extraordinary!" he exclaimed, beginning to look disconcerted. "All the time I've been with you I've had no trouble of this kind and now two jams in as many minutes. It's unbelievable. But never mind. Third time lucky!" He started the third and only spare magazine. In the same number of brief seconds the third magazine jammed.

"This is fantastic!" he cried, now thoroughly upset. "In all the years I've filmed this has never happened before. I'm afraid I'll have to go back to the camp, clear these magazines and fetch the remaining spares before I can go on."

While he and Cheruyiot returned to camp, we closed in on the base of the rocks, that now seemed to stare back at us in the swelling light and heat of day with a glimmer of grim satisfaction, and started to follow the rocky contour on the ground. Soon we found other fragments of painting. Indeed, where there was rock smooth enough for the purpose, there were inevitably traces of painting. On the whole they were not as vivid and clear as the great raised piece, perhaps because they were even older. The rock surfaces themselves had been destroyed by weather and time. The subjects were almost entirely animal, many of them of animals which, like the charging rhinoceros, no longer existed in that part of the world and belonged to the earliest period of Bushman painting when, like the fabulous world of Aesop, the artist's vision of himself and his nature were still utterly contained in the glittering mirror of animal life before him. In one deep bay in the cliffs we came across what must have been the master of masterpieces among the Slippery Hills. The rock rose smooth and sheer out of the sand and for a distance of about forty feet and twelve feet high, it was painted with a crowded scene of the animal world. Most of this immense frieze was faded, torn or semi-obliterated, but there was enough clear detail left to charge one's blood with excitement at the stature of the original conception and the complicated achievement of the artist. The presence in one corner of a tall, elongated man suggested that the art was later than the others. But how could one tell? I only know that from that morning I have been pursued by a vision of those hills as a great fortress of once living Bushman culture, a Louvre of the desert filled with treasure. I would have given a great deal to have seen those sullen, hurt rock faces in their original well-loved state, redeemed and glowing with ardent colour under a far blue Kalahari heaven while daily the golden hunters came home to them from the plain laden with game to sit securely round their fires, eating meat and honey, washing down a draught of mead with the rare water filtered through the creviccs, and perhaps discussing the latest picture hung in their absence in the contemporary wing of the gallery of time towering behind them.

From this old master we worked our way around the base of the hill for close on a mile, becoming so absorbed in the paintings that I forgot we were there also to look for Bushmen. A shout from Samutchoso, who had gone on well ahead, brought me back to my immediate task and the reality of the burning noonday hour. We found him in the midst of what was obviously the site of a recent Bushman encampment. There were the light screens of grass and acacia branches to shelter them against the sun and dew, and all around the sand was thickly strewn with broken and empty nutshells, wilted melon skins, rabbit fur, porcupine quills, tortoise shells and the hooves of animals. There were several fresh giraffe shin-bones cleared of every scrap of meat and sinew and the marrow the Bushman so relishes. Finally, there were the unscattered ashes of their fires, a torn leather satchel sewn with sinew and decorated with ostrich-egg shell beads which a Bushman hunter carries on his shoulder, as well as a broken four-stringed Bushman lyre.

"They've gone," Samutchoso told me, letting some nutshells trickle through his fingers. "They've gone until next winter. Left about a week ago!"

"Perhaps they've just moved round the hill to a new site nearer water?" I suggested.

"No, Master," Samutchoso answered firmly. "The main drinking water is in the rocks over there. It is only the ever-lasting water that is on the hill above it."

There and then, hot as it was, we climbed to both waters. The first, almost hidden by the hordes of bees drinking at it, filled the long narrow cleft that contained it, but one could tell from the slow drip through the veins in the rocks which fed it from above that, once emptied, it would not be filled again until the next rains. The "everlasting water," as was ex-pected by those who believed Samutchoso, led us to quite a different world.

We climbed up to it by a clearly defined track, the natural stepping stones worn smooth and shining with centuries of traffic. The moment one began to mount steeply one was aware that it was no ordinary track. It was too direct in its approach to be just another of the game tracks which, like the spokes of a sun-wheel from their hub, led from the hills through the plain to the far horizon. This track had been ex-tensively decorated. At several places where the rock pre-sented a smooth enough surface it was highly painted. One would lift oneself up from one shelf to another to find one-self staring into the face of a rhinoceros regarding one with-out fear or favour; or a tortoise, head out and cocked on one side as if listening to our wilful steps, would suddenly con-front one as if to imply a rebuke to the sweating procession climbing so frantically toward the summit. At another place we observed what must have been a crowded scene of the animal world, a farewell celebration, perhaps, to pilgrims on their way to the austere summit above. Finally, just below the last rim of rocks wherein the "everlasting water" lay, there was a group of vigilant painted animals assembled on a ledge rather like passport officers at a frontier. This, of course, was a subjective reaction, but perhaps, to some extent, it was also true objectively, and with this last painting an emotional circle was made complete for the painter. From the first clarion utterance of eland and giraffe on the raised rock to this final inspection on a far animal frontier, we seemed to be in the presence of a single system of spirit dedicated to the translation of flesh and blood into a greater idiom of the world beyond where fruit of true knowledge purported to grow by everlasting water. I even wondered whether, with our profane guns and prying cameras, we were not clambering over the forsaken altars of a great natural temple.

Samutchoso, anyway, had no doubts. The expression on his face was exalted. He was the first to go eagerly over the rim. I followed. Before us was a deep cup in the crown of the central hill. I just had time to see a gleam of water when a heart-rending sob broke from Samutchoso. He had stopped to kneel on a rock by the track and was raising his hands like a Musulman at his devotions when he overbalanced backwards so violently that he nearly fell. Both knees were bleeding, but it was not the injury that was troubling him.

"Did you see, Master?" he asked, profoundly troubled. "I was not even allowed to begin to pray!"

He pointed out two deep holes in the rock in which he had tried to kneel and a third somewhat apart on the left. It was there, he said, that the greatest spirit of all had knelt with his cruse of water to pray the day he created the world. Here also he, Samutchoso, himself had knelt to pray when he visited the hills before. Yet now he had not been allowed to do so. He had been pulled backwards. He was visibly anguished and I could say little to comfort him, but his instinctive obedience to the working of his fate still enabled him to lead us, like a man in a trance, to the pool of perennial water.

The grass around the edges of the pool was green and lush and the surface covered with growth and slime, for it was long since it had been disturbed. In that high place and in that arid desert its mere existence was a miracle. Dragonflies and butterflies gratefully made gay over it, and hip to hip the dark brown bees drank eagerly at its edges. Near by grew the "tree of true knowledge," as Samutchoso called it. From its branches hung large, round fruit like green navel oranges. Samutchoso announced they were still too green for eating and that fact, too, seemed to add to his foreboding. The fruit when ripe, he said, was more delicious than honey. I would have liked to bring some of it back for identification, but Samutchoso begged me not to pick any of it. I felt I had already so hurt his spirit that trying to film the fruit was as far as I could go.

Down the sides of the hill several distinct tracks of animals led to the water. Though there was no spoor in the earth, the rocks, as Samutchoso had foretold, were deeply impressed with the hoof-prints of the animals. He took us from one set to the other, and though my companions argued their own preferred explanations of the phenomenon far into the days to come, I will attempt none and merely add that I myself identified the spoor of eland, gemsbuck, giraffe and hartebeest embedded deeply in the rock.

Long before we reached this stage Duncan had rejoined us, his magazines replenished and his spirit undismayed. But once more, despite his skill and care, the frustration of the morning was repeated. As he was trying to film the "fruit of knowledge" the last magazine of six jammed. This renewed and continued set-back to filming, after all we had endured, was profoundly disheartening. Was I never to be allowed to make a film of the journey? Both Duncan and I refused to admit such a possibility. So he, Charles and I worked until late that night cleaning the magazines and camera parts, oiling, greasing and polishing them by our great fire, until Duncan in the end said with a defiant grin, "Well! I'd like to see anything stop me from filming tomorrow!"

But he was wrong. Again at first light we were invaded by bees and had to endure them until the sun rose, when they vanished as before. After that we returned to the hills, climbed up a precipitous cleft to the first painting and began to film it. Hardly had he started when the ominous blur in the precise mechanism of the camera announced another stoppage. So it went on all day. By nightfall everyone, except myself and Duncan, seemed convinced there was a permanent voodoo on us. Once more Duncan with all the tenacity of his race spent the evening overhauling his camera and spares. Charles and I left him to it and set up our Ferrograph and microphones to record some of the strange night sounds that wailed around the hills. Then we got an additional shock. The machine which before had worked so well now went dead on us. We tried every test prescribed in the makers' manual. We could find no fault in any of the parts but the machine was dead. By midnight we abandoned the effort without any sound recording. As we crawled into bed a strange wind rose, combining, with the carrion of the bush, to sing of annihilation and decay among the rocks now deep in sable against the dark.

The next day, from the invasion of bees at first light to the jamming of the camera before breakfast, the pattern was repeated. The snippets of filming we brought back testify to this day to the struggle that went on all the time, until in the afternoon, the forces working against us decided on the final blow. A steel swivel in the camera itself (a part so secure that no spare for it is ever carried) failed and brought abruptly to an end our filming with that particular camera. It seemed to me when that happened that the grim faces of the hills came near to laughter. The whole thing had so got on my nerves that I began to fear that our admirable Land-Rovers, which had never failed us, might also get caught up in the sinister cycle of misfortune and refuse to start. For clearly we now had to leave the place as quickly as possible.

My fear was not lessened by Samutchoso, who exclaimed in surprise, as he watched Cheruyiot deposit the camera in camp, "But surely, Master, you never expected those machines to work?"

"Of course I did," I answered heatedly. "Why not?"

"Would you like me to find out?" he asked.

"Please do," I answered curtly.

He asked me for a clean thread of white cotton with which he threaded a needle he produced from his bundle. He knotted the two ends of the thread together, turned the double thread around his fingers and placed the needle in the life line of the palm of his left hand. He then looked deeply into it.

By this time everyone in the camp knew something unusual was happening and all stopped working to crowd round the pair of us. Silently they watched Samutchoso. He stood gazing at his palm for about ten minutes and then in a voice we had not heard before, he began to speak to presences that only he could see, saying, "No, not you over there. Don't push so please. . . . Be so good as to make way for him that is behind you. . . . No, not you either, but the next please. . . ." And so on and on until at last a deep "Ah!" came from him as if he had found in a great multitude the one he sought. Then he fell silent and appeared to be listening intently. Another quarter of an hour passed thus, and then like a man awaking he rubbed his eyes, shook his head and seeing me again said slowly, "Yes! Master, it is as I thought, the spirits of the hills are very angry with you, so angry that if they had not known your intention in coming here was pure they would long since have killed you. They are angry because you have come here with blood on your hands. They are angry because you have not behaved like a leader of your men. You allowed men who are less than you to come into their presence before you did. You allowed them to trample all over the hills and drink of the water they provide for men and beasts without first saying their prayers and asking permission to do so. You should have come first with me and as the leader paid your respects to them. We should first have asked their permission and have made a sacrifice of food and said our prayers before taking of their waters. That is why they have broken your machines. And, Master, they have not done with you yet."

He said all this so quietly, without melodrama or any effort at effect, that it was deeply impressive. I saw a look of consternation on the listening black faces.

"What can I do to put it right?" I asked him.

He shook his grey head sadly, saying, "I do not know. Truly I do not know. They are angry with me, too. You saw how they threw me out of the place of prayer? They tell me they would have killed me if I had tried again."

And there for the moment I had to leave it. I got the camp busy preparing to run from the hills first thing in the morning. Our situation, from a practical point of view, was desperate. Our time was running out fast and in spite of Duncan's promising start at Muhembo I was not much nearer making the film I had contracted to make than when Spode left us. I had managed once, thanks to the steadfast support of Vyan and Ben, to lift the expedition out of one cycle of failure, but could I do it a second time? Again I would have to go a thousand miles and more into the civilized world beyond the desert and try to get Duncan's camera repaired. It was uncertain if I could get the spare parts, and Duncan thought even if I did the repair might take weeks. Could I count on everyone standing fast until I returned and once more taking up a task twice blighted by such abject failure? There in the silence of the impervious hills the answer seemed hopelessly problematical. And yet that was not what troubled me most. As the gloomy afternoon wore on, I found myself worrying more and more about what Samutchoso had told me of the spirits. I felt I could not leave the situation as it was. That seemed even more important than my own success or failure. Something more was demanded of me, and toward sunset I walked away with a gun once more to the gap in the hills to consider this strange persistent feeling.

When I came opposite the crimson cleft in the rocks, a movement in the bush brought my eyes out of their inner focus. Fifty yards away stood the kudu with the Viking horn and the long face that I had seen the first day. I stood still at once, and for some moments it remained immovable staring intently at me. I almost held my breath so close did the animal feel to me. Finally it just changed direction by calmly turning round and climbing back into the bush from whence it had come. It reminded me vivdly of the eland in the raised painting and that gave me an idea which sent me hurrying back to the camp to find Samutchoso.

"Suppose," I asked him, "I wrote a letter to the spirits to beg forgiveness and put it in a bottle and we buried it at the foot of the painting of the eland for the spirits to read, would that help, d'you think?"

He did not think long. With a light I had not seen in his eyes since the day afer our meeting with the buffalo, he exclaimed, "Master, it's a very good plan!"

While he stood beside me I sat down at once to write the letter. I wrote quickly, for in some odd way it seemed already written inside myself, but at the same time I felt it important to make it as formal and correct as possible. This, as near as I can remember, is how it ran:

In camp,
Sunset,
Thursday, October — 1955

To The Spirits,
    The Tsodilo Hills
    We beg most humbly the pardon of the great spirits
of these Slippery Hills for any disrespect we may have
shown them unintentionally and for any disturbance we
may have caused in their ancient resting place. At the
foot of this great painting, which is such clear evidence
of their presence and of their power to make flesh and
blood create beyond its immediate self, we bury this letter as an act of profound contrition, hoping they will read
it and forgive us. We beg that anyone coming after us,
finding this letter and reading it too, will be moved by it
to show them greater respect than we have done.

When it was written I read it out aloud to my companions,
some of whom thought it was going a bit too far. Nonetheless, I made them all sign it. That done we sealed it in an en-
velope which I addressed to "The Spirits, Tsodilo Hills." We
placed it in a lime juice bottle and at first light the next day
Samutchoso and I climbed up for the last time to the painting that had first caught our eyes. The eland and giraffe
over the signature of those gay young hands glowed with a
clear, warm, ruby light in the shadows, and almost at the
place where the forgotten artist must have stood to paint
them, we found a crack in the ledge with sand enough to
bury the letter.
    "Do you think that all will be well now?" I asked Samut-
choso when we stood up.
    "Would you like me to find out?" he asked.
    "Please," I requested.
    Thereupon he took out his needle and thread again and

stood there once more, with bowed head, looking deep into the life line in his hand. For some time I watched that grey head in the oldest attitude of communion with a spirit beyond his and my own tight round of knowing, moved as I had seldom been before. Below us the dawn came up fast, its light breaking over the vast plains like wave upon wave of some multitudinous sea incarnadine.

Then Samutchoso looked up quickly to say in a voice trembling with emotion, "All is well, Master. The spirits ask me to say that henceforth all will be well with you. Only they warn me that when you get to the next place to which you are going you will find one more unhappiness waiting for you. They ask you not to be discouraged by it because it will be an unhappiness that belongs not to the future but the past."

We returned in silence to camp. For the first time no bees came to attack us. Our Land-Rovers started up and took us promptly from the presence of the hills without hitch. We took Samutchoso to his home, and when I left him I was sad to see that although I might be free of the experience he had not yet done with it. I knew he felt as near to me as was possible to someone not of his race. He had treated me as a friend and I am certain wished me well. Yet there was a strange compelling note of regret in his voice when on saying farewell he remarked, "The spirits of the hills are not what they were, Master. They are losing their power. Ten years ago they would have killed you all for coming to them in that manner."

It was a cry straight from his heart and the final utterance of an experience which seemed to me to be an example of the injury the coming of the European had done to the being and spirit of Africa. Samutchoso's gods were dying from a contagion brought by us and against which he and his kind had not our inborn immunities. Now to whom and to what could he turn? For even he, illiterate and unimpressive in the rags and tatters of our civilization, knew that without his gods life would lose its meaning and inevitably lead toward disaster. His face and his cry rode with me all the hundreds of miles on the hard journey to Maun.

We arrived at Maun on another wide, white, glittering Sunday afternoon. I had decided at the last moment to go to Maun instead of Muhembo because I thought it would give my party more comfort and company while I was away trying again to get my film venture going, and so help them over what was going to be another tedious test of their good-will. On arrival Charles volunteered to seek out the D.C. and ask for mail. On his return I knew by his expression that he brought bad news. One of his letters was an urgent appeal from his mother begging him to come home because his father had died some days before. When he told me, the face of "He who was left after reaping," with his prophecy of "one more unhappiness," was as clear as if it had been staring at me over Charles's shoulder.

Chapter 9

THE HUNTER AT THE WELL

I HAVE tried so far to keep only to an account
of the strange sequence of events at the Slippery Hills and to
suppress the need for interpreting them which assailed my
mind whenever it was free of immediate duties. I have no
intention of attempting to explain these events now except
to mention one main fact of their consequences within myself.

From the moment of burying the letter at the foot of the
painting I had a feeling of having broken through one dimension of life that was full of accident and frustration, into a
more positive one. The feeling not only persisted but daily
gathered strength, so that although my return journey to
Johannesburg on this occasion was as difficult as the previous
one, yet I felt rid of all anxiety and conflict. Good seemed to
come even out of Charles's tragedy.

I took Charles with me in order that he might see his family and without him I might not have been able to deal with

my film problem in time. There were no planes available at Maun, and the organization of the Mines were not expecting one for days, so on the morning after our arrival we were compelled to set out across the four-hundred-mile strip of the northern Kalahari between Maun and Francistown in a diesel truck. Half-way across the desert between the wide, white horns of the great Makarikari salt lake and miles from any drinking water, the truck broke down. The driver was unable to mend it and had it not been for Charles, who went to work in his characteristic way, I don't know when, if ever, we would have arrived.

The same good fortune protected me in Johannesburg. I found a remarkable old German connoisseur of precision instruments who promised to do the necessary spare part for Duncan's camera within a week. He also told me of a rumour going round his specialized circle that a new camera of the same make had appeared in the city in the past week or so. By telephone, on foot and in endless taxis, I set out on the trail of that camera like the master detective in a boy's fiction story. In a few days I had tracked down the owner. He asked of me what, even today, seems an almost bloodthirsty fee. However, life for him had not been easy and my own need was desperate, so I consented without even bargaining. Leaving Charles to wait for Duncan's repaired camera and to follow at leisure, I caught the night train to Mafeking. There in the early evening Spencer Minchin, a lawyer and an old friend, took me on in his small plane. We spent the afternoon three hundred miles away at a D.C.'s court where Minchin had a client to defend; that night we flew further north, and early the next morning he flew me back into the Kalahari by way of Francistown, Bushman Pits and Maun. There I was glad to hear that Vyan and Ben, in good heart, had moved on some days before with all four Land-Rovers in order to meet me, according to our prearranged plan, at

Gemsbok Pan on the brink of the central desert. At Maun we stayed only long enough to refuel and took off into a sky so filled with the sulphur of summer and so bereft of life and substance of air that we cleared a notoriously difficult airstrip with little to spare. I had a brief glimpse of the copper water of the swamp, looked down on Lake Ngami, swollen wider by the floods than it had been for a generation, and noticed that the Kalahari veld around it had already been burned brown and black by the sun. Some two hours later the plane, bucking like an unbroken horse over the wild waves of heat tearing over the sandveld, circled the small isolated administrative outpost of Gemsbok Pan. The sound of the engines brought my companions running out from beneath the trees of my old camping ground to man the Land-Rovers. They met me in an exhilarated mood at the landing strip because they had not expected me for days. They themselves had arrived only the evening before, but already they had been busy.

Ben, Vyan and I have many friends among the older inhabitants of the small cattle-farming community which is scattered around the few permanent water-points of Ghanzis and Gemsbok Pan. On their way to Gemsbok Pan they had called in at one home after the other where they had been given a warm welcome. All the farms had "tame" Bushmen, the descendants of pure aboriginal ancestors, working for them. Their number is always a variable quantity because, as I have indicated, even the Bushman born on these few remote European farms wearies from time to time of the iron tyranny of our minds and rediscover the need for a long "walk-about" in the vast desert around him. Only by protracted disappearances of such a kind at seasonal intervals does he find it possible to endure our wilful ways. The urge is greatest in the early summer when the rains break.

Knowing the news would please me, Ben now said with

one of his rare smiles, "We've hit a perfect moment. You won't find a Bushman inside the central desert now who hasn't been born and bred there and knows where to sip the sands for water."

Also, aware of the little time left us before the rains, Ben had already persuaded one of the oldest pioneering households to part with one of their most trusted Bushman servants to help us on the journey deep into the desert as tracker, interpreter and adviser. He was a man of between fifty and sixty, born when the Europeans first burst into the Ghanzis area and so had the past tradition of his people sufficiently near to him to mould his mind and imagination. Ben himself had known him all his life.

When first I saw him standing diffidently by our campfire I was startled. He might have been a younger brother of the little old men I had known. Despite half a century of fierce Kalahari sun his skin was the classical light yellow Bushman colour; he was little more than five feet high, his shoulders broad, hips narrow, behind firm, full and clearly defined. His hands and feet were delicate and small, his eyes Mongolian, and face incredibly lined, wrinkled and sensitive, his ears neat and pointed. But there was not much laughter in his vivid eyes which, in repose, tended to look hurt and sometimes unreservedly bitter.

When I greeted him and asked his name he answered softly, as if even the right to possess a name of his own might be held against him, "I am Dabe, Master."

We were now at our final supply point and had to load our Land-Rovers to full capacity before we could move safely into the waterless plains of sand and flame around us. It was dark before we'd finished, but water and fuel tanks were full, our essential supplies replenished and all four vehicles sunk deeply into their springs. We had to resign ourselves to starting early the following morning and spent the evening round the fire going over for the last time the best possible line of advance.

Since time was shrinking fast, we could no longer contemplate the leisurely sweep around the central desert that I had originally intended. We had to make at once for the most likely area. Pooling our experience we concluded we could not do better than "have a stab," as Vyan put it, direct at the heart of the desert contained between what must once have been the mighty watercourses of the Bhuitsivango and Okwa. Both were perennially dry, but I remembered clearly that one summer just after the breaking of the rains I had come across Bushman shelters in a bend of the remote Bhuitsivango. These shelters, between high, sandy banks, had been newly abandoned and so well made that they suggested a permanent refuge in the lean, testing seasons of the desert. Moreover, Ben said that his memory was constantly pricked by a recollection of a small pure Bushman community grouped round some sip-wells which he and his father, on a reckless and almost disastrous traverse of the desert, had stumbled on in the same area. Although he had been only a young boy at the time, he had never forgotten the track they had taken from Gemsbok Pan and had a feeling he could find his way back there.

I had ample experience of how precise Ben's imponderable feelings about the Kalahari could prove in practice. That, and his mention of sip-wells, decided me. We all were convinced that the sort of community we were seeking could only exist if in possession of some secret supply of permanent water. All the open permanent waters in the Kalahari had long since been stolen from the Bushman by the encroaching races, and the only sources left to him were those hidden securely under the deep sands of the central desert. The location of these sip-wells was a secret shared only with his own trusted kind, and on all my journeys, over many

years, I had never found one. I might, indeed, have dis-
missed the constant talk of sip-wells as fantastic if Ben had
not vouched for their existence. Also, one of the old pioneers
of Ghanzis had once described to me in detail how, when lost
and dying of thirst, his life had been saved by a Bushman
woman who had dragged him to some place where she had
sucked water out of a hollow stick inserted in the hot sands
and squirted it directly from her mouth into his.

"We'll follow Ben's hunch first," I decided at the end of the
evening.

There is no need now to go over the detail of the journey
that followed deeper and deeper into the desert, the slow progress through the deep sand and the monotonous task of
breaking our way through scrub and bush under a direct and
pitiless sun in a cloudless blue sky, with only Ben's memory
to bring us back to course, like a compass keeping a helmsman
in safety on the high seas. What matters is that in the heat of a
blinding day we met a small group of little people of mixed
blood making their way out as fast as their parched and emaciated bodies could carry them to shelter at some frontier
cattle-post. They confirmed that we were not very far from
a group of true Bushmen with access to secret water. With a
reward of food and tobacco we did persuade one of them to
come and put us on the right way, but it was clear from the
start that he feared the commission. I was not surprised,
therefore, that when a barrier of impenetrable thorn halted
us and forced us to reconnoitre on foot, he abandoned us and
vanished into the desert bush. However, we took it as a good
sign that the direction in which he had set us conformed to
the magnetic bearing in Ben's memory. Finally, at about three
on a baking afternoon, we got convincing confirmation.
Dabe, who had run ahead to scout through a difficult bit of
bush, suddenly called us to him. He pointed at a set of small
human footprints in the sand. They could have been dupli-

cates of those I had seen in clay at the foot of the great storm-tree years before. Once again, it seemed I heard the voice of the old 'Suto servant from my childhood saying clearly, "You have only to see his small footprints once never to forget it and to know it always from the spoor of other men."

I looked at Dabe, whose eyes then were neither sad nor bitter.

He anticipated the obvious question. "Wild Bushman, Master," he said. "Came by here this morning to walk so! . . ." He pointed in the general direction we had followed all day.

From there onwards we followed closely to the footprints. Mile by mile they became fresher. Hope rose fast in me like a tide in flood. Finally, toward evening we climbed out of the scrub and bush onto the crest of a high ridge of sand. We looked down onto the deep heart of the desert and the empty bed of a broad, winding old watercourse far below. The sun was low behind us and already lining the watercourse with shadow. A strange hot wind blew in our faces. We climbed onto the roofs of our Land-Rovers and looked further into that remote world sealed with red sand and spread out as still as the water of a locked ocean. It looked utterly empty, without smoke or even a spiral of dervish dust that dances daily more and more demoniacally before the terrible court the drought holds in its desert as the time for rain approaches. Yet there before us were the set of prints clearly leading down into the depression below us.

"The place I had in mind," Ben said slowly, "was somewhere down there . . . I'm certain. . . ."

He was interrupted by Dabe, his voice blurred with emotion, exclaiming, "Oh, look! There's a wild man down there."

"Down there" was so far away that it took me some time

to see a small black blob bobbing up and down in the shining waves of grass.

I have often wondered since what would have happened if the wind had not been blowing away the sounds of our approach, and if the sun had not been turned to blind any eyes raised in our direction. By these means we were enabled to drop so quietly down the sandy slope that we were almost upon the Bushman before he knew we were through the secret portals of his castle of sand. Long before he saw us, we were able to identify the bare head of a young Bushman working energetically at something in the grass. When he heard us, he shot upright like an arrow out of the grass and grabbed his spear, but already Dabe was calling out loudly the ancient Bushman greeting, "Good day. I saw you from afar and I am dying of hunger."

The young man stuck his spear in the sand and with his right hand raised, palm open and fingers up, walked shyly toward us, saying in a tone I had never heard before, "Good day! I have been dead, but now that you have come, I live again."

We had made contact at last! I was so overwhelmed by the fact that for a moment I barely knew what to do. It was the young man who, after the exchange of greetings in his own tongue, a drink of our best water and a smoke of tobacco, put us all at our ease with his command of natural manners.

He was no taller than Dabe but slighter, with fine bones, and, of course, much younger. Nor was there any sign of bitterness or hurt in his eyes. His features were regular and sensitive in the classical Bushman model. His eyes were wide and large and looked steadily into mine when I asked him a question. They had the same vivid light in them which occasionally one sees in Europe on the faces of gypsies in Spain. He was naked, with a loin strap made of duiker skin around his middle, and his skin of a fresh apricot colour was still stained in places with the blood of an animal recently killed. All in all he had a wonderful wild beauty about him. Even his smell was astringent with the essences of untamed earth and wild animal-being. It was a smell as archaic and provocative in its way as the Mona Lisa's smile intense. But one of us, I forget which, at the first sharp whiff made a grimace of distaste. I rebuked him sharply fearing the alert young Bushman would interpret it only too accurately.

His name, he told us, was Nxou. It signified, according to Dabe, a "wooden bowl for food." He and his people lived near by, and he said that if we would give him time to finish what he had been doing, he would show us a camping place near his home and in the morning take us to his people. We watched him, probing holes in the sand with a pliable rod about twenty feet long and a sharp pointed hook at the end of it. The holes were made by spring-hares and soon he had hunted out his quarry and killed it deftly with a wooden club lying ready beside him. That done, he collected his spear, a bow and quiver full of arrows, a leather shoulder satchel containing some ostrich eggs filled with water, picked up his club and the dead hare and declared himself ready.

Any fears I had that he might decide to run from us in the dark were shamed by the air of trust with which he committed himself to us. We had no room in any of our Land-Rovers but he, who had never seen a motor before, unhesitatingly seated himself with his belongings on the spare wheel on the bonnet of my vehicle and in this way, just as the luminous, pure twilight descended, he calmly brought us to a place where the bush was re-forming its ranks beyond the frontier of grass favoured by the dunes and the wide depression. There, he said, we would have wood for fire by night and some shade in the day. Promising to return early in the morning, he bade us a grave good night or, to translate literally from Bushman *Txhaiisai-xhum*, beseeched us to "rest well." Then he walked away from us into the brown of evening, so supple in limb that I had only seen his equal in the wild dog whose inexhaustible capacity for movement carries him over land like a ripple across a pool.

"Is it wise to let him go like that?" Duncan asked, anxious for his film. "D'you really expect ever to see him again?"

I had no hesitation in replying, "We'll see him first thing in the morning."

No camping site in the central desert can ever be spectacular. This one was no exception and was, without doubt, the most uncomfortable we ever had. The trees in the dense thorn-bush around were little more than ten feet high and gave little shade. We had to make our home under a nylon tarpaulin stretched taut between our Land-Rovers and there in the long days to come we hoped to hold out against the Kalahari extremes of sun and weather. The site did not even offer the normal compensation of a generous view over the desert, because there was a restricted ring of tough thorn-trees and brief glades of red sand and grass about us. Yet we were more content than we had ever been. There one felt curiously close to the secret world into which we had broken, as if clasped in its arms and held close to its warm and deeply breathing bosom. We had made contact! It is impossible to exaggerate what that meant to us all who had been disappointed so often, and travelled so many thousands of vain, hot, uncomfortable miles. Ben, after his incredible feat of tracking by childhood memory, talked eloquently about his experiences of the desert and its animals and people. Vyan joined in as freely and disclosed how in vain he had tried to persuade his government to use Bushmen as trackers against Mau Mau because he was convinced they were the best in the world. I was sad that Charles wasn't there to share the moment with us, but judged it appropriate to produce some of the "surprises" I carry for special occasions.

With Jeremiah's assistance I gave them a special dinner, printing this menu in block letters by the fire-light:

> HOTEL KALAHARI
> Propriétaire, le bon Dieu
> Consommé Lyonnaise (dehydrated)
> Bacon, Saffron Rice and Raisins
> Peaches and Cream (both tinned)
> Coffee
> Chef: Jeremiah Muwenda
> Maître d'Hôtel: John Raouthagall

Although tired, we talked until late in the night, Dabe and all our staunch African companions crowding around to listen. The only warning note came from me. Remembering the grimace made at Nxou's smell, I felt compelled to utter a warning. I begged them to remember in the days to come that we were there not to teach the Bushman but solely to learn all we could from him: his ways, his spirit and the terms he had made with his own life in a world so harsh that even the greediest among us had shunned it. We could do that only if we set aside our own bias and preferences and prepared ourselves to listen and observe. Also we would have to tread delicately so as to inflict no vital injury on the Bushman's natural values.

I was shaving by torch-light in the morning, listening to the distant roar of a lion fading solemn as a shooting star, when a new sound fell on my ears. Jeremiah, too, heard it and stopped tending the fire to listen. Somewhere in the dark bush between us and the first sear of red in the sky, we heard music. It rose and fell, growing steadily louder, a tune in the wayfarer's nostalgic pattern, as sad with arrival as departure, but gay with the lift of spirit provided by the journey in between. Soon Nxou emerged into the fire-light, a cloak of skin like a Roman toga about him, playing as he walked, head bowed over one of the oldest instruments in the world. It was shaped like a long bow with only one string, bound in the middle, to the back. One end rested on his parted lips, the other in his left hand while he beat the taut string on either side with a small stick and, catching the reverberations in his open mouth, shaped them between his lips to produce the notes. Behind him walked another who could have been a sturdier brother, hunting bow in hand and shaft of the spear stuck into a quiverful of poisoned arrows. He was Bauxhau— "Stone-axe"—and although not of as fine texture as Nxou he was as authentically Bushman and more vividly handsome. They were close friends, and with the good Bushman manners that they expected of others, they squatted down at the edge of the fire-light waiting to be greeted before they came into the centre of our camp. Once by our fire they did not speak unless spoken to, but Nxou went on playing his instrument and Bauxhau listened.

"I see the hotel has an orchestra," Duncan remarked when I woke him with coffee, obviously relieved at the sight of his Bushman by the fire. "All modern conveniences in fact."

"This is the last convenience of the day," I told him, laughing, as I handed him his cup. "From now on you'll have to work as you've never worked before."

As soon as we had eaten we went to visit Nxou's people. Those of us who had expected a large settlement were immediately disappointed. We were among the first four shelters before we had even seen them, so discreetly were they made and so naturally did they blend with the growth and colour around them. Basically they were of the same beehive design as the other shelters we had encountered in the Slippery Hills but more solidly built and more carefully roofed with branches of thorn and tufts of grass. Each had a tree at the back to support it and from some of the branches hung strips of venison drying in the wind and shade. The floors of the shelters were scooped out in places to make them more comfortable for the hips of the people sleeping in them; the interiors were almost bare of decoration or utensils. But where the women slept hung strings of the white beads and ivory headbands made out of the shells of ostrich eggs, and along the sides of the shelters were rows of ostrich-egg shells securely placed upright in the sand, plugged with grass and presumably filled with water.

Outside the first shelter a middle-aged woman sat diligently pounding the seeds of the *tsamma*, the Kalahari melon which sustains man and beast with food and moisture in the long, hot months between the rains. The stamping block is the Bushman woman's most precious possession: a large pestle and mortar carved out of ironwood. Wherever she goes she carries it with her to make meal out of nuts and seeds of melons and grass, and to pulverize dried meat for toothless children and old people. As the woman pounded it the block made a curious drum-like sound which travelled a surprising distance and in the days to come greeted us from afar like a quickened beat of our hearts at the realization that after a harsh day, home was near.

In front of the second shelter sat Nxou's father stringing a bow; his wife at his side was cooking something in a small clay pot on a tiny fire which hardly made any smoke. At the third shelter another middle-aged man was repairing one of the long rods used to fish in holes in the ground for springhares, porcupines, badgers, ground squirrels and other animals that live underneath the Kalahari sand. Outside the last of the shelters sat two of the oldest people I have ever seen.

They were Nxou's grandparents, and the skins of both were so creased and stained with life, weather and time that they might have been dark brown parchment covered with some close Oriental script. Both had serene expressions on their faces, and they look continually from one to the other as if in constant need of reassurance that the miracle of being together after so many years was indeed still real. They seemed to have grown old in the right way, they and their spirit being contained within their age as naturally as a nut is enclosed within a shell and only when fully ripened falling obediently to the need for a renewal of life.

The old lady, I could see, was already beginning to feel the heat. From time to time she put her hand deep into a hole beside her to pull out a handful of cool sand which she scattered over her naked body for relief. I have often seen elephants do the same thing with their trunks. She did this as daintily as some Mongol lady fanning herself, and was as shy as a young girl, immediately looking away from us when she caught our eye, and then glancing coyly back out of the corner of her slanted eyes when her curiosity became too great. Her husband, however, regarded us as if trying to get into focus something seen from an immense distance.

When I asked if that was the whole community Nxou shook his head. The young women and children he said were already out in the desert looking for food. The other half of his people were grouped around five similar shelters about a mile away. All told, there were about thirty persons, though it was difficult to determine the exact number because from time to time relations would suddenly appear like reflections in a distorting mirror out of the vast quicksilver day around them, stay for a week or ten days, and then as suddenly vanish again into the desert. But during our stay the number was seldom less than thirty, though often more. I did not press Nxou to elaborate on the answers to my questions because I noticed they tended to make him uneasy. Instead I followed him on foot and in silence to the other shelters.

They were almost exact copies of the first, with people doing the same sorts of things, except that one man was busy re-dipping his arrows in newly prepared poison, and another softening a duiker skin with incredible swiftness by squeezing the juice of a large bulb onto it and wringing the moist skin between his hands. While we were there the younger women began coming home. They were all naked except for a leather wrap each hung by a strap from one shoulder and tied round her waist. The hem of the wrap was decorated with ostrich-shell beads, and around the smooth yellow necks of the younger women hung rows of necklaces made of the same beads. In that sun, against those apricot skins, the necklaces shone like jewels. Each woman carried a shawl of skin tied into a bundle which she placed on the sand and undid, taking out the amazing variety of roots and tubers they had collected in the desert, as well as dozens of ostrich-egg shells filled with water. Like everyone else they appeared to be of pure Bushman stock and in their truly feminine way possessed the same wild beauty that made Nxou and Bauxhau so attractive. Indeed, one of the younger women might have been the model of the girl figuring in one of the most impressive rock paintings. Her dress of draped skin, and the circle of beads below her left knee, was exactly like that of her ancient painted prototype, only she did not walk with a flower in her hand, though her step was as high and her carriage as full of grace. Her name was Xhooxham, signifying as we gathered with difficulty from Dabe, the equivalent of "lips of finest fat" because fat in that harsh land is one of the rarest and greatest of all delicacies.

Only one of the women had a child, a baby she carried in a skin on her hip. It was her first, Nxou said, and when she sat down in a patch of shade to feed it and the plump little body was tugging sleepily at her full round breast, the look of unimpeded tenderness on her face was so intense that she might well have had a halo around her Mongolian head. But apart from that one little suckling, there appeared to be no other babies. I had always been told that the Bushman had small families, that the Bushman was, in fact, to use the language of animal husbandry applied to him in my country, a "shy breeder," but even so this lack of children was excessive. I questioned Nxou and he said there were four more children but that was all. Just then a woman came from the back of a shelter with a little boy. He could hardly walk and was naked except for one string of beads shining like pearls around his fat tummy. Any slight doubts we might have had about the authenticity of the people around us were removed by the vision of the infant man openly displaying his *qhwai-xkhwe*, the ancient badge of his race.

"Look at that little chap, Duncan," I told him, "and you'll see why the Bushman calls himself *Qhwai-xkhwe*."

Duncan was amazed. "Surely he can't keep it up for long?" he asked.

"From birth to death," I told him, and though Duncan tried to prove the impossibility of the statement, the little boy remained a picture-book illustration of the national male condition, and figured so in all our films, even in the climax of midnight dancing.

We were still discussing the little boy when a woman called out something to her companions. They all stopped what they were doing and began jumping up and down, clasping and unclasping their hands in gestures of instinctive gratitude, and chanting what I learned later to be a hunter's praise in such clear and melodious voices that my nerves resounded like violin strings with the sound. Another young man, a little taller than Nxou and almost as attractive, came running into our midst, a small buck like a boa around his neck. His name was Txexchi, signifying a "powerful wilde-beest," and he, Nxou and Bauxhau were so much together that inevitably we christened them "the Three Musketeers."

So the day went quickly by. At noon we did not halt for food but went from one group of shelters to the other meet-ing new arrivals and making ourselves better known to the old. At each shelter we left a small present of tobacco and the promise to help them hunt for more food. Whatever appre-hensions may have been felt about our arrival were, I believe, largely vanquished by that calm, leisurely coming and going between our camp and their shelters. I was not naïve enough to imagine all reservations had been conquered. But when, toward evening, I mentioned the critical matter of water and Nxou and Bauxhau immediately offered to show us how they themselves dealt with the problem, I felt the major battle of our first contact had been won.

In the cool of the evening they and Xhooxham, "Lips of Finest Fat," led us some miles away to the deepest part of the old watercourse between dunes yellow in the sun. There we found several shallow excavations dug for water in am-pler seasons, but the supply which never failed them was hid-den, safe from evaporation of sun and wind, deep beneath the sand. Near the deepest excavation Bauxhau knelt down and dug into the sand to arm's length. Toward the end some moist sand but no water appeared. Then he took a tube al-most five feet long made out of the stem of a bush with a soft core, wound about four inches of dry grass lightly around one end presumably to act as a kind of filter against the fine drift sand, inserted it into the hole and packed the sand back into it, stamping it down with his feet. He then took some empty ostrich-egg shells from Xhooxham and wedged them upright into the sand beside the tube, produced a little stick, one end of which he inserted into the opening in the shell and the other into the corner of his mouth. Then he put his lips to the tube. For about two minutes he sucked mightily without any result. His broad shoulders heaved with the immense effort and sweat began to run like water down his back. But at last the miracle happened and so suddenly that Jeremiah gasped and I had an impulse loudly to cheer. A bubble of pure bright water came out of the corner of Bauxhau's mouth, clung to the little stick and ran straight down its side into the shell without spilling one precious drop!

So it continued, faster and faster until shell after shell was filled, Bauxhau's whole being and strength joined in the single function of drawing water out of the sand and pumping it up into the light of day. Why he didn't fall down with exhaustion I don't know. I tried to do it, and though my shoulders are broad and my lungs good, I couldn't extract a single drop from the sand. We named that place, where we saw one of the oldest of legends about the Bushman become a miraculous twentieth-century fact, "the Sip-wells." Were it not for the water we extracted we could not have stayed there in the central desert but would have had continually to go laboriously back and forth between it and our own remote waterpoints. And of course without the sip-wells Nxou and his people could not have survived there at all between the rains.

We were on our way back from the sip-wells, the dunes in the west sharply outlined against a crimson sky, and I was feeling not only content but also warmed and illumined as with revelation, when we came upon another astonishing sight. The bush and plain was just beginning to resound with call of nightjars, the melancholy cry of carrion birds and mournful bark of jackals. One would have thought that all good Bushmen would have been sitting around the fires at the mouths of their shelters seeking safety from lion or leopard. But on the edge of the bush, a mile from our camp, we caught up with a brave little procession made up of three of the four children, all up to their ears in thorn and grass. A little boy, grubbing stick in hand, led the procession with a bundle full of roots, tubers, caterpillars and succulent grubs in his hand.

A small girl, whose name meant "spoor of gazelle," followed with a bundle of wild and sun-dried berries and rare ground-nuts. She was already clearly a little mother to her companions because, although she followed the boy in front dutifully like a wife, she made sure by constant backward glances and affectionate exhortations that the youngest of all, who was in the rear, stayed close to her. He carried a large tortoise in a hand held level with his shoulder, and was breathless with the conflicting efforts of supporting it and keeping up with his elders in front.

Nxou's face when he saw them was instantly warm with affectionate delight. He went on his knees beside them, peered into their bundles and uttered such sounds of astonishment and appreciation that the children, who clearly loved him dearly, stood shaking with laughter of sheer joy despite their fatigue. When Nxou took up the tortoise he made a great fuss over it and, according to Dabe, told the little boy that if he gave that to his grandmother she would certainly tell him a bedtime story that would last well into the night.

In their company we came home, the light of our fires red on the leaves of the trees standing solemnly under the darkness which was about to crush the last glimmer of a great day. All evening long we sat by our fires comparing our impressions and I was not surprised that we all shared the main one. None of us doubted that we had struck a pure Bushman community living their Stone Age life. Even I, who was most ready to distrust the conventional portrait of the Bushman and the grotesque caricature of his life drawn in our histories, had not imagined it would be like this. I had not expected anything so comely, dignified and orderly. In the past, wherever I had broken through into lonely communities in remote regions of Africa, some clear demonstration of the impact and excitement of the arrival of a rare stranger, particularly a red stranger, had always greeted me. Here there had been none, just everywhere a formal exchange of greetings and welcome. Of course Nxou had prepared his people for our coming and this must have had something to do with the calmness of their response. Yet I did believe that to be the whole story. I suspect it went much deeper than that and had to do with fundamental questions of birth and breeding in the spirit of an ancient-centred people. In the days that followed the suspicion sharpened and gradually became certainty.

Daily the lies and the distortions of the past were thrown more firmly into our faces by this small but self-contained Stone Age example. Daily I became more convinced that in this regard our version of history was largely rationalization and justification of our own lack of scruple and excess of greed, and that the models drawn upon by historians and artists must have been the Bushmen nearest them who had already been wrenched out of their own authentic pattern to become debased by insecurity and degraded by helplessness against our well-armed selfishness. I could not explain on any other basis the stories of Bushman excess and apathy handed down as universal facts. One story, for instance, which I have seen repeated in many an anthropological and scientific treatise, states that the Bushman is so unconscious a creature that after gorging himself with food, like a python he will go to sleep and, when the pangs of hunger again begin to stir, he will merely draw the band of skin tighter and tighter around his stomach until at last only death from starvation serves to make him conscious enough to go out once more to hunt.

This certainly was not true of our sip-well community or

the few other little groups we found on our rounds while based with them in the central desert. When they killed more game than usual they would certainly treat the occasion as a feast day, eat largely and perhaps sleep through the day. But on the whole they were contained in a natural sense of discipline and proportion and curiously adjusted to the harsh desert reality. They never ate all their meat at one sitting. Whenever possible they set something aside for a leaner day. Later on, their stories clearly showed us that they had considered the ways of the ant and bee and had been made wise thereby. Most of the meat was immediately cut into strips and skilfully dried in the shade and wind to become for them what pemmican was to Eskimo and Red Indian. It was most impressive to see them skin and cut up game. Nothing was wasted or discarded except the gall and dung in the stomach. The entrails were cleaned and preserved, and even the half-digested grasses in the paunch were wrung out like washing for the juices they contained and these collected in the skin and drunk by the hunters to save their precious water. In case of need they even stored water in ostrich-egg shells on the extreme perimeter of their permanent base at the sip-wells. One day out hunting with Nxou and Bauxhau some seventy miles from the sip-wells I was puzzled to see them break away from the spoor we were following in the terrible heat of the day and make for particular scrub which, to me, was exactly like the desert of scrub around us. They dug into the sand and disclosed a cache of six ostrich-egg shells filled with water from which they emptied two before covering the rest carefully again with sand. The same foresight and sense of economy seemed to go into their building of fires, which they made in the classical way by rotating a round rod of hard wood between their hands in a hole in a small board of softer wood at their feet. There was never any shortage of fire-wood. It is one of my greatest joys to build big campfires in the desert and sit in the night in a Gothic structure of tall aspiring fire-light, with my companions grouped around for comfort and conversation. They were, I suspect, shocked by this extravagance; their own fires were so discreet, neat and unwasteful of wood.

Nor, when fed, did they lie apathetically all day long round their shelters. They were always going about work of some kind. The younger men like Nxou, Bauxhau and Txexchi were constantly out hunting for game. Nxou, who was not only the moving spirit among the three but the outstanding personality in the little community and clearly destined to become its leader, was utterly dedicated to his hunter's role. We soon saw why he was called "Bowl of Food" for that is what he was as hunter to the bodies and as musician to the spirit of his people.

Daily, too, the younger women and children went out with their grubbing sticks to look for food in the sands of the desert. Whenever I accompanied them the intelligence, diligence and speed with which they harvested the earth never ceased to astonish me. A tiny leaf almost invisible in grass and thorn just above the surface of the red sand, and to me indistinguishable from many others, would cause them to kneel down and grub deftly with their wooden digging sticks to produce what I, in my ignorance of Kalahari botany, called wild carrots, potatoes, leeks, turnips, sweet potatoes and artichokes. One of their greatest delicacies was a groundnut which, when roasted on their fires, would eliminate all rivals from cocktail counters. And, of course, they loved the wild tsamma melon in all forms, and highly prized the eland cucumber. This last was so near to its European counterpart in flavour and texture, despite the fact that it was protected with formidable thorn on the outside, that out of it Jeremiah made salad and vegetable dishes for us. All this was achieved at the worst time of the year. I longed to see the riches that could be garnered in the full harvest of summer.

While the hunters were out, the older people did the maintenance work of the community: repaired the bows and arrows, the long "fishing-rods," and prepared the poisons used in hunting. This they did out of a deadly compound of a mysterious grub found in summer at the end-root of a certain desert bush, powdered cobra poison and a gum produced by chewing a special aloe blade in the mouth and then mixing the extract in a wooden cup with the other powders. They also cured and tanned the skins of the buck brought home by the hunters. When I looked back on the laborious methods used in our own farms, I was amazed at the speed and skill with which they worked. They were natural botanists and chemists and had an unbelievable knowledge of the properties of desert plants. A bulb gave them the acid to remove the hair from the skin without damage, another softened it in a remarkably short time. This activity was of particular importance to the community. These skins produced for them the "iron" they used for their arrows, spears and knives. From time to time one of them would vanish with a parcel of skins to contact someone who had a definite link with an African or European outpost where these things could be bartered.

They also made the tough Bushman rope used in their bows, snares and daily round of living. They did this by extracting from wild Kalahari sisal long silky threads which they plaited and spun into rope of all lengths and thickness. We watched one of them producing a length of rope with only a springbuck horn and his toes and fingers as instruments, and using his thighs as work-table. When finished we had a bet on its quality, and set Nxou and the maker tugging against each other to try and break it. But they failed.

Swift and neat efficiency really was an impressive feature of this community. Whenever called upon to do so, they worked with devotion and will. Their arrows, spears, skins, ropes and snares were not merely functional but beautifully marked in a manner which showed that they were also an image of spirit. The older women, in their spare moments, made beads out of broken ostrich-egg shells and strung them into necklaces or the broad shining bands which they wore around their heads for ceremonial occasions. Hour after hour they would sit chipping nimbly and delicately with the sharp end of a springbuck ram's bone at a fragment of shell in order to produce one little round white disk from the brittle and fragile raw material. According to Dabe they seldom got more than three beads out of one huge shell, and as a headband needed hundreds of beads, the task obviously was prodigiously exacting and long. Yet they kept at it diligently, the same look on their faces that I've seen in the eyes of silversmiths at work in the bazaars of Aleppo and Damascus. Every woman and girl child possessed several necklaces and at least one glittering headband, apart from the beads used to decorate the leather wrap, shawl and shoulder satchel which were their only covering. Sometimes, too, they carved greater beads out of a crimson root and amber wood and this combination of ivory-white shell, crimson and amber jewellery on the smooth apricot skins between the firm round breasts of the younger women seemed to me as truly belonging as a ruby garland against the skin of a Hindu deity. Some of the men, particularly Bauxhau, patiently carved abstract patterns into the ostrich-egg shells that were their drinking vessels. The designs were either dyed ink-black with some vegetable extract, or burnt in with fire.

But alas! the Bushman no longer painted. The dream that I had carried with me since childhood of seeing a Bushman artist painting had to join the haunted world of the unfulfilled. When I asked them about painting, sombrely they shook their heads. I had reproductions of some of the beautiful copies the selfless Stow had made of Bushman paintings in my native Free State. When I showed these to our sip-well community the two old people, man and woman, began crying as if their hearts would break and hid their heads in their arms. But the younger men instantly crowded around and exploded with sounds of astonishment as if suddenly they saw confirmed something that, until then, had been only rumour. I have myself a favourite copy of a herd of eland resting in the heat of the day. I call it "Stone Age Conversation Piece" because the grace and ease of the grouping are so striking that it might almost be some eighteenth-century family depicted in a salon at their country-seat in a France great under its "Sun King" and oblivious of revolution and disaster to come.

"Look at that old bull," Nxou now said to Bauxhau, making him giggle like a girl. "Do you see the glint in his eyes? He has had enough of that old cow at his side and is thinking of what he can do with that young heifer over there! But you see those young bulls there? They are thinking the same thing! He'll have to fight them if he is to have his way. And do you think he'll win? And look at that mother licking the face of her child! Surely, it must be her first for her heart to cry so much for it?" And so it went on every time they asked me to show them the pictures.

They loved also to play. I was told by Dabe they had a game of chequers that the men played on squares in the sand, but I never saw them do it. Once, when we had helped them to hunt for food, they played another game which we called "Bushman badminton." The shuttlecock was made of a single wing-tip feather of the giant bustard tied to a long leather lash and fastened to the heavy and rare *marayamma* nut. One man would fold the shuttle in the middle and hang it over the end of a long, pliable rod which he held in his right hand. He would then flick the shuttle high in the air, and all the other men equipped with rods of their own, would race for the spot on which it was descending, like a parachute, out of the blue. The whole object of the game was to be the first to catch the shuttle in the air with a sideways cut of the rod, hold it briefly for a moment and then flick it upwards in some unexpected direction. The game would sway backwards and forwards over grass, bush and spiked thorns with great speed and skill, the women looking on from the shade, and the little boy with his unashamed *qhwai-xkhwe* imitating the movements of the men. Sometimes I, too, joined in to the great satisfaction and merriment of all because I played it so much less well, though I found it good exercise and fun. I didn't realize until later that it had also been good tactics. Not being afraid to look the fool, apparently, helped greatly to give them confidence in me.

Sometimes, too, they had a mimic war. The pantomime was based on some half-forgotten historical fact, but the only detail that was clear was that the war had started in the old Homeric way: some comely young Bushman archer from one group had ravished the apricot Helen of a middle-aged and prickly Menelaus in another, and enticed her to leave her home and people with him. The result had been a war between the two groups, but a war with a difference. For no sooner was Helen reclaimed and the ravishing Bushman killed than both sides were filled with fear and revulsion against their deed, as if suddenly among the acacias of their vast Kalahari garden the voice of God himself had made the leaves tremble as He reprimanded them for their mutual sin. They instantly sat down to talk to one another and resolved that it must never happen again. Accordingly they divided the desert into two zones, promising never to cross the demarcation line between them. They, and Dabe too, assured me that none of them to this day would go from one zone to the other.

"But how d'you know which zone is which?" I asked

thinking of the thousands of square miles of identical sand, dune and bush.

They laughed at my innocence with that wonderful Bushman laugh which rises sheer from the stomach, a laugh you never hear among civilized people. Did I not know, they exclaimed when the explosion of merriment died down, that there was not a tree, expanse of sand or bush that was alike? They knew the frontier tree by tree and grass by grass.

When these people performed their pantomime of the war, they divided into two teams facing each other on their knees in the sand, about fifteen yards apart. They would then taunt one another with the challenges and battle-cries of another age, the shouts and movements getting louder and more violent until at last they were twisting and turning with thrust, parry, counter-thrust and evasive action as though indeed spears and arrows were raining down upon them. Though they never moved from their knees, the gesture of heads and bodies, the expressions on their faces, and the cries of the wounded and dying, enabled me to relive vividly the atmosphere of a battle of their past. I was reminded at once of a story Peter Scott had told me about the Eskimos. After he had described some incident of the last war to them, they had exclaimed with horror, "But do you Europeans actually go out and kill people you've never met?" Our Bushman, too, apparently felt they could not be tempted to go out and "kill people they had never met." So they observed religiously the rule of their frontiers.

The women, of course, had other games. They played a sort of rounders which was as graceful and compelling as any I have ever seen. They used the round tsamma melon as ball. They would go round in circles about five yards from one another, the one who had the melon unexpectedly throwing it, without a backward turn of the head, to the girl behind. She not only had to catch it but, as she caught it, she had to imitate the movement of the animal then being mentioned in the words of the tune they were singing. They sang in lovely clear voices, the pace and rhythm growing faster and the movements of the animal they were imitating getting more lively. I could always recognize the animal from this vivid abstract they made of his total movement. Toward the climax of the game they would be running fast and so easily that Xhooxham was like a kind of Atalanta running her fateful races in the Hesperides. This is as near as I could get to the idiom of the song from Dabe's translation:

I went out into the veld
to look for melons;
And on the way: what do you
think I saw?
I saw a blue Wildebeest
But the blue Wildebeest just
flicked his heels at
me and ran away.

I went on and on across
the veld and what do you
think I saw?
I saw a Hartebeest and called
Out: "Oh! Hartebeest, come to me,"
But it just flicked its
heels and ran away.

Then I saw a Gemsbok,
and I cried: "Oh! Gemsbok, I am
hungry, come to me."
But it just flicked its heels
and ran away.

So it went on, right through the rich variety of buck and four-hooved creatures of the desert until darkness or the day's work called them away.

Sometimes the women would sit together beside their shelters, in the long level light of the evening sun, their beads and necklaces like gold upon them. Each would hold a handful of long, straight, dry grass and sing all together, beating time with the grass and stroking the stems with the tips of their fingers like the strings of a guitar. The melody was charged with all the inexpressible feelings that come to one at the going down of the sun over the great earth of Africa. They called the song "The Grass Song" and with the difficulty of interpretation neither Dabe nor the singers could readily explain it. I can only recall the feeling and render the words inadequately:

> *This grass in my hand before it was cut*
> *Cried in the wind for the rain to come:*
> *All day my heart cries in the sun*
> *For my hunter to come.*

They would sing this over and over again, the song becoming more charged and meaningful by repetition, as if the heart, too, was enjoined to a constant act of importunity as in the New Testament injunction to prayer, in order to make life and its powers accessible to its deepest entreaties. The song put us all under a spell, so that I was not surprised that often the young men hearing its crescendo of longing could contain themselves no longer. They would drop what they were doing and come out of the bush, their feet pounding the desert sand like a drum, their hands stretched wide and their chests heaving with emotion, crying as if the sound had been torn alive and bleeding from the centre of their being, "Oh, look, like the eagle, I come!"

Also, these Bushmen made music. Nxou was constantly at it, and the instrument which he played was like a bow and most popular. In his hands it seemed to become a greater kind of bow, hunting meaning in the wasteland of sound not with arrows of flint and iron but with darts of ordered notes flying out at the silence. All the men could play the instrument but none like Nxou. Over and over again I saw him come back tired from the hunt, throw down his kill and spears and arrows, and reach at once for his musical instrument. The women would sit for hours, the full look of peace upon them, listening to him. Even walking between one group of shelters and another, he was constantly making his favourite music. Hardly a dawn came in which I did not shave to it, and one very early morning, in a temporary camp pitched while hunting far away, I heard it at a wonderful moment. It was still dark. I had just awakened and was realising with a quickening pulse that I was actually seeing star after star rising over the rim of the desert, so clear was it and so great the view. I have, of course, seen sun and moon rise countless times, never though, even at sea, witnessed such a rising of stars. At that moment, suddenly Nxou began playing one of his endless journeying tunes. The rhythm, and the sound, and the pulse of far starlight, as well as the undulations of the great swell of darkness breaking into foam and spray on the rock of the Milky Way, sounded so at one with each other that I reacted as I did when I first heard Beethoven's Ninth Symphony, the full chorus of human voices rising undismayed to the final height of resolution in their discovery of a universal meaning in the tragedy of an individual fate.

The thing that did surprise me, however, was that the Bushman had no drums. They asserted the basic rhythm of their musical occasions by beating it out with an explosion of sound between half-cupped hands, or as in their dancing by pounding the earth constantly and vigorously with their feet.

But they had a more evolved instrument, a four-stringed lyre exactly like the one we had seen broken at the foot of the Slippery Hills. Only the women played this, a young girl usually tapping the strings with a small stick and an elder woman conditioning the sound by deftly stroking the string as the girl beat it with her thumb.

We found that this love of music was not peculiar to our own close group but characteristic of all these people in the desert, bearing out the tradition of the Bushman's skill as a musician and his deep devotion to music. Once, far away from our sip-wells, while resting in the middle of a hunt in the heat of a terrible day, I heard cries for help. We all sat up alarmed, and soon there came staggering through the bush a little group of Bushmen in grave difficulties. They had seen the smoke of the fire made for our noonday tea and come straight to it. They had had no water for many days and were weak and hungry, their eyes bright with a light I had last seen on the faces of my starving fellow-prisoners in a Japanese prisoner-of-war camp. As they sat down in our shade a woman started scraping with a bone at the one desert bulb left, catching the scrapings in her hand and wringing some thick white drops from it straight into the mouth of a child with black, cracked lips. I tried it and it tasted like gall. They were still a day's march from permanent water and though Ben and Dabe said they could have made it on their own, I doubted it. But the moment they had drunk from our water they produced a lyre and began to make music.

"What is the music saying, Dabe?" I asked.

"It says 'thank you,' Master," he answered with a rare smile, waving his hands toward the sky and burning desert around us.

We concluded music was as vital as water, food and fire to them, for we never found a group so poor or desperate that they did not have some musical instrument with them.

And all their music, song, sense of rhythm and movement, achieved its greatest expression in their dancing. They passed their days and nights with purpose and energy, but dancing, too, played the same deep part in their lives as attributed to the Bushman of old in legend and history.

As we filmed and recorded all these activities I might easily have been trapped into a sense of satisfaction by the seeming ease with which we were accepted and the trust upon which we appeared to be taken. But I had one major set-back which made me aware of how delicately we had to proceed with the Bushman. Whenever I tried to ask Nxou and his people about their beliefs I came up against a blank wall of resistance. They not only pretended to be unaware of what I was talking about, but refused resolutely to discuss my question and became quickly so restless and uneasy that I desisted. Although Nxou, in my presence, had suggested to the little boy that he could bribe his grandmother with his tortoise into telling him a bedtime story, when I asked him or the others to tell me their stories they said they did not know what I meant by "stories." When I explained what I meant they said they knew no stories. One evening I surprised an old lady in the act of telling stories to the three children. But the moment she saw me she stopped. When I asked her to continue and to allow me to listen as well, she pretended to be too deaf to hear what I said.

"It's perfectly true! She's too deaf to hear," the others cried, crowding around and instinctively supporting her.

"There!" the old lady told me, a look of relief on her wrinkled face. "You see? It's as they say, I'm too deaf to hear."

Of course, they, she and I all laughed loud and long at the manner in which she had given herself away. I was moved at the essential innocence of minds that could behave like that when they felt themselves at bay. My childhood and long years in the company of primitive people had taught me, too, that this fear could show me where their real treasure lay. Their food, the secrets of their water, the daily round could be shared, but the contents of their spirit were different. Also I remembered that Stow reported a Bushman, when pressed for details of a story, as saying, "It is forbidden to talk of these things except by men who have been initiated in the mysteries of the dance."

So instantly I stopped all questioning and forbade the practice among my companions as well. I thought I would leave it until we had danced together. However, when I suggested dancing, I felt the same uncompromising reserve in them and had to drop that subject as well. I suspected there was a deeper trust they had to discover in us and themselves before these things would be possible, and I was certain that could only come with time and patient living. Unfortunately my time was limited. I never regretted more our wasted weeks in the north than I did then. All I could do, however, was to identify myself as deeply as possible with the life of the Bushman and hope for the best. I thought I could do this most effectively by joining their hunters and helping to provide the food they needed. So as soon as we seemed to be accepted on this level by the little community, we began going out with the hunters.

That immediately produced its own exciting set of revelations. The historical picture of the Bushman as a hunter was quickly verified and surpassed. Day after day we saw how easily and truly Nxou and his companions read the marks left by the animals, birds and insects, as well as weather and time, in the sands of the desert. I myself had just enough insight into the ancient science to appreciate what masters they were. They could tell very quickly how long it was since the buck, lion, leopard, bird, reptile or insect had signed his timesheet in the sand. No two hoof-prints were alike to them, for all spoor, like finger-prints to a Scotland Yard sleuth, were distinct and individual. They would pick out one from fifty, and deduce accurately the size, sex, build and mood of the great antelope that had just made it. They knew their world as much by this subtle script in the sand as by its more imposing physical appearances. When they met a new person their minds instinctively recorded not only the look on his face but also his footprint in the sand. On our first morning at the sip-wells I drew Nxou's attention to what I thought was a strange footprint near by. He laughed and teased me, asking if I really was so stupid as not to know my own cook's spoor, for it, indeed, was Jeremiah's foot-mark in the sand. Another time, when many miles from home and separated from the rest, Nxou and I, on the track of a wounded buck, suddenly found another set of prints and spoor joining our own. He gave a deep grunt of satisfaction and said it was Bauxhau's foot-marks made not many minutes before. He declared Bauxhau was running fast and that we would soon see him and the animal. We topped the dune in front of us and there was Bauxhau, already skinning the animal.

On another occasion Vyan wounded a springbuck. He immediately set out after it with Bauxhau and myself. At first we ourselves had no difficulty in following the spoor because of the occasional smear of blood on the grass beside it. Soon, however, the wounded animal joined his herd, also fleeing from us. The spoor became one of hundreds, the grass too trampled and dusty for any show of blood. But Bauxhau never wavered. His eyes picked out the one spoor in the maze of hundreds and held fast to it. Two miles further on he turned aside from the main stream of hoof-prints to show us again the solitary spoor and before long great splashes of blood led us to where the animal lay in the shade of a thorn-tree, where Vyan quickly put it out of pain.

Always at the beginning of any particular hunt there was

one solemn ceremony to perform: an earnest consultation between all hunters as to which spoor was most worth-while following. The Bushmen would sit on their heels, like elder statesmen, discussing the size, mood, sex and direction of the animals, study the wind, the sun, the hour and the weather generally. When they had picked out one particular spoor they revealed their decision by flicking their hands over it loosely from their wrists and making a sound like the wind between their teeth. They would do that, too, whenever a spoor was fresh and promising, and the gesture came so clearly from a background of meaning that we never saw it without an immediate quickening of our own pulses. The decision made, they would set out at a steady trot, until the spoor told them the quarry was near. Sometimes they would stalk it, first on their knees and finally flat on the stomach, until the animal came within range of their bows. Frequently, if seen, they would make no effort to hide themselves but go slowly, hands behind their backs, imitating the movements of ostriches pecking casually at food in the veld. When hunting in a group they seemed to prefer shooting in pairs, coming up together to their knees like shadows within a bush. Without a word being spoken, but by some process of wordless intercommunion of purpose, simultaneously they would let fly their arrows at the animal, the bowstrings resounding with a wild harp-like twang. That done, they would stand up at leisure. They never expected the animal to drop dead at once, knowing they would have to wait until the poison began to do its deadly work. But the first thing to establish was that the arrows had found their mark. The arrows were made in three sections for this very reason. First, the poisoned head was made in one short hollowed piece which fitted into another slightly larger one, which was joined to the main shaft notched at the far end to take the bowstring without slipping or fumbling. This made certain that the wounded animal would be unable to rid itself of the arrow by rubbing its wounded place against a tree, for in this way the arrow-shaft either parted from the arrow-head on impact, or else as soon as the animal started rubbing itself against trunks and thorn-bushes. If the hunters recovered the arrows intact, of course, they made no attempt to follow the alerted quarry. But if they found only the shaft they would take up the spoor at once and the real business of the hunt began. How long it took before they closed in for the kill with their spears on an animal already half-paralyzed by poison depended on the sort of poison used, the size of the animal, the nature and place of the wound. Sometimes the chase would last only an hour or two, but with the greatest of all quarries, the eland, it sometimes took a whole day. Indeed, Nxou told me he had once followed an eland for two and a half days from the time he hit it to the moment he killed it with his spear.

I have never seen a killing which seemed more innocent. It was killing in order to live. On their faces there was always an expression of profound relief and gratitude when the hunter's quest had been fulfilled. There was also a desire to complete the killing as quickly as possible. Invariably Nxou, when he caught up with his quarry, would stab straight into its heart and work his spear-head vigorously round in order to help the animal as quickly as possible to its end. I've watched their faces many times while performing this deed and I could see only the strain of the hunt, the signs of the fatigue from running all day under a cloudless sky in a high temperature, together with a kind of dedicated expression; but no gloating, or killing for the sake of killing. In the whole process they seemed able to call on unbelievable reserves of spirit and energy. We had a breath-taking illustration of it in the greatest of all our hunts which brought about a fundamental change in our relationship with the whole community: that was the day we killed the great eland bull.

Chapter 10

THE SONG OF THE RAIN

UP TO this moment we had kept ourselves
and our hosts well supplied with game. We had helped them
to kill steenbuck, duiker, an ostrich, hartebeest, springbuck, a
wart-hog and guinea fowl. Physically, the Bushman now
looked less spare and stronger than when we had first met.
But no hunt seemed to end without the nostalgic wish, expressed aloud, that the quarry had been an eland.

I have mentioned before the extraordinary meaning of the
eland in the Bushman's life and imagination; indeed I propose
dealing with its significance more fully in another volume. All
I need say here is that among our little hosts it was clear that
the consummation we sought in our hunting could only be
achieved by killing an eland. There were plenty around. We
found their spoor over and over again. We caught lovely
glimpses of their superb shapes moving with a flicker of purple flame through the diamond glitter of desert distances, or
swiftly crowning with glory a crest of red sand. Sometimes,

briefly, they would even stand still at the end of a natural av-
enue of storm-trees in serenely royal pose. But they had held
the little hunter's imagination so fruitfully throughout the
ages just because they were too observant, intelligent and
well organized to allow us ever to get really near them.
When it became clear that we had to provide our Bushmen
with the eland for which their spirits even more than bodies
yearned so strongly, we were forced to devote our days to
nothing else.

One morning, soon after sunrise, we came on the fresh
spoor of a herd of about fifty eland. When I saw Nxou's
wrists flicking over it as he found it, I had a feeling that our
hunter's day had really come. We followed the spoor resolutely all morning into the climax of the day without catching up with the herd. Nxou, Bauxhau, and Txexchi kept hard
at it, trotting silently beside the spoor in the scarlet sand.
From time to time I joined them but could not have kept up
except for repeated rests in my Land-Rover. About three in
the afternoon they drew near enough to have a shot at the
herd. I happened to have dropped back at the time to try and
persuade a ten-foot mamba with the biggest eyes I had ever
seen to pose for the camera, and when I caught up again I
found that the herd had gone off so fast into the east that there
had been no time to find out whether they had been hit. But
from that moment the hunters raced after the great antelope.

I had seen them run many times before, yet never with
this reserve of power nor with such length and ease of stride.
I am certain they ran as only the Greek who brought the
news of Marathon to Athens could have run. Their minds
were entirely enclosed in the chase and impervious to fatigue
or other claims on their senses. With Ben driving at his best
through bush, scrub and over hyena and ant-bear holes, with
the Land-Rover momentarily airborne and going over each
obstacle like a steeplechaser over a hurdle, we only just man-

aged to keep close to Nxou, who was in the lead. At one point I was horrified to see a bright yellow and deadly Kalahari cobra uncoiling like a twist of saffron rope from behind a bush and, hood extended, rise swiftly to strike at Nxou. Without a hesitation or swerve he rose like a hurdler high into the air and sailed over the angry head from which a forked tongue, shining with spittle, flickered like lightning. He didn't even look back at the snake but held on straight to the freshening spoor.

From the point where the final chase began to where we caught a glimpse of the full herd again, they ran thus without pause, for twelve miles according to Ben's speedometer. And the final mile was an all-out sprint. So fast did they go on this stretch that they passed momentarily out of our straining vision. We were climbing up a steep dune through a thick matted bush of thorn and the finest and deepest of blood-red sand underneath. Large ant-bear and spring-hare holes pitted the dune like shell holes on a ridge of modern battle. Superbly as Ben led us in his Land-Rover, we were inevitably slowed down. For the first time I feared the chase would fail. From the smoking tracks of the eland in the sensitive sand and the clearly defined length of stride they recorded on it, it was obvious that the herd was thoroughly alarmed and running full out. Yet they were not over-far ahead: the spoor was so fresh that it glistened darkly in the crumbling sand. That, and the fact that our Bushman hunters had suddenly spurted ahead, alone, checked my fears.

Then suddenly we broke out of the thorn on the crest of the dune, to see Ben and Vyan, guns in hand, tumbling out of their Land-Rover abruptly halted. I drew up sharply, snatched my rifle from Dabe and jumped out to run over to join them. The sun was low and its full light flowing like a broad, flashing stream down an immense dried-up watercourse coming out of the west and going due east. The watercourse was bare of trees and covered with long yellow grass. Immediately below us, running full out as if the race had only just begun, were our hunters, their sweating shoulders copper and gold above the erect grass. And most wonderful of all, half-way up the bank opposite us was the whole herd of eland purple and silver in the sun and drawn by their fear into one tight motionless ring, staring out of their wide eyes in our direction. Though they were five hundred yards or more from us, it was impossible for people who knew them as well as we did not to read in the angle of their heads and the close formation into which they were formed, their dismay that after so long a chase they should still be pursued.

"They'll be off in a second," Ben cried out in alarm. "Far as it is we'll have to shoot at once if we're to get our Bushman their meat."

As he spoke, a great bull broke out of the paralytic ring of the herd with an enormous bound high into the air. He might have been a lithe springbuck, instead of a creature weighing nearly a ton, for the ease with which he did it. A spurt of red dust rose in the yellow grass as his feet found the earth and immediately he led off with the speed of a race-horse straight up the side of the dune. So fast did the rest of the herd come out of their huddle and follow on one another's heels in single file that the herd went over the grass-gold dune on the far side like a single twist of silk.

Fastidious hunters that they were, fearful of hitting the eland women and their young, Vyan and Ben fired almost simultaneously at the flying bull, but the distance was great and the target erratic, and though they tried again and again he vanished unscathed over the dune.

I very nearly joined in to fire at the same target but something in me had already marked the fact that our Bushman hunters were not making for the main herd. Excited as I was by seeing the magnificent bull leading his herd out of their trance and the noise of Ben and Vyan opening up on him, I checked my impulse long enough to have another look at our hunters. Then I saw it all: another great bull, nearly two hundred yards behind the main herd, was coming out of the bed of the watercourse on the farthest side. He too, the moment the firing started, bounded forward but much more slowly than the rest of the herd. In one so great and massive as he it could only mean that he was wounded and that despite the length and speed of the chase Nxou and Bauxhau had read his condition accurately from the spoor in the sand and made him their special quarry. Nonetheless, the bull was still going strongly enough to prolong the chase for an hour or more, since the sun was dangerously low. I shot at him immediately and managed to hit him in the hindquarters. He faltered, walked on holding his head all the higher in the instinctive pride of so noble a breed that it makes the male scorn all sense of physical injury, but he suddenly sank back onto his hindquarters into the grass. Even then he went on holding his head up to look steadily at the little hunters closing in on him with their spears.

Running toward them, gun in hand, as fast as I could go, I still had time to notice how small they looked beside him as they went in spear in hand for the kill. They drove their spears straight at his heart, and when I came up to them Nxou was working his round in the heart of the bull to help him as quickly as possible over the end. But it's a law of life observed devoutly by the great animal kingdom of Africa: that one does not die unless one must. Great as was his pain and hopeless as the cause of life was for him, this lone bull still observed the royal law and would not accept the release of death. So I motioned our Bushman away and put a bullet in his head.

Hardly was he dead than Nxou and Bauxhau started skinning the bull. That was the amazing part of the chase; without pause or break for rest, they were fresh enough at the end to plunge straight away into the formidable task of skinning and cutting up the heavy animal.

As we watched them do it in the closing hour of the day, we noticed an expression on their faces that we had not seen before. Suddenly a deep laugh broke from Nxou. His arms covered with blood, he stood up from his work and said something to Bauxhau, who giggled like an excited girl. Dabe, hearing them, threw the round, shabby little European hat he insisted on wearing high into the air, and in the grip of the same excitement called out in wild approval, "Oh, you child of a Bushman, you!"

I asked him what it all meant.

"Master," he said almost beside himself, "now we are going to dance!"

I turned to Nxou and asked, "Why now?"

Because, he said, with a freedom I had not experienced before, always, ever since the days of the first Bushman, no hunter had ever killed an eland without thanking it with a dance.

Now the place where we killed the eland was about fifty miles from the sip-wells. The trail had twisted and turned so much that I had no idea where we were or in which direction our camp lay. But Nxou and his companions had no doubt. That was another of the many impressive things about them. They were always centred. They knew, without conscious effort, where their home was, as we had seen proved on many other more baffling occasions. Once, indeed, more than a hundred and fifty miles from home, when asked where it lay, they had instantly turned and pointed out the direction. I had taken a compass bearing of our course and checked it. Nxou's pointing arm might have been the magnetic needle of the instrument itself, so truly did it register. So now, turning for home, I only had to consult Nxou and follow his directions.

But this was not yet the end of a wonderful day. Something very remarkable happened on the way back. We drove home slowly, for the going was rough and our Land-Rovers deeply loaded with meat. The sun was down and the sky before us so red that Ben exclaimed in Afrikaans, "Dear Lord, isn't that a perfect sunset to end a hunter's day? It looks really as if the Master Hunter up there, *die ou Baas Jagter daar bo*, has just killed his eland too."

Struck by this glimpse of the poet in Ben, which was rarely exposed, I was about to answer when he went on, "You know, I once saw a little Bushman imprisoned in one of our jails because he killed a giant bustard which, according to the police, was a crime since the bird was royal game and protected. He was dying because he couldn't bear being shut in and having his freedom of movement stopped. When asked why he was ill he could only say that he missed seeing the sun set over the Kalahari! Physically, the doctor couldn't find anything wrong with him but he died nonetheless!"

We were silent for a while, and then trying to break out of the gloom I said, "I wonder what they'll say at the sip-wells when they learn that we've killed an eland?"

"Excuse me, Master," Dabe said, bolder than I had ever known him, "they already know."

"What on earth do you mean?" I asked.

"They know by wire," he declared, the English word "wire" on his Bushman tongue making me start with its unexpectedness.

"Wire?" I exclaimed.

"Yes. A wire, Master. I have seen my own master go many times to the D.C. at Gemsbok Pan and get him to send a wire to the buyers telling them when he is going to trek out to them with his cattle. We Bushman have a wire here," he tapped his chest, "that brings us news."

More than that I couldn't get out of him, but even before

we were home it was clear that our sceptical minds were about to be humbled. From afar in the dark, long before our fires were visible from a place where we stopped to adjust our heavy load, the black silence was broken by a glitter of new song from the women.

"Do you hear that, oh, my Master?" Dabe said, whistling between his teeth. "Do you hear? They're singing 'The Eland Song.'"

Whether by "wire," or by what mysterious means, they did know at the sip-wells, and were preparing to give their hunters the greatest of welcomes. By that time we ourselves were so identified in deed as well as mind with our hosts that, despite the vast differences of upbringing and culture, their exalted mood also became our own.

Accordingly I woke up the next morning with a feeling of profound achievement. Jeremiah, John, Cheruyiot, as they set about cutting up the fat of the great eland brisket to sweeten our hard fare, seemed to be purring with satisfaction. My European companions emerged from their sleep in similar mood, and I'd never seen a camp happier than we were that morning and prepared for the dance that was to come. "The first ball of the season" Duncan called it.

Apart from this it was also one of those Kalahari days which seemed to be charged with a meaning of its own. I felt as if it had been shaped by some master designer to carry forward into a new dimension the pattern that had been achieved on the previous evening.

Hitherto, in the rush of recording human events, I have neglected to tell of the unfolding of the seasons which accompanied them. All the time at the Sip-wells it had been growing steadily and frighteningly hotter. The sun had long ceased to be a friend, and the scorched earth, which had daily shrunk back into its last reserve of shade, had steadily darkened until at noonday the leaves of the gallant thorn-trees looked as if they were about to crumble to ashes and greeted the sunset with a sigh of relief that was echoed in our own exhausted senses. Often at noon, I would see Nxou and his companions throw themselves down beside us in shade that was little more than a paler form of sunlight and instantly go to sleep, more weary with heat than with distances run. This was perhaps the most moving of all their gestures, this instant act of trust between them and the harsh desert earth which, though too harsh for us, had been kinder to them in its pagan heart than we had ever been. They lay there securely clasped to the earth and nourished with sleep at its unfailing bosom. But when they woke they instantly stood up to scan the sky for cloud and other signs of rain as if even in their deep sleep they had felt the Mother Earth exclaim: "Dear God, will such dryness never end?"

Daily too, on our far-hunting round, we noticed that the surface of the desert became more churned and pitted where buck and other animals had dug, with hoof and claw, to get at the roots and tubers which could give them the relief of moisture that the heavens increasingly denied. No European can know how deep this need and anxiety of the wasteland of Africa enters into the blood and mind of its children. Here at the sip-wells it was no laughing matter. Nxou and his people did not fear for their store of water supply, which was deep in the sand and protected against the sun. But they feared what the lack of rain would do to the grasses and the game on which they lived. They alone knew what kind of disaster could come if the rains failed. I am certain many a Bushman community has perished from drought and famine in the Kalahari, unknown to anyone, with only a vortex of vultures in the blue to mark the place of their going, and only the hyena and jackal to sing their funeral song. Daily the shadow of this deep fear lengthened in our awareness as sun after sun went down without a cloud in the sky, and night upon night came and went without the hope-giving flicker of lightning below the star-uneasy horizon.

One night round the fire, all of us obsessed with this discharge of disquiet in our blood, Ben told us something which perhaps shows how deeply contained is the natural Bushman in the rhythm of the seasons, and how much he is a part of their great plans. Ben told us that the little man's womenfolk would become sterile during periods of drought and until the rains broke would cease to conceive. He knew this from his own experience and from that of great hunters before him. That was one reason why the Bushman had such small families. Had we not noticed, he asked, that there were no pregnant women around? Where else in Africa would we see so many married and vigorous young women and not one in the family way? Yet this fear of drought went even deeper than that. If a woman had conceived in a fall of rain that was not maintained and bore a child in a period of drought which threatened the survival of all, immediately at birth the child was taken from her, before as Dabe confirmed, "it could cry in her heart," and was killed by the other women. The anguish and bitterness with which those who loved children performed this deed, Ben said, proved how necessary it was. Also, he thought it would silence those who condemned them from their arm-chairs of plush and plenty. We went to bed with a new dimension added to our view of the dark necessities among which this rare flame of Stone Age life burned.

But on this particular morning there was a first real promise of rain in the air. The atmosphere was silver-dim with sudden moisture and heavy with electricity and heat. Soon after breakfast a cloud no larger than the Old Testament's hand of man appeared with a flag of wind at its head. It was soon followed by others, and all morning long we watched with growing excitement cloud upon cumulus cloud piling up like towers and palaces over some enchanted "Tempest" island. Were we to be privileged to celebrate the hunter's fulfilment not only with meat that was the food of his gods, but also with the water that was wine to his earth? As the day wore on the answer seemed likely to be positive. Yet even so, I, who had seen so many promises of rain snatched away at the last minute from the cracked lips of the African earth, was afraid to hope until, at long last, the thunder began to mutter on a darkening horizon. By the time the first dancers started coming into our camp the rumble of thunder was constant and rolling slowly nearer like the noise of a great battle. Suddenly it made our small camp look puny and exposed. Yet it added to the jubilation of the dancers in the clearing we had made for them.

How lovely they looked! The women had rubbed some fat into their skins and their bodies were a-glitter. Their jewellery, too, seemed to have been polished and flashed in the sun which moved on, undismayed, to grapple with the giant cloud rising in the west. The women walked toward us already attuned to the music humming, quivering and swaying with its rhythm and song. As they arrived they quickly collected on the edge of the clearing and began singing aloud, beating time with their feet and hands. Occasionally one of the older women would run out into the open, her arms stretched like the wings of a bird, her mincing steps and jeering song mocking the men, who had not yet appeared from the bush, for their tardiness.

The men, however, held back out of sight, obedient to their own part in the over-all pattern of the dance to come. They seemed, deliberately, to provoke the women to a greater and greater frenzy of singing and longing. When at last they came, it was because they could no longer keep away and were compelled almost against their will. Then a moan as of great pain broke from them. Arms stretched out, feet ceaselessly pounding and re-pounding the earth, they came bounding out of the bush with that cry of theirs: "Oh, look, like birds we come!"

When this happened the triumph in the women's voices soared like a star in the night and brought about a new intensity of passion to their singing. The men became so drawn into the mood of the music that it was nearly impossible to recognize their individuality. An archaic mask sat on all faces as they began to sing and dance the theme of the eland. I have seen many primitive dances. They are invariably communal affairs and tend to have a bold, often violent and fairly obvious pattern. But this music was rich, varied, tender and filled with unworldly longing. It had a curious weave and rhythm to it, some deep-river movement of life, turning and twisting, swirling and eddying back upon itself in order to round some invisible objects in its profound bed as it swept on to the sea.

In this manner they danced their way into the life of their beloved eland and their mystical participation in his being. They danced him in the herd, his cows, heifers and children around him. They danced him in his courting, right up to the moment where, fastidious animal that he is, he vanishes alone, with his woman, for his love-making in the bush. They danced him grown old, challenged, and about to be displaced by the young bulls in the herd. Quite naturally the older men became the challenged, the younger the challengers. The movements of the dancers, the expression on their faces, and the voices crying "Oh!" from far down in their throats and straight from the source where the first man had his being, greatly moved us. We saw the lust for battle in the young faces, the look of perplexity in the eyes of the women torn between loyalty to a former lord and obedience to the urge of new life within them, as well as the agony of impending defeat in the expression of the old bulls. And we saw life decide the battle, the old cast out from the herd while the young, with unbelievable tenderness, put an arm around the shoulders of a woman, become suddenly still with the acceptance of her fate, and so move inexorably together toward the oncoming night.

The darkness fell quickly because of the rising storm, and the dance of the eland naturally made way for the greatest of all the Bushman dances: "The Fire Dance." Here the women without a pause grouped themselves singing in the centre of the clearing. Quickly they piled a fire there, lit it the classical way and then an uncle of Nxou's led the men in a ring dancing around the fire. They danced the first Bushman soul setting out in the darkness, before mind or matter, to look for substance for fire. They looked in vain for its spoor in the sand, as if fire were some subtle animal. Hour after hour they went round and round in the same circle without finding it. They called on the sun, moon and stars to give them fire. Then we saw them leading the blind companions who in some prehistoric period of the quest had gone too near the scorching flames. Because it was a sacred dance we noticed how in the progress of his search the seeker now acquired the power of healing. Suddenly he would break off his dancing to stand behind a moaning woman and with trembling hands draw out of her the spirit that was causing her unrest, emitting in the process the cry of the animal with which the alien invader was identified. That done, he would return to join the magic circle still dancing in search of fire. How the dancers found the power to go on ever faster and faster, hour after hour, seemed beyond explanation or belief. They danced so hard and long that the circle in the sand became a groove, then the groove a ditch high up to their calves. Long before the end they seemed to pass over into a dimension of reality far out of reach of my understanding, and to a moment and a place which belonged only technically to the desert in which we were all gathered. Indeed, so obsessed did the men become by this search for fire that they were drawn nearer and nearer to the flames beside which the woman sat. Then suddenly they halved the circle and went dancing with their bare feet through the middle of the flames. But even that was not the end of the quest. Now, the longing became so intense that two of the elder women were kept constantly busy preventing some fire-obsessed man from breaking out of the circle and hurling himself head first straight into the flames, like a moth overcome by excess of longing for the light. Indeed, one man did break through and before he could be stopped had scooped up a handful of burning coals and attempted to swallow them whole.

All the while, in the ebb of the music rising and falling like a tide around us, the noise of the thunder rose louder in our ears. The lightning began to play incessantly overhead and to wash the dancers yellow in a *Nibelungen* gold. It sounded as if the whole of nature was being mobilized to participate in this expression of man's first and still unfulfilled quest. The jackalls, hyenas, the shriek owls, the male ostriches booming, all seemed stirred to howl and scream as never before, and beyond the sip-wells the lions roared back deeply and most strangely at them, at us, and at the storm. Toward the end the men's feet, together, were beating the earth so fast and regularly that it was difficult to believe that the noise was made by the feet of many men and not by a single automatic piston.

At last here and there a dancer began to fall in his tracks. The two older women would pick him up and carry him aside where he lay moaning in a trance of fatigue in the darkness. Then, almost on the second of midnight, the hero of the dance, Nxou's slender and comely uncle, suddenly found fire the way it was meant to be found. He knelt down reverently beside it, the singing died away in one last sob of utter exhaustion, the dancers sank to the earth while the man picked up the coals in his naked hands and arose to scatter them far and wide for all the world to share. He stood there swaying on his feet, the sweat of an unimaginable exertion like silk tight upon his skin, dazed with the anguish of near disaster in doom of eternal darkness as well as by the climax of deliverance. Swaying, he made a gesture and uttered words of prayer to the night around him. What the words were I never knew, except that Dabe said they were too ancient for him to understand. All I do know is that I myself felt very near the presence of a god and my eyes seemed blinded as if by sudden revelation. In the darkness beyond the sip-wells, on the high dunes at the back of the heroic dancer, the lightning struck with a savage, creese-like cut at the trembling earth, so near that the crackle of its fire and the explosion of the thunder sounded simultaneously in my ear. And at that moment the rain fell.

It rained all night. I thought I had never heard a sweeter sound than it made on the tarpaulin over my head and in the sand within reach of my hand. So close had my search in the past few weeks brought me to the earth, its elements and its natural children that throughout the rest of the eventful night, in my half-waking condition, I felt I had rediscovered the first language of all things and could hear plainly the deep murmur of the earth taking the rain into her like a woman taking a lover into her arms, all the more ardently because secretly she had doubted that he would ever come. I went on lying there in the darkness as if in the presence of gods and Titans. All around me the voice of the thunder, now deafening with nearness, now solemn with distance, was like the voice Moses heard on his mountain-top in the desert of Sinai. When the dawn broke, it was still raining heavily, and already there was a bloom of quickening new life in leaf, grass and bark.

For once Nxou did not come to me at dawn. He appeared with Bauxhau about noon, both of them running and laughing with joy at their pretended dismay at the cold impact of the rain on their warm, naked skins. We took them into our shelter and there, over mugs of hot coffee, it happened. Suddenly with the two of them I had the same feeling that I'd had with the earth and rain in the previous night. For the first time since I had met them we had access to the same language of meaning.

On the impulse I asked, "Nxou, who was the first Bushman in the world?"

The old look of reserve flickered for a second over his fine-drawn face. Then his eyes cleared and he said, "If someone told me his name was Oeng-oeng, I would not know how to say no."

"So the first Bushman was called Oeng-oeng?" I quickly followed up.

"Yes! Oh, yes! Yes!" he answered, his eyes shining as if he was even more pleased than I that at last the barrier was down. "His name was Oeng-oeng."

"Indeed," said Bauxhau grinning, "he was Oeng-oeng."

Then it all poured out. We sat there for the rest of the day listening to their stories. Charles, who had come back with Ben and Vyan some days before after they had gone out to one of our supply points to re-fuel and re-provision, happier than ever to be with us, moved quietly in the background to record all they told us. In the days that followed, whenever we had leisure from hunting or filming, the process went on, from the first version of creation and Nxou's Shaksperian assertion that there was "a dream dreaming us," to the last tangled and tortured expression of spirit when his forefathers were brutally torn from the main trunk of their race and flung far out into the desert. Happy at last to be able to share with us what was also most precious to them, they poured out all before us. I would have loved to question and elucidate, but I was afraid, unwittingly, to intrude and cause damage. Already with our radioactive intellects we had hurt so deeply the first spirit of Africa. So I just listened, entranced.

They spoke fluently, vividly and with great variety of tone and gesture. Often I could tell what they were saying before Dabe and Ben could translate it. For instance on a hot afternoon Nxou was telling me one of his favourite stories, a tale of an eland, the first man, his greedy children, a turtle-dove and an unfailing source of honey, all full of magic and resolved with a miracle of resurrection out of a corruption of worm and dust in the earth. Now, the toes of the eland are long and elastic so that they can splay out the hoof like a palm of a hand to make his going over the desert sand easier, and as he lifts his majestic foot the toes snap back into position with a wonderful electric click. When Nxou came to the part where the god-like eland is going unwittingly to his doom, he imitated the sound the eland makes when he walks in the silences of the desert so vividly that Ben, who had dozed off in the heat, woke, jumped up and seized his gun, saying, "Quick! Did you hear that? There must be eland just behind that bush!"

The Bushman stories and mythology I must record at another time. But I will mention just one of their beliefs because it played a practical role during our visit at the sip-wells. We all, of course, know the myth of Cupid armed with a bow and arrow. To me it was an archaic symbol of no great consequence to the spirit of my own time. But to the Bushman it has a living and immediate meaning. In a hunter's community the imagery of the bow naturally went deep, and there was still magic in it. The bow was as much an instrument of the spirit as a weapon of the chase. The Bushman clearly believed that with a bow he could not only kill game but project his wishes and exercise his influence at a great distance from himself. Our history has recorded only the destructive aspects of the bow, namely, the Bushman's belief that with its magic he could kill from a safe distance all that stood between him and his wishes. History has called it "the Bushman's Revolver" and given no hint that it had also a gentler mission. Here at the sip-wells we found that the Bushman made also a special bow, a "love-bow," as much an instrument of love between men and women as Cupid's bow was in the affairs of gods and ancient heroes. A Bushman in love carved a tiny little bow and arrow out of a sliver of the bone of a gemsbok, a great and noble animal with a lovely sweep of long crescent horn on its proud head. The bow was most beautifully made, about three inches long and matched with tiny arrows made out of stems of a sturdy grass that grew near water. The minute quiver was made from the quill of a giant bustard, the largest flying bird in the desert. The Bushman would stain the head of his arrows with a special potion and set out to stalk the lady of his choice. When he had done this successfully he would then shoot an arrow into her rump. If, on impact, she pulled out and destroyed the arrow, it was a sign that his courtship had failed. If she kept it intact then it was proof that he had succeeded.

When I heard this I was most anxious to film the scene, but we immediately encountered difficulties that at first seemed insuperable. The Bushmen were frankly afraid of the idea, but after living with it for a day or two they seemed prepared to attempt it. Unfortunately the most beautiful Bushman girl had got married just before our arrival. Yet Duncan was most anxious she and Nxou should act the parts together. It was not difficult to explain what we wanted because of their own games and drama of make-believe. We talked first, of course, to the girl and her husband. They thought it over for days and then the man said shyly that she would be allowed to play the part. We then asked Nxou to play the husband, but for the first time he looked angry with us. Over and over again Dabe explained patiently that it would be sheer make-believe. Nxou appeared incapable of drawing the distinction and resolutely refused the part. In the end everyone began to get angry, accusing him of "stupidity" and "ingratitude," but I was touched by his obvious signs of deep conflict.

"Enough, Dabe," I said. "Ask him why he won't do it. Tell him I'd be grateful to know."

Relieved, Nxou turned his back on the others to say almost pleadingly to me, "Look! That man is my friend. I have known him all my life. Although he says he does not mind, I know his heart will be hurt to see his woman pretending to be mine."

He stood there resolute, naked, his skin stained with dust and the blood of many an animal, a smell upon him that was too strong for most civilized noses, but to me, at that moment, he seemed truly clothed in manly value and delicacy.

I turned to Duncan. "There! He won't even pretend to be in love with his friend's wife! Take off your hat to him, all of you!"

So we chose a secondary star for our film. Successful as it has been in the outside world, the scene still seems to me to be a reluctant and self-conscious affair and I'm not at all certain I was right to inflict even that little unreality upon them.

In those days, too, with the first rain still falling, I heard new music. The plucked sound of the lyre met me one twilight evening as I walked toward the Bushman shelters, and a woman sang to this effect:

> *Under the sun*
> *The earth is dry,*
> *By the fire*
> *Alone I cry.*
> *All day long*
> *The earth cries*

For the rain to come.
All night my heart cries
For my hunter to come
And take me away.

Suddenly from somewhere out of sight a man heard the song and his whole male being knew the reply. With tenderness that I know in no other primitive singing, he sang back:

Oh! Listen to the wind,
You woman there;
The time is coming
The rain is near.
Listen to your heart,
Your hunter is here.

We called it "The Song of the Rain" and it is for ever associated in my mind with that sudden reflowering of the desert which arose from the coming of the rains. Even the thorn quickened and its iron branches budded. I do not know the names of all the flowers that appeared in the grass standing so erectly and proudly around us. We spoke of May to describe the branches of white blossom, dazzling against the purified blue above us; we called the wonderful white lilies near the sip-wells, amaryllis; the sharp-spiked purple and red blooms in the bush, Kalahari iris; and the shy, shade-loving primulas, primroses. There were wild Bauhinia, curved and carved along the edges and folded in at the ends like Botticelli sea-shells; wild protolarias, mimosa and dozens of other blooms sunflower bold and love-mist fine. The song of birds building their nests became almost deafening, and in the distance the male ostriches, their black and white Macedon shirts repleated, began to trip fantastic, courting dances in circles round one another, booming ceaselessly to relieve the sudden fire of longing within. One day I came across two giant bustards harsh with passion and so busy bowing, curtsying and tripping to each other that they refused to acknowledge me though I came within five yards of them. I caught a rare glimpse in an earth hole of a baby hyena in purple fur; at another place I saw a tiny jackal of burnished gold, and at yet another walked a bleating, trembling, newly dropped springbuck kid whose mother had been taken by lion.

It was all beautiful but, like autumn and death, spring and new love too have their own unrest. Daily I was aware of a new and growing restlessness which passed from "Spoor of Gazelle," from Nxou, from the oldest of the Bushmen, from Dabe and Ben, to me. I found Ben increasingly silent, nightly examining the sky and remarking how the lightning showed the tide of the rainy season daily surging nearer to where his lands lay, still unploughed, far away down south. I knew it was unfair to keep him a day longer than was necessary, and one night I was constrained to explain, "I won't stay here a minute longer than necessary to finish the film I promised to make, Ben."

"Of course. I know." His answer was genuine enough but I could feel the natural unrest within it.

Vyan, though not by hint or word would he have added to the pressure which he knew was already great in me, discussed increasingly with Ben the complexities of animal husbandry. He was homesick for his humpbacked cattle and the view of the Northern Frontier Province hills on the far rim of his ranch. Jeremiah, too, took out the under-exposed and well-nigh illegible snapshot of his "very, very clever son" and stared at it overlong by the fire. I was forced to recognize that spring is not the natural time for completion but rather the moment of life's re-beginnings.

Duncan, alone, was blissfully happy working from dawn to sunset, photographing, filming and tending his cameras. He was an endless source of amusement to the Bushmen because time and again he would forget everything except his camera and walk straight into a tree, or fall backwards into a bush of thorn, to emerge without his hat. But behind their merriment I knew they, too, were daily more anxious to be off on one of their mysterious "walk-abouts" to the rare places of desert life of which they alone knew. This was evident in the eyes of the mothers as well as the children that they now brought to me to doctor for minor ailments. But our coming, too, had laid many of their fears to rest, and some of them looked at us as if to say: "Stay with us for ever. With your magic and your guns we'll make heaven of this desert earth."

I, myself, would gladly have stayed on much longer. There was so much more to learn and so much else I wanted to do. There was, for instance, the great gathering of Bushman clans at which Nxou hinted one day. We were speaking of dancing and he said the best dances always were in a full summer after the rains at some great pan in the deepest part of the desert, where all people came to play and dance and eat and "make glad together." I took a compass bearing of the direction in which he pointed and longed with all my heart to be able to stay for the great occasion. But I knew it was impossible to do so without loss of honour. All situations in life have an inner as well as an outer shape which is uniquely their own, and one does violence to either at one's peril. I feared that perhaps I had already been greedy, trying to force more out of the situation than it naturally contained. That fear in the end preserved me.

As the end of the filming of the love-bow ritual came in sight, and comforting myself with the hope that if I were obedient to the true proportions of the occasion, one day life might reward me with the chance for a longer and more fruitful journey, I asked Ben and Vyan to go out to our nearest supply point for the last time. I asked them to bring back not only enough water and petrol to carry us across the heart of the great desert to the railway on the far eastern boundary, but also to bring back some farewell presents for our Bushmen.

This matter of presents gave us many an anxious moment. We were humiliated by the realization of how little there was we could give to the Bushmen. Almost everything seemed likely to make life more difficult for them by adding to the litter and weight of their daily round. They themselves had practically no possessions: a loin strap, a skin blanket and a leather satchel. There was nothing that they could not assemble in one minute, wrap in their blankets and carry on their shoulders for a journey of a thousand miles. They had no sense of possession. When first I offered to cut up and divide fairly between them a buck that we had killed they merely looked puzzled and said, "Yes, by all means if you wish it. But why go to that unnecessary trouble? If one eats all eat; if one is hungry all are hungry." When I gave one of them a cigarette, after three puffs it was passed to the next, and so travelled backwards and forwards, three puffs at a time, among all of them. With such a people I had long since realized there was only one way of truly giving, and that was to give them a place in our hearts and imaginations, to see beyond the dialectical obsession with externals that bedevil our minds to where stood these authentically caring and cruelly uncared-for children of life. Only in that way could they have a part in our lives and not vanish as so many others had done before them. I feared even to give a small present of glass beads to the women in case it made them dissatisfied with their own ostrich shell, stained roots and coloured woods. Yet my instinct was strong that some free gift from us was needed in order to seal both in their minds and ours the fact that this encounter was different from any other between our races: a meeting of hunters at a well in a desert, all fol-

lowing the same perilous spoor of greater meaning and becoming. We decided, therefore, to give presents of a handful
of beads and a vivid kerchief to each of the women which, in
deference to the absence of a sense of individual property,
was to be equal from the youngest to the oldest. We got each
of the men a hunter's knife and a plug of tobacco.

On the last evening we set up our one table on the edge of
the clearing, piled our presents on it, brewed buckets of coffee
made mellow with the last of our preserved milk and satu-
rated with sugar, and invited all the Bushmen to join us.
While another hunter's sunset glorified the sky we gave them
each their presents. They accepted them as in a dream, with a
look of wonder and also, I thought, a touch of sadness that
this was the end. They dispersed quietly, only Nxou making
some attempt to sing the wayfarer's song we knew so well.

Watching them go, Ben said, "They, too, will be off soon."
He waved his hand to the far south where a god-like head of
thunder-cloud was beginning to send out lightning in the
darkening sky.

"But these old people, how will they get on?" I asked,
pointing to the ancient couple I had met the first morning,
now slowly following in the wake of the others.

"They'll go as far as they can," Ben answered. "But a day
will come when they can't go on. Then, weeping bitterly, all
will gather round them. They'll give them all the food and
water they can spare. They'll build a thick shelter of thorn to
protect them against wild animals. Still weeping, the rest of
the band, like the life that asks it of them, will move on.
Sooner or later, probably before their water or food is finished, a leopard, but more commonly hyena, will break
through and eat them. It's always been like that, they tell me,
for those who survive the hazards of the desert to grow truly
old. But they'll do it without a whimper."

Remembering the untroubled expressions on the two wrinkled old faces, it was almost more than I could bear to hear.

"Do they know all this, Ben?" I asked.

"Yes, they know it all right. They've had to do it to others before them," he answered, swinging around sharply on his heel to go back to the fire, as if in the darkness beyond he had seen a gathering shadow he did not wish to face.

I sat for some time by myself thinking over what he had told me. Life was only possible for all of us because, in our past, there had been those who had put the claims of life itself before all else. Did it really matter whether the end came from the crab within or the hyena without? We will have the courage to meet it and give meaning to the manner of our dying, provided we, like these humble, wrinkled old Bushmen, have not set a part of ourselves above the wholeness of life.

We broke camp early the next morning, all the Bushmen, the women wearing their vivid new kerchiefs, crowding round our last fire to watch us. Their eyes as they followed us seemed uncomprehending and to me almost accusing. I know we all felt sad. I heard Vyan mutter to Ben, "You know, an old hunter up north once said to me, 'Wherever you camp in the bush you leave a part of yourself behind.' I feel it more about this place than any other."

For once I moved off first because I wanted to get the break over quickly. Just before I got into my Land-Rover, "Spoor of Gazelle" broke out of the bush, the kerchief round her neck streaming out like a flag of fire behind her, and ran up to put an ostrich egg full of water in my hand as I had so often seen her do to other hunters setting off on a long chase. "Bowl of Food" (Nxou), "Stone-axe" (Bauxhau), "Powerful Wildebeest" (Txexchi) and "Lips of Finest Fat" (Xhooxham) were sitting silently beside the fire watching us intently. As I slammed the door of the car they all stood up and raised their hands as Nxou had done the evening I first met him. I drove past the silent huddle of little men and women all standing upright with hands raised above their heads. As I waved to them I felt as if all my rediscovered childhood was dying within me. I drove up past the sip-wells and up to the high dunes behind them. On the crest I stopped, got out and looked back. The remaining three Land-Rovers were just crossing the dry watercourse. Beyond them there was no smoke over our old camp, no visible sign of man or human habitation. The desert looked as empty as it had ever been. Yet in that vast world behind the glitter of pointed leaves and in the miracle of sand made alive, and thorn of steel set alight with flower by the rain, the child in me had become reconciled to the man. The desert could never be empty again. For there my aboriginal heart now had living kinsmen and a home on which to turn. I got back into my Land-Rover. I drove over the crest and began the long, harsh journey back to our twentieth-century world beyond the timeless Kalahari blue.

·